P9-DNQ-850

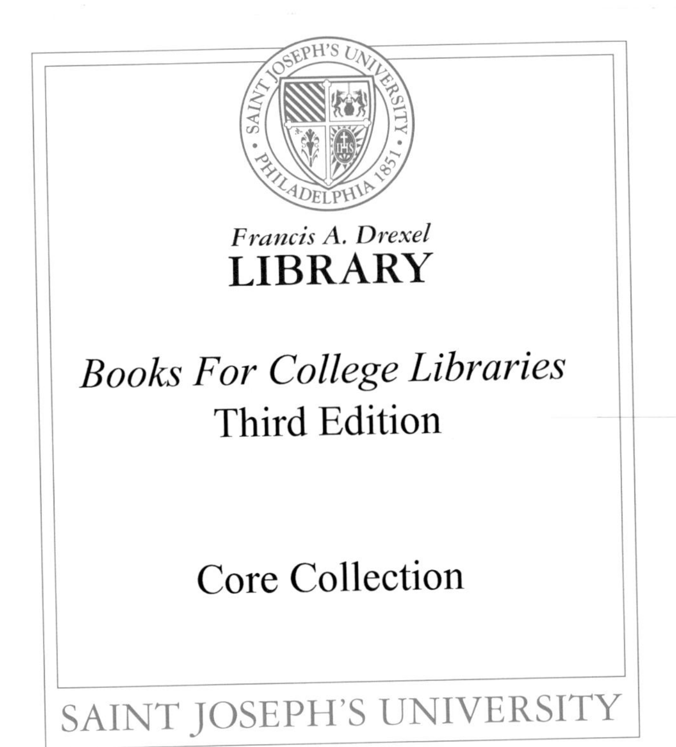
SAINT JOSEPH'S UNIVERSITY
PHILADELPHIA 1851
IHS

ON THE MARGINS OF THE GOOD EARTH

ON THE MARGINS OF THE GOOD EARTH

The South Australian Wheat Frontier
1869–1884

D. W. MEINIG

Syracuse University

Second in the Monograph Series

Published for

The Association of American Geographers

by

Rand McNally & Company

Chicago

The Monograph Series of the
Association of American Geographers

Printed in the U.S.A. by Rand McNally & Company
Library of Congress Catalogue Card Number 62-7266

EDITOR'S NOTE

FROM THE TIME of our earliest archeological records of western civilization, one of the most important and interesting kinds of geographical line has been that between "the desert and the sown." This boundary, between land used by man for the grazing or hunting of animals that live on steppe grass or desert shrub and land plowed and used for the growing of crops, rarely has been fixed in any area for long periods of time. The greatest stability has been evident on the borders of lands irrigated by exotic rivers running through deserts; the least in the case of mid-latitude grasslands in which crop yields are characteristically high in periods of good rainfall, but in which the occurrence of such periods is notoriously capricious. Across such boundaries the herdsmen and farmers have often faced each other in suspicion and uneasy truce, interrupted occasionally by political or military conflict or, more rarely yet, by periods of cooperative peace.

There has been great interest in the study of such boundaries of past millennia but, in most cases, we have had little evidence about their establishment. Only in the records of recent penetration of arid lands for irrigated agriculture, and of grasslands for both herding and farming, can we study their origin as, often at substantial economic and social costs, they became defined empirically. In such a study of development we may hope for a more profound understanding of their nature.

This monograph is a detailed report on such a resolution of the margin between two competing forms of land use in the colony of South Australia in the later nineteenth century. The author long has been a student of similar processes and problems in a not grossly dissimilar area of the Pacific Northwest of the United States. In his preface he describes the nature of his study with precision but with a fine disregard for formula, tradition or the taxonomy of academic pigeonholes. As a geographer with strong historical interests, he simply has undertaken the description and interpretation of changes in the patterns of settlement and land use in the area from what information he could glean from field and archive.

The result is a study, executed with imagination, grace and skill, that the Selection Board of the Monograph Series presents to the Association and the whole scholarly world with pride and confidence. The editor would only add that he has found the performance of his duties a most pleasant and profitable task.

ANDREW H. CLARK
Madison, Wisconsin

PREFACE

THIS STUDY IS neither a history nor a geography in the usual sense, but an historical inquiry into certain features of geographical interest. That is to say that it does not attempt to describe and analyze the whole complex of interrelated factors in the colonization of the northern wheatlands of South Australia, nor the whole range of geographical changes which resulted from that movement. It does attempt to relate some portions of that history, to map some of the basic patterns which were developed, and to examine with some care selected features in the colonization process.

That it does no more than this is because of my own limitations in time, knowledge, training, and interest. Clearly, it was quite impossible to exhaust the full volume of relevant materials or to acquire any full familiarity with each locality. Some topics, as surely, were beyond my competence, and others received less attention because of personal inclinations. I have written of those things which interested me and which seemed most important within my particular frame of reference and have not attempted to follow any kind of comprehensive program for the geographical study of colonization.

Despite such restrictions, I would like to think that the over-all result does have some balance and cohesiveness. I have tried to write for those interested especially in South Australia and those whose concern is for broader matters related to this kind of colonization. In the main these are no doubt quite separate groups and I have been conscious of the fact that the very attempt to serve both raises the danger of satisfying neither. The one may well despair of the seeming morass of local details, the other may view the attempts to set the over-all context of the inquiry as extraneous and my summary coverage of South Australian developments before and after this colonization period as hopelessly superficial. But I make no apology for these features, for I believe that both the general and the particular are equally important to the interests of both groups.

The opportunity of spending nearly a year in South Australia offered me the chance of gaining an enlarged perspective upon a long-standing interest in the history of colonization and regional development in the American West. The settlement of the northern wheatlands in South Australia was remarkably parallel in general with that of the area I was most familiar with, the Columbia Interior of the Pacific Northwest. Rather than attempt to trace comparisons among numerous individual features, it seemed far more sound to try to immerse myself, as far as possible, in the whole story of that South Australian colonization for at least a brief period. I believe this to be the "basic research" technique most appropriate to this kind of historical geography, wherein not only the specific items, but their relationships, the whole character of the times, and often quite unexpected features are revealed. Thus this study is really a by-product of a more general interest, and elsewhere I have suggested some of the likenesses and differences apparent in the colonizations of these two regions.[1] But, though I have tried to suggest something of its broader relevance, the main body of this volume is rigidly focused upon South Australia. To make available some detailed coverage of this important but neglected era of South Australian history and interesting but little known area of agricultural colonization, has seemed likely to result in the most useful contribution.

It is as pleasant to acknowledge the help received in the travel, research, and preparation of this study as it is difficult to keep the

[1] Donald W. Meinig, "Colonization of Wheatlands: Some Australian and American Comparisons," *The Australian Geographer,* VII (August, 1959), 205–13.

list within reasonable bounds of space. I wish to thank, first of all, Professor Graham H. Lawton of the Department of Geography, University of Adelaide, for the invitation to come to South Australia, and the United States Educational Foundation for the Fulbright Research Scholarship which made it possible to accept. It was Professor Lawton who first introduced me to the field of historical geography, and to join him a decade later in his homeland and have a try at applying some of the things I had learned from him was an unusually gratifying opportunity. The entire departmental staff at Adelaide received me with a hospitality far greater than any visitor would dare hope to expect, and I thank Mrs. T. J. Marshall and Dr. Keith Thomson, especially, for their sustained aid and interest in all my work. It was a special privilege to have the sympathetic critique of Dr. Douglas H. Pike and Dr. A. Grenfell Price. I also thank Mr. F. G. N. Cawte for his interest and support.

The staffs of the Barr Smith Library of the University of Adelaide, the Royal Geographical Society of Australasia (S. A. Branch), the South Australian Department of Agriculture, and, especially, Mrs. A. A. Wamersley and her assistants in the Newspaper Reading Room of the South Australian Public Library, facilitated my work in every possible way. I thank the Surveyor General of South Australia, Mr. Harold L. Fisk, and members of his Department for their interest in and patience with my antiquarian requests and the South Australian Archives for supplying the historic photographs.

The first draft of this study was prepared in Australia; its revision for publication in this series was greatly aided by the suggestions of the members of the A. A. G. Monograph Committee. The skilled hand of my incisive and benevolent editor, Andrew H. Clark, has markedly improved every page.

I would like to thank the editor of *Agricultural History* for permission to use certain of my materials relating to Goyder's Line which appeared originally in the October 1961 issue of that journal.

I wish to express my gratitude to those at the University of Utah, and especially Professor H. Bowman Hawkes, whose encouragement and willingness to make special arrangements enabled me to go to Australia. It is quite impossible to make specific mention of the many friends in South Australia who assisted in so many ways, but I wish to thank particularly the Roy C. Sandow family of "Koomarlie," Hoyleton, and the Maurice Dolling family of Wokurna and Mt. Lofty for their hospitality and for showing us how very pleasant South Australian country life can be. Finally, special thanks to Lee, to Laurel, Kristin, and Alison, and to Nelda, for their characteristic patience and good cheer which made the journey and the stay so very enjoyable.

D. W. Meinig
Syracuse University, March 1961

CONTENTS

LIST OF MAPS

LIST OF FIGURES

I.

Colonization: The Context of Inquiry

Another object is — by being thoroughly provincial — to broaden the view . . . .
— Douglas Pike
Paradise of Dissent, Preface

The agricultural colonizations of the nineteenth century are of compelling geographical interest. Because, on any close view, colonization is by its very nature not a mere event but a complex process, its geographical study is necessarily concerned with "the *evolution* of space content on the earth's surface"; and, again because of its very nature, such a study becomes necessarily in some way "a report on a revolutionary change in the character of a region."[1]

Such statements neither explicitly set a particular framework nor define just what is to be studied, but both presume a focus upon areal changes involving physical, biotic, and cultural processes. Agricultural colonization is a particularly important geographical topic simply because it necessarily produces abrupt and decisive changes through this whole range of processes. By definition it involves the radical replacement of one vegetative cover by another, the radical disturbance of the soil, and the alteration of

[1] The quotations are from, respectively, Edward A. Ackerman, *Geography as a Fundamental Research Discipline,* Department of Geography Research Paper No. 53, University of Chicago (June, 1958), p. 28, and Andrew H. Clark, *The Invasion of New Zealand by People, Plants and Animals, The South Island,* Rutgers University Studies in Geography No. 1 (New Brunswick, 1949), p. v. The first study is an influential theoretical statement of the essential need for the historical dimension in geographic research, the second an influential example of the contributions so obtained.

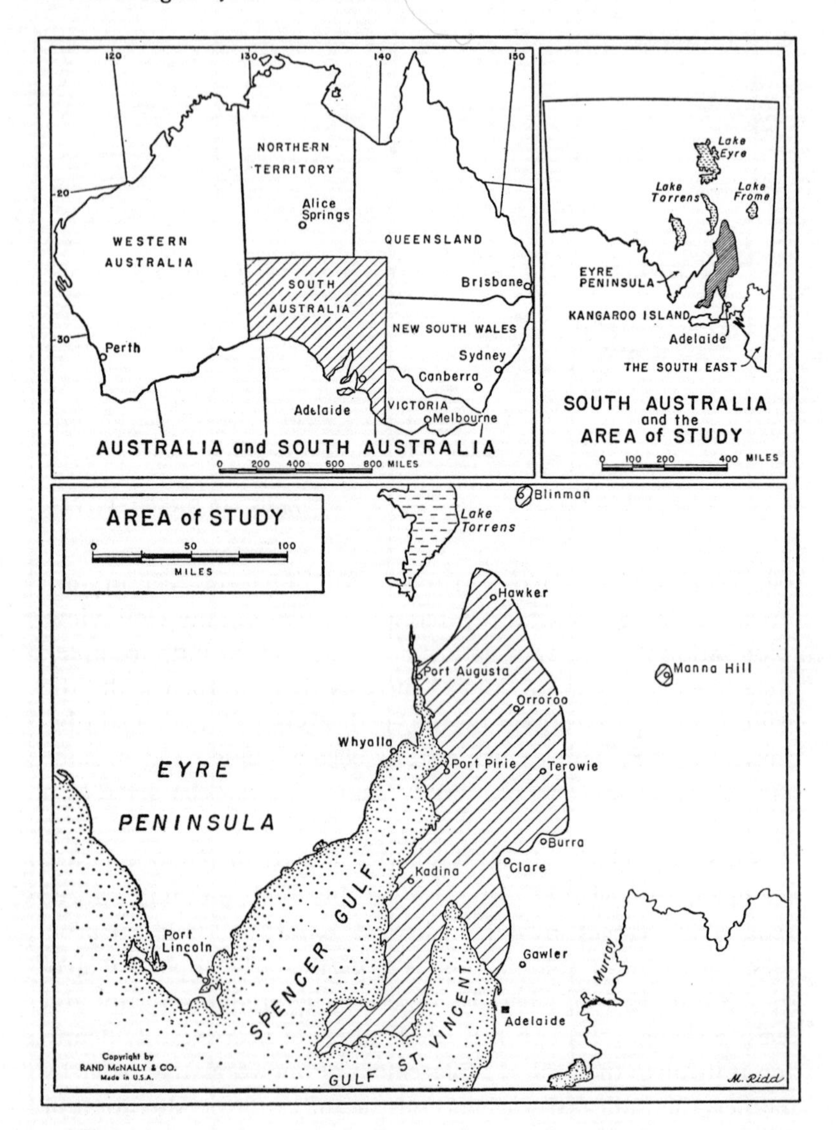
120
130
140
150
20
30
NORTHERN
TERRITORY
Alice
Springs
WESTERN
AUSTRALIA
QUEENSLAND
SOUTH
AUSTRALIA
Brisbane
NEW SOUTH WALES
Perth
Sydney
Canberra
Adelaide
VICTORIA
Melbourne
AUSTRALIA and SOUTH AUSTRALIA
0 200 400 600 800 MILES
Lake
Eyre
Lake
Torrens
Lake
Frome
EYRE
PENINSULA
KANGAROO ISLAND
Adelaide
THE SOUTH EAST
SOUTH AUSTRALIA
and the
AREA of STUDY
0 100 200 400 MILES
AREA of STUDY
0 50 100
MILES
Blinman
Lake
Torrens
Hawker
Port Augusta
Manna Hill
Orroroo
Whyalla
Port Pirie
Terowie
EYRE
PENINSULA
Burra
Clare
Kadina
SPENCER GULF
Port
Lincoln
Gawler
R. Murray
Adelaide
GULF ST. VINCENT
M. Ridd

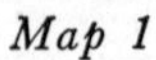

Map 1

a host of other less apparent but no less important ecological features. Likewise, by definition, it involves the imposition of a new plan of organization upon the land, the creation of new resources out of nature's materials, the spread of a new volume of population unevenly over the surface, the development of a new network of routeways, and the initiation of a new pulse and pattern of circulation throughout the region. In short, it necessarily results in a radically new geography.[2]

This is a study of some of these processes which did create a new geography in a particular portion of the earth (Map 1). Though localized in space it has a wider relevance for the study of its time, for this colonization was not an isolated, unique expansion but part of a world-wide movement. And though localized in time, it has a wider relevance for the study of this particular place, for the patterns established in these few years set a framework which endures in many respects to the present. Thus despite the narrow focus there are broader implications, both generic and genetic, and though these are not explored in this specialized study they do constitute the general context of inquiry. Before examing this particular tree, therefore, it will be well to reconnoiter, if but hastily, the general forest.

At the very time when the South Australian pioneer was experimenting with the northern wheatlands in his colony, other pioneers on other continents were doing essentially the same thing: in western Kansas and central Dakota; in Manitoba and Assiniboia; in the Walla Walla and the San Joaquin; in the eastern Ukraine and western Siberia; in the inner Pampa and on the High Veld. Obviously each of these colonizations had its peculiarities in land and people, institutions and processes, but, as obviously, each was not only concordant in time but comparable in type.[3] Nor need the selection of counterparts be so restricted

[2] For a more formal statement of such basic processes in "the evolution of space content" see Ackerman, *op. cit.*

[3] And such similarities are not only apparent in academic retrospect but were recognized by South Australians of that time who followed the progress of their counterparts and wheat-growing competitors elsewhere in the world with an intense, and somewhat fearful, interest. Some evidence of their concern will be related in subsequent chapters, but such references will no more than hint at the amount of attention devoted to the topic in the rural press of the day.

as to era and areas in the search for useful generalizations. On the other hand, the comparative study of such colonizations does require that special care be given to the selection of examples at comparable scales.

South Australia is the youngest offspring of the Australian branch of the British family, a child of the nineteenth century, reared in a remote, dry-summer subtropical environment. Such general facts of parentage, timing, and locale suggest the gross context of her development. Thus as a culture area South Australia is but one small segment of the "Neo-European World" – that heterogeneous collection of regions created by the transplanting of European peoples and institutions into positions of dominance in once alien lands.[4] But her parentage is not only European but British, and not only British but more narrowly of a particular segment of British society. South Australia obviously occupies a different place within the geographical patterns of cultural variation over the globe at each level within this hierarchy. Thus in the largest view her colonization may be measured against the commonplaces of European overseas settlement; at another level it may be compared with the general character of British practices; while more narrowly it is one of a half-dozen Australian ventures.

That this was a nineteenth-century colonization adds a further dimension to the context and another hierarchy for generalizations. The complexities of that great era of change defy summary statement, but developments in technology may be isolated for special emphasis. The concept of the Industrial Revolution, by itself, sets only the grossest kind of framework. But that revolution is an ongoing complex of changes so dynamic that each decade – indeed one might almost say each year – has been provided with a new set of tools cumulatively ever more varied and voluminous, each with its own special implications to the speed and efficiency, over-all character and pattern of developments. Mumford's triad of stages, "eotechnic," "palaeotechnic," and "neotechnic," pro-

[4] The concept of the Neo-European as one of the great "culture worlds" is briefly noted and mapped in Donald W. Meinig, "Culture Blocs and Political Blocs: Emergent Patterns in World Affairs," *Western Humanities Review,* X (Summer, 1956), 203–22.

vides a useful general periodization of such technological eras which can be further subdivided to serve comparisons on a finer scale.[5] The colonization of the northern wheatlands of South Australia not only occurred during the late phase of the palaeotechnic, it was a characteristic expression of that phase and could hardly have taken place prior to the development of the particular technological and economic complexes of that time. The whole world-wide movement of which this colonization was but one small part was concomitant with the mass production of iron and steel, the perfection of the railway, and the elaboration of a new array of farming machinery. These, coupled with the particular stage of European population growth and market developments, allowed such remote lands to be transformed almost immediately into specialized grain regions rather than gradually evolving through various stages from subsistence farming. It was in just such areas at just this time that the railway had a peculiarly important significance; here it was not so much an intruder modifying older regional patterns as a pioneer tool for the creation of almost wholly new ones. Such colonizations not only resulted in new areas of agriculture but in new kinds of agricultural regions created through new kinds of processes, and thus a careful sense of history with a close attention to such nonrepetitive technological stages is an essential part of the context of comparative colonization studies.

A third basic hierarchy of categories pertains to locale, in the sense not of position but of physical qualities. In the broadest relevant view South Australia is but one part of the global pattern of sub-humid, middle-latitude, "open" countries, lands which in their pre-European state were expanses of plain or gentle hill country covered with grasses or scrub forests. Such areas taken together constitute an environmental type only in the most general, but for some purposes a highly significant, sense. More narrowly and more clearly, this corner of the world is but one member

[5] Lewis Mumford, *Technics and Civilization* (New York: Harcourt, 1934), especially Chapters 3–5. The latter two terms were coined by Patrick Geddes (as Mumford notes) but it remained for Mumford to enlarge the perspective, add the "eotechnic," greatly elaborate upon the character and implications of each stage, and append the prospect of a "biotechnic" era which he hoped to be incipient.

of the "Mediterranean" lands, an environmental family rather sharply distinct in climate and somewhat less so in some other physical characteristics. But the Australian Mediterranean regions have their own peculiarities, most notably in soil and vegetation and in special vagaries of weather and climate; further, these regions of this one continent can obviously be subdivided according to more local sets of features. Certainly comparisons as to how European colonists have dealt with similar kinds of country in different parts of the earth ought to yield valuable results, but it must be recognized that to compare the northern wheatlands of South Australia with, say, the Red River Valley and Assiniboia, Capetown and the Karoo, or Swanland, is to compare at three different scales of environmental generalization.[6]

The possibilities latent in the comparative study of agricultural colonizations defy enumeration. Certainly such eras and areas are especially relevant to some of the grand themes of long-standing geographical interest; they are times when "man's role in changing the face of the earth"[7] was especially vivid and intense, and because they have resulted in the creation of a whole new set of spatial patterns and functions they represent marked stages in the "sequent occupance" of these regions.[8] In addition, these colonizations are intimately related to other great themes which have so far been neglected by geographers. Dawson's model "life

[6] Care in the selection of such analogues may seem an obvious kind of caution, but one need not select examples from the literature very carefully to suggest that, as obviously, it has been commonly abused. Marvin W. Mikesell has recently emphasized this point as well as many other matters relevant to the themes here emphasized in "Comparative Studies in Frontier History," *Annals of the Association of American Geographers,* L (March, 1960), 62–74.

[7] The volume by that name (Chicago: University of Chicago Press, 1956), edited by William L. Thomas, Jr., with the collaboration of Carl O. Sauer, Marston Bates, and Lewis Mumford, suggests the enormous range of fields of study and great variety of themes related to such a topic.

[8] The term "sequent occupance" was coined by Derwent Whittlesey. For further reference to this and to other themes and methods prominent in historical geography research see Andrew H. Clark, "Historical Geography," in Preston E. James and Clarence F. Jones, *American Geography: Inventory and Prospect* (Syracuse: Syracuse University Press, 1954), Chapter 3. In addition, Clark's major studies on New Zealand (*op. cit.*) and Prince Edward Island (*Three Centuries and the Island* [Toronto: University of Toronto Press, 1959]) are outstanding examples of colonization studies organized within a consistent general context.

cycle of a pioneer region,"[9] Turner's famous "influence of the frontier,"[10] and Webb's global concept of the "Great Frontier"[11] are merely a few of the more prominent examples on a local, national, and world scale, respectively. Each of these is a hypothesis which not only has profound geographical implications but which needs to be tested and illuminated by geographical research.[12]

But if regions may be logically analogous in general, more narrowly they are inherently unique. Though it is important that South Australia be viewed within a broadly-constructed context, it is just as essential that the details of her own local experience be carefully examined, for, ultimately, all generalizations must be grounded upon what actually happened when a particular group of people colonized a particular part of the earth in a particular manner at a particular time. Which is simply to say that, basically, history and geography must be written "not from the top down, but from the bottom up," and therefore local studies are "not only respectable, [they are] vital to sound" studies at any level.[13] Because this phase of South Australian colonization has not been so examined before, this study offers an array of new details which may serve to refine and alter prevailing general conclusions about such movements which have heretofore been based only upon a limited number of the possible examples. It is precisely in this way that "by being thoroughly provincial," one may hope "to broaden the view."

[9] C. A. Dawson, assisted by R. W. Murchie, *The Settlement of the Peace River Country* (Toronto: Macmillan, 1934), pp. 1–13, Vol. 6 of W. A. Mackintosh and W. L. G. Joerg, eds., *Canadian Frontiers of Settlement* (9 Vols.; Toronto: Macmillan, 1934–40). Dawson specifically restricts his model to the Anglo-American grasslands, but its applicability elsewhere needs to be explored.

[10] Frederick Jackson Turner, "The Significance of the Frontier in American History," *Annual Report of the American Historical Association for 1893* (Washington, D. C., 1894), pp. 199–227. The literature on the Turner thesis is of course voluminous. A recent excellent bibliography is that in Ray Allen Billington, *Westward Expansion,* (2nd ed.; New York: Macmillan, 1960), pp. 762–64.

[11] Walter Prescott Webb, *The Great Frontier* (Boston: Houghton, 1951–52).

[12] Mikesell's article, *op. cit.,* gives special attention to the Turner thesis as a theme in comparative colonization studies.

[13] Because I believe that the nature of geography is fundamentally analogous to that of history, I have joined it with history in these phrases taken from James Malin's succinct statement "On the Nature of Local History," *Wisconsin Magazine of History* (Summer, 1957), 227–30.

II.

Colonization: The South Australian Context[1]

> Other parts of Australia may muddle through in the best British tradition: South Australians zealously attach themselves to some conscious theoretical purpose . . .
>
> — DOUGLAS PIKE
> *Paradise of Dissent,* p. v

FORMULATION AND INITIATION

South Australia may be said to have been rationalized in plan before it was discovered on land. Just as Terra Australis was theorized upon the map before its existence was known in fact, so the idea of a colony such as South Australia was conceived in theory without regard for the eventual place of birth. Only quite fortuitously did the southern coast of the great southern continent soon appear as an auspicious locale for parturition. This matter of beginnings is important because an unusual emphasis upon theoretical planning became the most distinguishing feature of the colony, and it established a heritage which continued to shape developments long after the founding years.

Although Douglas Pike's observation that "a great part of the writing of South Australian history has been devoted to finding the founder" implicitly warns of the complexity of origins, any

[1] The resumé of the background and early years of the colony is based primarily upon A. Grenfell Price, *The Foundation and Settlement of South Australia 1829–1845* (Adelaide: Preece, 1924) and Douglas Pike, *Paradise of Dissent, South Australia 1829–1857* (London: Longmans, 1957). See Bibliographic Note for further comment.

summary statement must concentrate on the role of Edward Gibbon Wakefield. Wakefield first turned his attention to the problems of colonization during a sojourn in a London prison in the late 1820's. His narrow escape from having been transported to an Australian penal colony may well have initiated his interest, but the general topic was a lively one in England at the time. The grievous social and economic disruptions of the homeland and the perplexing problem of rationalizing a highly varied and widely scattered imperial domain were insistent challenges to practicing politicians and social theorists alike. To some, an orderly scheme of colonization appeared to offer at least a partial solution to both problems.

The English were certainly not short on experience in colonization, yet it was impossible to find any precedent among all their efforts which might serve as a model of success. All the varied American colonizations were overshadowed by the spectre of political revolt. Canada offered no reliable prescription, the recent Albany scheme in Cape Colony was already a disappointment, while the Australian penal colonies were the despair of any social theorist. The freshest example, the Swan River colony on the west coast of Australia, seemed clearly to expose certain basic flaws. There an enormous extent of land had been sold to English speculators, but no provisions had been made to induce emigration and the scheme was faced with utter stagnation. In 1829 Wakefield gave close attention to this venture, consulted and corresponded with many men of like interests, and began to piece together his theory of "systematic colonization." Largely by his initiative the National Colonization Society was formed in 1830, numbering among its members or informal associates such prominent men as Jeremy Bentham and John Stuart Mill.

The basic principles of colonization which came to be identified as the "Wakefield theory"[2] were as follows:

1. Land should be sold at a fixed minimum price or above.
2. The proceeds of land sales should be used primarily to subsidize the emigration of *bona fide* colonists.

[2] Wakefield was an eclectic and by no means responsible for each idea, yet he, more than any of his colleagues, sought a comprehensive balanced "system."

3. The volume and pace of emigration should be closely correlated with the amount of land available.
4. Settlement should expand in contiguous blocks (the principle of "concentration").
5. A large measure of local self-government in matters of selection of officials, land sales, emigration, and revenue was essential.

Implicit were the doctrine of prior survey and an emphasis upon family colonization to prevent the evils of "squatting," speculation, and the involuntary emigration of prisoners and bond-servants. Numerous other features also appeared as these ideas were elaborated in theory and faced the prospect of actual test. Ultimately, it has been noted, Wakefield "envisioned the transplanting, not of a seedling, but of the full grown tree of English society, root, trunk, and branch."[3]

As the theory took shape its enthusiasts sought some virgin ground where it could be given a fair trial. Australia had from the first been an area of special interest, and when word was received late in 1830 that Captain Charles Sturt had traced a great river debouching near Gulf St. Vincent on the southern coast, the promoters seized upon this as a most eligible locale. "What is known of the climate, soil, capacity of production, and local situation of Gulf Vincent is of the most flattering nature," wrote Wakefield in his famous *First Paper* of December, 1830.[4] Actually, precious little was yet known about such matters, but the idea of a colony in southern Australia was firmly established from this date. With both a plan and a place in hand the next move was to gain the approval of the British government. After nearly four years of difficult negotiation an act to establish South Australia as a British province was obtained.[5] But this success was achieved only at the expense of serious compromise. Most of the basic elements of the Wakefield theory remained intact, but the principle of self-government was denied, and a set of Crown-appointed officials was superimposed upon the colonization company. Thus the

[3] Pike, *op. cit.*, p. 495.
[4] Quoted from a portion reproduced as the frontispiece in Price, *op. cit.*
[5] The most important provisions of the act are reprinted in C. M. H. Clark, *Select Documents in Australian History* (Sydney: Angus, 1950), Vol. I, pp. 204–8.

theorists lost control over the management of the delicately complex land, emigration, and revenue system, and this was to prove a seriously disruptive factor. Further, an unforeseen speculative element was introduced to meet the Crown requirement of an advance deposit of certain cash guarantees. Such money could be raised only by special privileged land sales and these compromised not only the land-emigration balance but also, through provisions for "special surveys," the doctrine of concentration. Nevertheless, with the passage of this act in 1834 intensive preparations for the actual colonization were undertaken with great expectations. Bentham's proposal to christen the new land "Felicitania" had not been accepted, but the exuberant idealism it symbolized flourished unabated under the more prosaic "South Australia."

Considerably more detailed information about the area had been obtained during these years of negotiation. Sturt, the most knowledgeable of the explorers, had been directly consulted. His evaluations of the general area were favorable and he recommended specifically the lands along the east side of the Gulf St. Vincent as the best location for initial settlement. On the basis of diverse accumulations of fact, opinion, and inference, various influential leaders of the colony soon became vociferous promoters of other locales. Port Lincoln, Kangaroo Island, and the Murray mouth were the leading alternatives to Sturt's proposal (Map 2). The final decision, however, rested solely upon the Surveyor General, Colonel William Light, who arrived with the vanguard in late 1836. After an intensive but hurried reconnaissance Light selected the site of Adelaide, at the margin of the plains near the base of Mt. Lofty, six miles inland from Gulf St. Vincent. In January, 1837, he began to lay out the design of the capital and to block out control points for the survey of rural settlement areas in the uplands to the south.

Light's choice of the site for Adelaide, the crucial geographical decision of the whole venture, was based upon careful reasoning. The Surveyor General was not only well trained for the tasks of his office, but was also a veteran of considerable experience in southern Europe which gave him a valuable insight into the kind of country with which he was dealing. Water, soils, forests, the

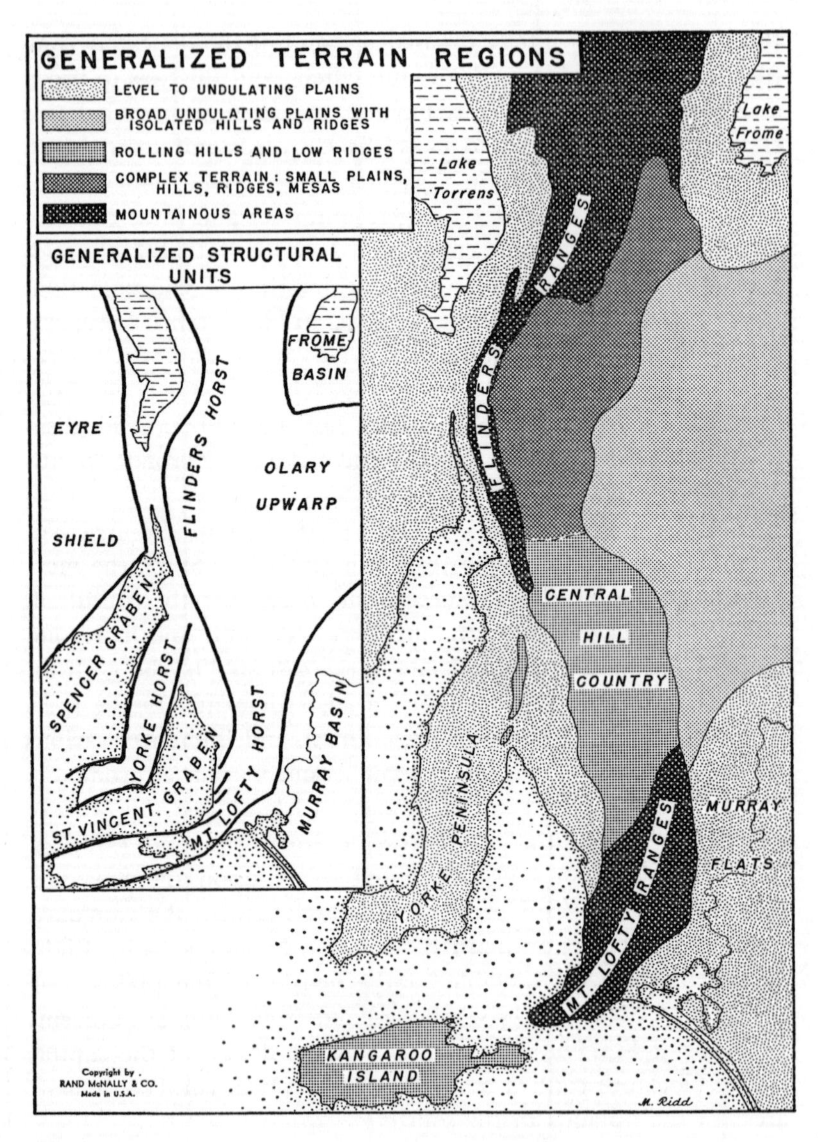
GENERALIZED TERRAIN REGIONS
LEVEL TO UNDULATING PLAINS
BROAD UNDULATING PLAINS WITH ISOLATED HILLS AND RIDGES
ROLLING HILLS AND LOW RIDGES
COMPLEX TERRAIN: SMALL PLAINS, HILLS, RIDGES, MESAS
MOUNTAINOUS AREAS
GENERALIZED STRUCTURAL UNITS
FROME BASIN
EYRE
SHIELD
FLINDERS HORST
OLARY UPWARP
SPENCER GRABEN
YORKE HORST
ST. VINCENT GRABEN
MT. LOFTY HORST
MURRAY BASIN
Lake Torrens
Lake Frome
FLINDERS RANGES
CENTRAL HILL COUNTRY
YORKE PENINSULA
MT. LOFTY RANGES
MURRAY FLATS
KANGAROO ISLAND
M. Ridd

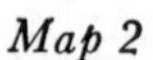

Map 2

"lay of the land," and the adjacency of a good natural harbor were basic local criteria, but inferences about the probable climatic pattern and the productivity of and accessibility to an extensive hinterland were also important considerations.

THE PHYSICAL SETTING

A fairly accurate impression of the general surficial physical patterns of coastal South Australia was gained within a few months of arrival, and inland reconnaissances soon extended the limits of knowledge. Many of these readily apparent features reflected the gross structure of what has become known as the South Australian "shatter belt," a complex series of north-south trending faults east of the stable shield of Eyre Peninsula. These have resulted in a sequence of narrow, longitudinal embayments, peninsulas, and mountain ranges which are a striking anomaly along the generally smooth southern coastline of the continent. From west to east the main components of this system are the graben occupied by Spencer Gulf in the south and Lake Torrens in the north; the narrow horst of Yorke Peninsula; the St. Vincent graben; and the major uplift curving northward from Kangaroo Island through the Mt. Lofty and Flinders ranges. East of the latter lie the extensive alluvial basins of the Murray and Lake Frome, separated by the broad gentle upwarp of Olary Ridge (Map 2, inset).[6] These several physical units display a considerable variety of land surfaces. Yorke Peninsula is a low, gently undulating strip about 125 miles long and 20–25 miles wide. It is nearly devoid of streams, which adds to the monotony of its texture. At its northeastern base the Barunga Range, a long, narrow, rounded ridge, marks its structural connection with the mainland. The Mt. Lofty ranges, on the other hand, present an abrupt face to the sea along the Fleurieu Peninsula and stand as a continuous highland, locally downfaulted and eroded into small basins and valleys, with an

[6] The material on physical features and structure has been based upon Charles Fenner, *South Australia: A Geographical Study* (Melbourne and Sydney: Whitcomb & Tombs, 1931), M. F. Glaessner and L. W. Parkin, eds., *The Geology of South Australia* (Melbourne: Melbourne University Press, 1958), and A. K. Lobeck, Joseph Gentilli, Rhodes W. Fairbridge, *Physiographic Diagram of Australia* (New York: The Geographical Press, Columbia University, 1951).

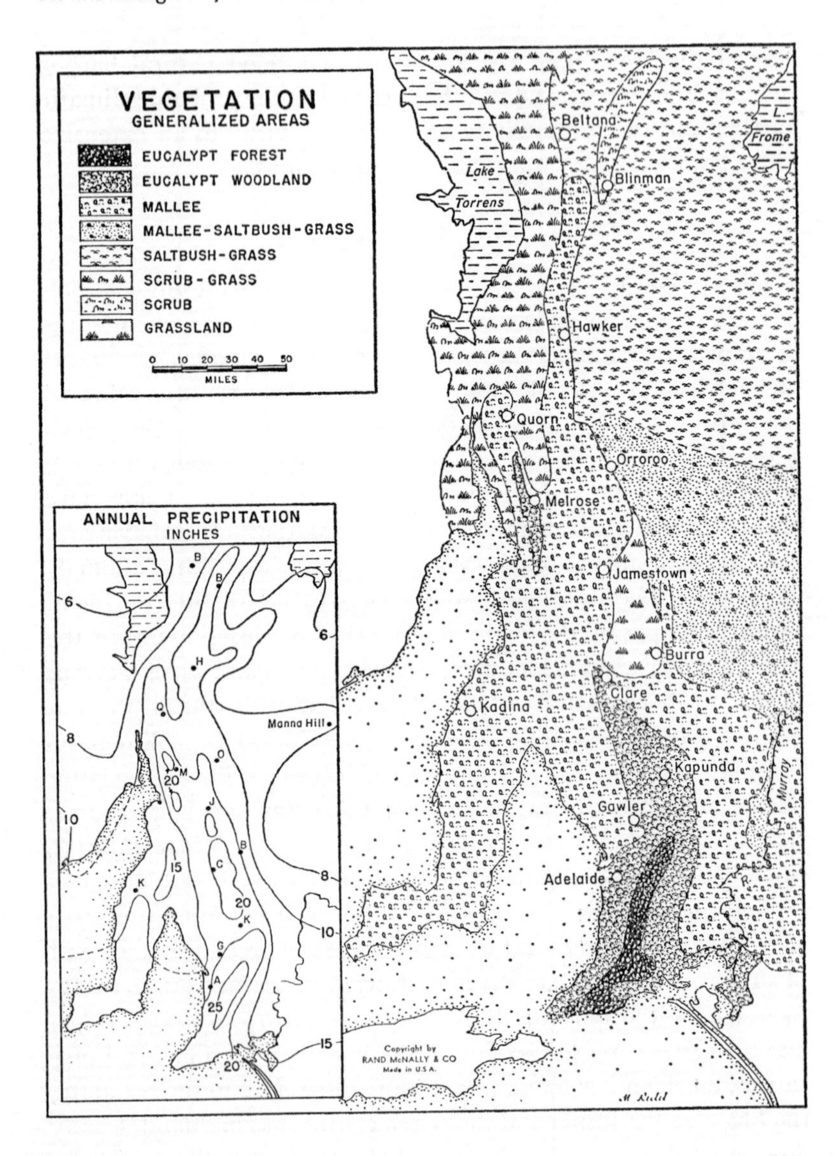
VEGETATION
GENERALIZED AREAS
EUCALYPT FOREST
EUCALYPT WOODLAND
MALLEE
MALLEE-SALTBUSH-GRASS
SALTBUSH-GRASS
SCRUB-GRASS
SCRUB
GRASSLAND
0 10 20 30 40 50
MILES
ANNUAL PRECIPITATION
INCHES
Manna Hill
Lake
Torrens
L.
Frome
Beltana
Blinman
Hawker
Quorn
Orroroo
Melrose
Jamestown
Burra
Clare
Kadina
Kapunda
Gawler
Adelaide
Murray
Copyright by
RAND McNALLY & CO
Made in U.S.A.

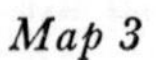
Map 3

average crestline of about 1500 feet. Northward this western scarp continues to be sharply apparent for some sixty miles, fronted now by the broadening, gently rolling alluvial plains which have filled the upper end of the St. Vincent embayment (Fig. 1). Farther north the character of this highland changes. The underlying base is upwarped, while the general highland relief diminishes, resulting in a hill country marked by a series of disconnected, parallel, low ridges, intervening alluvial basins, and an intricate pattern of somewhat trellised minor stream courses. Beginning near the head of Spencer Gulf, the Flinders Range stands as a third section of this highland system. Here an even more abrupt western escarpment, higher elevation, and sharp-angled arid erosion combine to present a more truly mountainous appearance. The eastern sides of both the Mt. Lofty and Flinders ranges are less sharply marked than the western. The Flinders section, especially, frays out into a complex of local ridges, mesas, residual hills, and broad arid basins (Fig. 2).

A general Mediterranean type of climate had been inferred for this area in the early years of exploration. The mild wet winters and hot dry summers had been likened to the seasons of southern Europe, prompting the promoters of the colony to envision the production of such characteristic crops as citrus, olives, and wine-grapes. However, initial impressions of Eyre and Yorke peninsulas and Kangaroo Island and the common scarcity of surface waters immediately raised concern over the generally arid appearances. That this dryness intensified northward was obvious at any season. If indeed "Mediterranean," too much of South Australia seemed to have more in common with Tripolitania than Tuscany. Both Sturt and Light reasoned that the Mt. Lofty ranges would have a marked effect upon the pattern of precipitation, and the choice of the windward plains and the southern highland for initial settlement was dictated strongly by a desire for the security of the most humid country. This inference about the precipitation pattern was soon confirmed by experience (Map 3, inset).[7]

[7] This isohyetal map is based upon "Map of South Australia Showing the Principal Land Utilization Zones, June 1959," Department of Lands, South Australia.

The Mediterranean character of the seasons was also confirmed by experience and, while it bolstered the promise of certain kinds of agricultural productions, it also imposed some rather severe problems of adjustment. The proper calendar rhythms of farming practices had to be worked out by experiment; less critical but more taxing upon all was the adjustment of attitudes and the commonplace routines of living. The long summer drought with its brilliant sunshine and temperatures which soared well past 100°F were a searing experience, a season "more like gehenna than paradise" for these English migrants who "quickly stopped sighing for the summer sun and yearned for the first winter rains."[8] Through a long portion of the year customary clothing and shelter were drastically inappropriate, fresh food quickly spoiled, carefully nurtured flowers and shrubs from home withered, water vanished into the air, and a spark was a fearful agent of destruction in the brittle-dry countryside. This radically different climate and calendar (how incongruous a sweltering Christmas must have seemed) should have been an insistent warning that no matter how carefully and thoroughly designed was the colonization theory, one could not really make a "little England" out of such a land.

The natural vegetation provides some further basis for the early inferences about the patterns of climate and contributed to the strangeness of the countryside. The immediate locale of Adelaide was an open woodland area, almost savannah-like; the density of the trees increased along the lower highland slopes and the forest became almost continuous at higher elevations (Map 3).[9] The climatic implications of this vegetation-elevation relationship were commonplace, but the actual appearance of these

[8] Pike, *op. cit.*, p. 498.

[9] Published maps of Australian vegetation vary greatly in categories and regional boundaries. I have drawn primarily upon the work of J. G. Wood, "The Vegetation of South Australia," in Rupert J. Best, ed., *Introducing South Australia* (Adelaide: Australia and New Zealand Association for the Advancement of Science, 1958), pp. 84–95, and R. T. Williams, "Vegetation Region," map and commentary, in the *Atlas of Australian Resources* (Canberra: Department of National Development, 1955). My colleague, Professor David J. de Laubenfels, also gave valuable advice on many points. None of these sources, however, are responsible for the generalized categories and boundaries shown; these have been chosen solely to depict the kinds of regional differences which are most significant to this particular study.

landscapes was not, for unless they had already touched some other Australian shore the colonists could have seen nothing which closely resembled the towering, branching, slender-leaved gum trees (eucalyptus) which dominated all such country. To the English settlers these woodlands presented a strangely shaggy and disheveled appearance, and when they began to put them to use their twisted, iron-like trunks seemed an exasperatingly intractable material. Even more unusual, however, was the growth on the plains, North of Adelaide, on Yorke Peninsula, in much of the central hill country, and east of the ranges toward the Murray, the lowlands were covered by the "mallee," a scrub forest of peculiar eucalypts which branch from a thick, shallow root into an umbrella-like cluster of stems and canopy. Varying in height from six to twenty-five feet, and in density from a near thicket to an open scattering, these trees, together with lesser bushes and grass, mantled the plains with a cover uniquely Australian (Fig. 3). In a few localities north of Adelaide and in the central hills north of the Mt. Lofty ranges, the mallee markedly thinned and gave way to patches of grassland. Much farther north and northeast it was replaced by other types of scrub forest or by saltbush, but such lands were well beyond the reach of the early settlers.

The relative scarcity of reliable streams was yet another strikingly different feature of this new homeland. Only the Mt. Lofty ranges support a fairly dense succession of perennial streams; but they are short, small, and even the more lengthy, from the Torrens to the Wakefield, ooze sluggishly across the lower plains with hardly sufficient volume or velocity to reach the sea (Map 4). The central hill country is drained by the River Broughton, which has a more extensive basin than any to the south, but with so little water that through much of the year many of its tributaries are little more than a tracing of gullies shallowly incised into the red earth. Farther north the Flinders arc trends so near the coast that its westward drainage is but a series of small creeks. In its lee Willochra Creek drains northward to a series of small plains, bending through a gap in the range to Lake Torrens – but creek and lake carry water only in the wet season. Along the whole eastern margin of the uplands there is a disconnected sequence of intermittent stream courses which quickly dwindle and merge

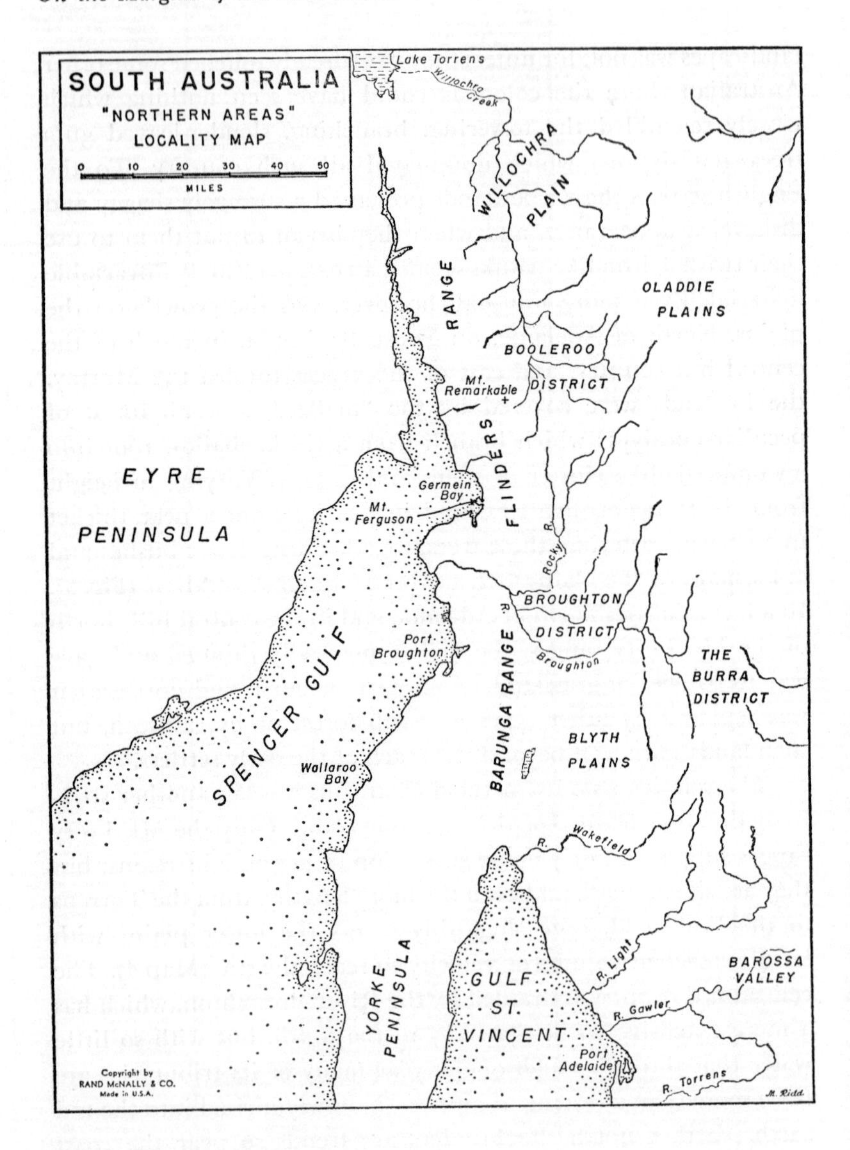
SOUTH AUSTRALIA
"NORTHERN AREAS"
LOCALITY MAP
0 10 20 30 40 50
MILES
Lake Torrens
Willochra Creek
WILLOCHRA
PLAIN
RANGE
OLADDIE
PLAINS
BOOLEROO
DISTRICT
Mt.
Remarkable
FLINDERS
EYRE
PENINSULA
Germein
Bay
Mt.
Ferguson
Rocky R.
BROUGHTON
DISTRICT
R. Broughton
Port
Broughton
THE
BURRA
DISTRICT
SPENCER GULF
BARUNGA RANGE
BLYTH
PLAINS
Wallaroo
Bay
R. Wakefield
YORKE
PENINSULA
GULF
ST.
VINCENT
R. Light
BAROSSA
VALLEY
R. Gawler
Port
Adelaide
R. Torrens
Copyright by
RAND McNALLY & CO.
Made in U.S.A.
M. Ridd

Map 4

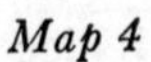

Fig. 1 The alluvial plains northeast from the head of St. Vincent Gulf. The view is from the edge of the Central Hill Country overlooking Hoyleton station westward to the Barunga Range on the horizon. (1958)

Fig. 2 The Booleroo district, a local plains section lying between the Flinders Range and a series of residual hills and ridges to the east, as appear in the distant background. (1958)

Fig. 3 Mallee northeast of Port Broughton, in a small area of sandy soil either never cleared or at least not farmed for many decades. (1958)

into the broad plains surface. By any English standard water was nowhere plentiful; beyond the southern highlands it was at least seasonally scarce; and at no great distance to the north or east true aridity impinged with increasing severity.

EARLY DEVELOPMENTS

Altogether it was a strange kind of land to its colonists. Inevitably some were bitterly disappointed from the moment of disembarking; many dismissed the whole region as suitable only for grazing; but others set to work to test the soil and seasons. Actually, for two years the rigidities of the land allocation system and the utterly inadequate provisions for surveying delayed rural settlement and little more than garden plots in Adelaide were attempted. Not until about 1842 could agriculture be said to have gotten well underway. By that time some crops had been dismissed as unsuitable (e.g., bananas, pineapples, dates) others appeared promising (e.g., oranges and wine-grapes), and one, wheat, was clearly established as a basic local if not as yet an export agricultural staple. Considerable numbers of sheep and cattle had also been shipped in or driven overland from eastern Australia. All this initial effort was concentrated either in the immediate vicinity of the capital or in the valleys and vales of the uplands to the south. As these districts yielded well there was no inducement to test the plains country northward. The disinclination to turn any efforts in that direction was further strengthened by the reports of explorations further inland. Early encounters with the plains to the east and with the dismal salt beds and desolation of the Lake Torrens vicinity gave rise to the "fertile island" theory which viewed the colony as a small nucleus bound to the southern hills, narrowly separated by a periphery of poor grazing lands from the boundless deserts of the interior. Momentarily, in the early 1840's, it was believed by many in the colony as well as in England that the supply of arable land would soon be exhausted.

This narrow outlook coincided with, or perhaps was partly a reflection of, a more general crisis in the colony. The "mischief of double government," an inflexible adherence to some of the theoretical features of the plan which proved unrealistic in practice, together with a host of special problems had resulted in the financial bankruptcy of the original program, the cessation of emigration, and the imposition of complete Crown control in 1842. Actually the over-all ideal of the founders lay at the root of much of the difficulty. The vision of directly transplanting rather than gradually evolving a full social order inevitably led to an overemphasis upon the creation of a model capital city with a full urban society, and the comparative neglect of rural industries. The result was a top-heavy superstructure unsupported by sufficient primary production. Of the total population of 16,000 in 1842, half lived in Adelaide while those in the countryside were still scratching out a bare subsistence in the initial phases of agricultural pioneering. A drastic reduction in this overhead was essential and while it was a severe blow to the subsidized urban economy it did drive more people onto the land to the ultimate benefit of all.

In retrospect the whole scheme actually appears remarkably successful. Colonial beginnings are always difficult, but the observation that "in Australia every beginning has not only been difficult, but scarred with human agony and squalor"[10] hardly rings true for South Australia. Despite financial distress, administrative confusion, and environmental experimentation, a solid nucleus was established in these first years which, compared with other beginnings on the continent, was quite exceptional: a family-based, self-consciously Christian, middle-class society, diverse in skills, imbued with energy, untainted by either the evils of gross speculation or penal servitude. However far short of achieving their full ideal, South Australians, by and large, ever thereafter would maintain a conscious pride in the distinctiveness of their heritage.

The stagnation of the early 1840's was short-lived. An important factor was the discovery and development of major copper deposits at Kapunda and Burra. These stimulated an inflow of people and capital once more and not only expanded the market for agricultural produce but for the first time focused settlement interests toward the more northerly hill country. Even more significant was the invention of a successful mechanical reaper by

[10] C. M. H. Clark, *op. cit.*, "Introduction," p. 94.

John Ridley in 1843.[11] This famous "stripper" was a radical "breakthrough" for agricultural progress, and over the next few years wheat rapidly gained on wool as a staple export.

In the next decade major gold discoveries in neighboring Victoria were a further stimulus to progress. Nearly half a million people flocked into that colony during the 1850's, the first big reverberation in the chain reaction of the California gold rush. Melbourne, Bendigo, and Ballarat mushroomed into excellent markets for South Australian produce. Adelaide was soon a major center of deposit and export of Victorian gold and thrived as a commercial entrepôt throughout the decade. Rural industries were stimulated not only because of the profitable outlets but because much of the profits of both farm and city were invested in land. Settlement expanded northward for the first time with any vigor, still slowly on the plains but rapidly in the hill country beyond the Barossa Valley. Just how much farther agriculture could be extended in that direction was debatable but certainly the pessimism of earlier years had been displaced. Beyond the farming zone, pastoralists had established flocks and stations over the whole of the gulf plains, the central hills, the southern Flinders, and along the margins of the Murray basin.

By the end of the decade the turmoil of the gold years was over and the contributions to progress were clearly evident. More than 350,000 acres were in cropland (75 per cent of it in wheat) and there were just under three million sheep. Population had doubled in ten years to a total of 125,000, with now but a third concentrated in the metropolis. Exports neared £2,000,000 and the balance of trade was markedly favorable. A broad-gauge (5′3″) railroad had been built from Port Adelaide to the capital and on northeastwardly to the copper district at Kapunda. Most important, perhaps, was the fact that developments had reached a sufficient scale and prosperity to engender the grant of local self-government in 1856. Thereafter, the designs for colonization expansion and development would be drawn up in South Australia's own legislature.

[11] A. R. Callaghan and A. J. Millington, *The Wheat Industry in Australia* (Sydney: Angus, 1956), pp. 337–43.

NEW PROBLEMS OF COLONIZATION

The pace of progress was slowed in the 1860's. The most dramatic event was a drought of unprecedented severity beginning in 1864. The farmers escaped relatively unscathed, but the pastoralists suffered severe losses. Their distress led to a comprehensive examination of the tenure regulations affecting the grazing lands. The deliberations largely consisted of an assessment of the facts and recommendations supplied by the Surveyor General, G. M. Goyder, who made an extensive reconnaissance of all the stricken pastoral districts. A revision of the laws was passed which established a qualitative classification of grazing lands, and nominal fixed rentals and rights of renewal on leases of Crown lands.[12] With this rationalization of the regulations and the relaxation of the drought the wool industry soon rebounded.

At the same time, however, a less dramatic but more important crisis was developing in the other major segment of the economy. Despite the fact that wool was more important in export value, wheat, not wool, was the prime concern of the colony.[13] Wool was profitable, but directly so only to a small portion of the population, and South Australia was far overshadowed in its production by other colonies; Victoria had twice and New South Wales three times as many sheep.[14] But in wheat South Australia was preeminent, with half the total acreage of the continent and twice that of Victoria, her nearest rival.[15] Wheat was being exported to Victoria, New South Wales, Queensland, Mauritius, and South Africa, and sporadic shipments to England had proved successful. The importance of wheat could not really be measured in purely commercial terms, however. Wheat was of prime concern simply because it was the farming staple, and in South Australia the farmer, not the stockman, was given priority of importance. Such a view obviously reflected the ideals of the founders in which the

[12] S. H. Roberts, *History of Australian Land Settlement (1788–1920)* (Melbourne: Melbourne University Press, 1924), pp. 254–55.

[13] The proportions of total exports by declared value in 1869 were: wool 33 per cent, wheat and flour 30 per cent, and minerals 21 per cent.

[14] Clark, *op. cit.*, Vol. II, p. 176. These proportions refer to the middle 1860's.

[15] Edgars Dunsdorfs, *The Australian Wheat Growing Industry 1788–1948* (Melbourne: Melbourne University Press, 1956), p. 532. Unless otherwise noted, all comparative statistics on wheat in the several states are from this source.

family-sized freehold farm and concentrated rural settlement were basic. In contrast, the grazing industry, speculative, dispersed, often absentee-controlled, employing wage labor, and holding land by lease rather than title, was almost a contradiction of those ideals, and despite its economic significance it was never to have the great power and prestige it enjoyed in all the other Australian colonies. Wheat had been the firm foundation of development and it was regarded as the great medium of future progress: "the more they grew, . . . the sooner would their population increase, and the province be generally benefited."[16] It was, indeed, a prime governmental responsibility to foster a continual expansion of its production. To those few who had the temerity to suggest that "we are cultivating wheat in South Australia to too great an extent," the Chief Secretary replied bluntly: "I do not believe it possible to do so."[17] That he spoke for the great majority, the debates and votes in the legislature leave no doubt.

But the very fact of parliamentary concern over wheat was an indication that all was not well in the latter 1860's. Colonization had markedly slowed and in 1868 the statistics showed the distressing fact that the total acreage in wheat was actually less than in the previous year. That specific decline could be attributed to temporary causes, to drought and a heavy incidence of rust the year before. But what made the situation really serious was the realization that settlers were actually leaving the province, not because of any natural hazards, but in search of new farms on more liberal terms. In Victoria, especially, new land policies and the opening of the fertile lands of the Wimmera district had already lured a considerable number of some of South Australia's best farm families.[18] Moreover, concomitantly the market situa-

[16] *South Australian Parliamentary Debates,* Oct. 7, 1868, col. 575.

[17] *Ibid.,* Oct. 6, 1868, col. 532–33.

[18] *Ibid.,* 1868, cols. 532, 575, 659; *South Australian Parliamentary Paper No. 124* (1867). Many of these emigrants were Germans, who had the reputation of being the best farmers in the colony. This group was the only significant non-British element in the province, totaling about 7 per cent of the population at the time. The removal of the nucleus of this group to South Australia was sponsored and partially financed by George Fife Angas, one of the principal promoters of the Wakefield scheme. The initial settlements of these East German Lutherans were near Adelaide; later they also colonized the Barossa Valley and became leaders in viticulture and orcharding. A. Grenfell Price, *Founders and Pioneers of South Australia* (Adelaide: Preece, 1929),

tion would be adversely affected, for Victoria seemed certain to change quickly from an importer of wheat into a rival exporter. Of the other areas of disposal only England provided a rapidly expanding market. Yet there too, at this very time, South Australia was confronted with a formidable new competitor, for in the wake of the California gold rush the Sacramento Valley was becoming one of the world's important grain regions, with England as its principal market. Thus the scale and efficiency of Californian agriculture had become matters of pressing concern for South Australia.

A NEW LAW FOR NEW LANDS

These threatening rivalries became the central issue before Parliament in the spring of 1868:

> As compared with other colonies and with the large wheat-growing country of California, the circumstances of South Australia have so far changed that it becomes necessary for us to consider carefully our present position. (Cheers).[19]

It was a time for some changes, perhaps, yet certainly not for despair, for the positive advantages of South Australia seemed nature-given and secure:

> None of the Australian colonies were so suitable for growing wheat as this colony. They had a coast line, which removed much difficulty as to the cost of transit, their climate was well adapted for the use of the reaping machine, and their wheat was got off the land in better condition for shipment than that of California. Now, the colony was pre-eminently an agricultural country, and if the same facilities were given here for cultivation as were in Victoria, New South Wales, and California, South Australia would take the leading place for agriculture.[20]

The principal "facilities" needed were new land policies which would attract large numbers of farmer colonists by means of liberal allotments at low cost. Were such a change made, it was

Chapters 3 and 8; Charles A. Price, *German Settlers in South Australia* (Melbourne: Melbourne University Press, 1945); Glen D. Weaver and H. F. Raup, "Colonial Germans in South Australia," *Journal of Geography*, LVIII (November, 1959), 369–80. Keith W. Thomson, "The Settlement Pattern of the Barossa Valley, South Australia," *The Australian Geographer*, VII (November, 1957), 51–58, discusses the German imprint upon that area.

[19] Statement of the Chief Secretary, *S. A. Parl. Debates*, Oct. 6, 1868, col. 530.

[20] *Ibid.*, col. 568.

confidently assumed that there would remain "nothing to prevent our growing wheat at prices which would be ruinous to other places."[21]

The policy then current reflected its Wakefield heritage. The doctrine of survey prior to selection had been rigorously adhered to; several counties had been established, but sales were made only within "hundreds," a basic survey unit of approximately one hundred square miles which was further subdivided into farm units averaging about eighty acres. As new hundreds were normally "proclaimed" only in areas contiguous to older settlements the principle of concentration was maintained.[22] Land could only be purchased at cash auctions. The legal minimum offering price was £1 per acre, but the government was empowered to set a higher price for the better lands and the auction system usually further increased the price greatly. Although a few huge pastoral estates had been accumulated, generally these regulations had fostered the settlement of medium-sized family-operated freeholds as intended. Further, the government rather than private speculators had received the benefits of any initial competition for land, which funds were then available to subsidize public works. Yet it was apparent that high prices and prepayment were now strong deterrents to rapid colonization.

If the need for change was clear, the exact nature of the desirable change was highly controversial. Such a bewildering variety of plans was proposed that the delegate who observed that "there were as many schemes on the land question as there were members" was not far from the literal truth.[23] Few, however, supported any really radical departures from the basic philosophy of colonization. The extreme liberality of American practice was cited but rejected as inappropriate despite recognition of its enormous success in attracting immigrants.[24] And in large part it was unsuited, for the situation and importance of the pastoral industry was

[21] *Ibid.*, col. 533.

[22] The hundred was an ancient territorial division in some counties of England. See *S. A. Parl. Paper No. 158* (1860) on its origin and application locally.

[23] *S. A. Parl. Debates*, Oct. 7, 1868, col. 583.

[24] *Ibid.*, col. 575. The liberal American pre-emption laws were noted, though no one seems to have called attention to the recent Homestead Act which granted clear title to 160 acres at no cost after five years of residence.

markedly different in the two countries. Chiefly, however, their own heritage simply made the American system irrelevant, for the dynamic flux of American colonization must have seemed an unenviable maelstrom when compared to the Wakefield ideal of careful governmental control over the quality, quantity, pace, and direction of settlement.[25] What was wanted was simply the least modification of the old which would meet the new needs of the times.

The principal issues debated were: the level of the offering price; whether to have a fixed price or continue auctions; whether to adhere to cash prepayment or allow sales on credit, the optimum size of allotments, how to continue to encourage compact settlement, how to combat the evils of speculation, "dummying," and "peacocking,"[26] and how to arrange an orderly expansion of agriculture into areas of pastoral leases.

Out of a welter of proposals and lengthy debate a composite measure known officially as the Waste Lands Amendment Act, and popularly as the "Strangways Act," was finally passed in January, 1869.[27] Under this law a few localities of between twenty and one hundred square miles, carefully chosen so as to be comprised of land well suited for cultivation, were to be designated as "Agricultural Areas." Within these, farm blocks not exceeding 320 acres were to be surveyed; such units would be sold at auction, but the successful bidder need pay only 20 per cent initially and the balance at the end of four years. Each credit purchaser was limited to a maximum of 640 acres, all in a contiguous block,

[25] As a retrospective report noted a few years later, "the adoption of the Wakefield system by the founders of this colony naturally prevented us from following as a prototype the land laws in use in the United States." *S. A. Parl. Papers* (1879), Vol. III, pp. xiii–xiv, reprinted in Clark, *op. cit.,* Vol. II, pp. 136–42.

[26] "Dummying" referred to the practice of pastoralists using hired puppets to obtain land and so avoid any acreage restrictions placed upon a single owner. "Peacocking" referred to the practice of obtaining control over critically important localities, especially water holes and streams, without which utilization of extensive surrounding lands was made difficult or impossible. Popularly referred to as "picking the eyes out of the country," it could, under competitive unrestricted selection, enable a pastoralist to dominate a huge area, or a farmer or speculator to ruin a pastoral holding, depending upon which one got control. See Roberts, *op. cit.,* p. 399 and maps 204a, 220a.

[27] *South Australian Acts of Parliament, No. 14* (1868–69).

and he was to occupy his land within six months, and reside on it until his purchase was completed. Within these Agricultural Areas, township and peripheral suburban lots were also to be surveyed but, as heretofore, sold only at cash auctions. All of these lands would be encompassed within the framework of new hundreds to be proclaimed in lands now under pastoral leases, which leases would be terminated in an orderly manner. All lands in these new hundreds outside of the special Agricultural Areas would be subdivided into farm lots and sold at cash auction as before.

The increase in the average size of farm blocks to be made available was an important change. Despite a still strong prejudice in favor of the older standard of about eighty acres it was now generally admitted that the competitive conditions for commercial wheat growing required an enlarged scale.[28]

But the really important innovation was the approval of the sale of land on credit. This seemingly simple change was a major departure from tradition, and though applicable to but a few small areas, it would prove to be the opening wedge of a whole new era of land settlement.[29] And of course it opened a whole new area for settlement, in which hundreds of pioneers might hope to build a prosperous future. That such hopes were, in reality, a rather awesome gamble with a multitude of factors in an area untested for agriculture did not deter these people. Despite the gamble with the fertility of the soil, the variability of rainfall,

[28] *S. A. Parl. Debates,* Oct. 6, 1868, col. 543.

[29] It should be noted that this change in policy refers only to governmental practices. Actually in previous years some of the land had been bought from the Crown by land agents who then resold it on credit to farmers. Nevertheless, although some of these agents charged quite reasonable rates of interest such private marketing could not help but be a very different matter from direct credit sales by the government itself. I am indebted to Mr. Keith R. Bowes, a graduate student in the Department of History, Australian National University, Canberra, for calling my attention to the operations of private land agents. Mr. Bowes has made a detailed study of the politics and policies related to this colonization, but unfortunately it was not possible for me to consult the manuscript he is preparing on "Land Settlement in South Australia, 1857–1890." It is clear that his study will greatly expand, clarify, and in some instances correct some of my interpretations of these matters. I gratefully acknowledge his helpful comments and hope that his work will soon be available to the public.

the hot winds, wheat rust, grasshoppers, and, not least, the price established in a distant highly competitive market, these people pushed forward. Colonization was given an entirely fresh impetus, with the country north and west of the existing farm region as the major frontier.

III.

Settlement Expansion: 1869–1874

> There are many who seem to think that agricultural settlement has about reached its extreme limit in the North, but the present season seems like a practical refutation of such a theory. Some of the heaviest crops have been gathered on the border lands where the agricultural and squatting elements have been brought into collision.
>
> —*The Northern Argus* (Clare), Feb. 3, 1871

GEOGRAPHIC OVERVIEW, 1869

A long salient narrowing along an axis from Gawler to Clare marked the northern and western limits of compact agricultural settlement in 1869 (Map 5). This zone was almost wholly within the north-south trending hill country and was in the main but an extension contiguous in area and similar in type to the early core of the colony. It was now to become the threshold of a new frontier of colonization and that expansion would, for a time, be bound in part to the facilities and services already developed. Its roads and railroads would provide the avenues of contact; its outermost townships[1] would become the portals and supply centers.

[1] The term "township" in South Australia refers to agglomerated settlements having both retail and residential functions—to what would commonly be called a "town" in most (but not all) regions of America. I have tried to be generally consistent in my use of this term in the Australian sense, although at times I have used "village" and "hamlet" to refer to very small centers.

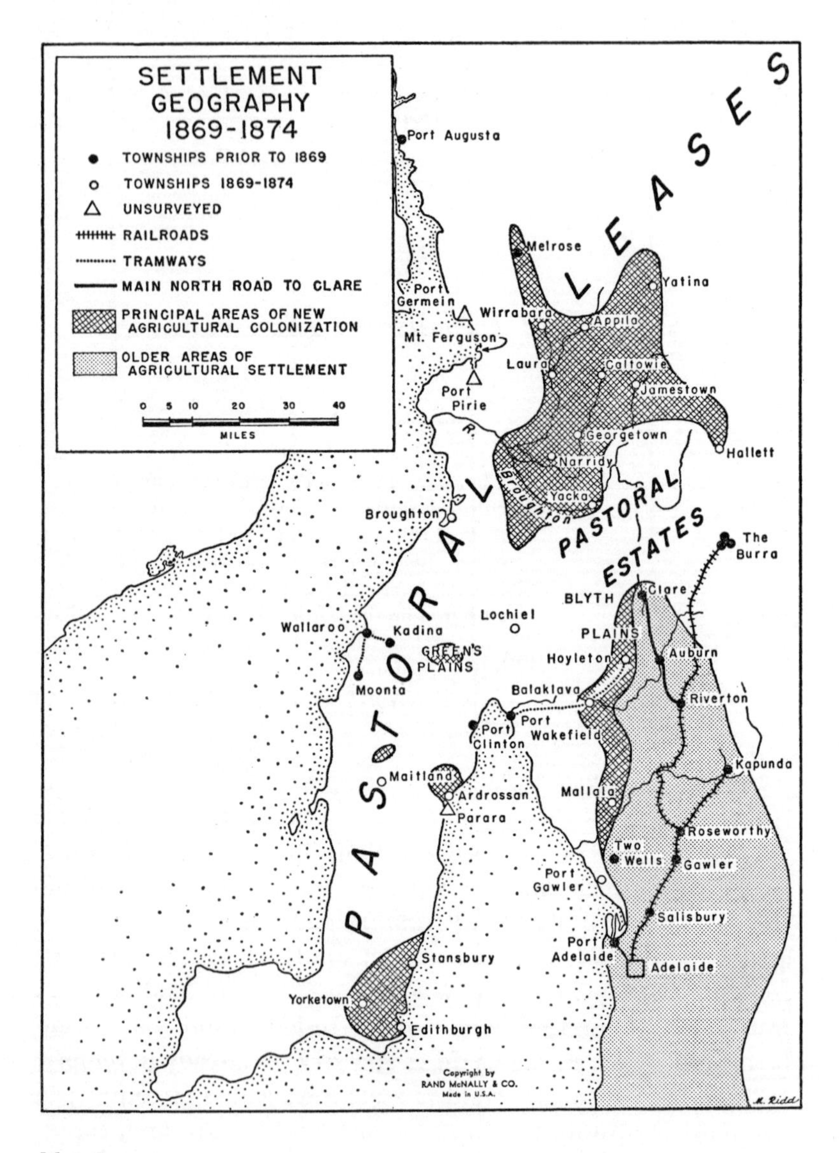
SETTLEMENT GEOGRAPHY 1869-1874
TOWNSHIPS PRIOR TO 1869
TOWNSHIPS 1869-1874
UNSURVEYED
RAILROADS
TRAMWAYS
MAIN NORTH ROAD TO CLARE
PRINCIPAL AREAS OF NEW AGRICULTURAL COLONIZATION
OLDER AREAS OF AGRICULTURAL SETTLEMENT
0 5 10 20 30 40
MILES
PASTORAL LEASES
PASTORAL ESTATES
Port Augusta
Melrose
Yatina
Port Germein
Wirrabara
Appila
Mt. Ferguson
Laura
Caltowie
Jamestown
Port Pirie
R.
Georgetown
Hallett
Narridy
Broughton
Yacka
Broughton
The Burra
BLYTH PLAINS
Clare
Lochiel
Wallaroo
Kadina
GREEN'S PLAINS
Hoyleton
Auburn
Moonta
Balaklava
Riverton
Port Clinton
Port Wakefield
Kapunda
Maitland
Ardrossan
Parara
Mallala
Roseworthy
Two Wells
Gawler
Port Gawler
Salisbury
Port Adelaide
Adelaide
Stansbury
Yorketown
Edithburgh
Copyright by RAND McNALLY & CO. Made in U.S.A.
M. Ridd

Map 5

Most of this area had been settled for a decade or more. On the farms much of the land was fenced and in crop, and good stone houses dotted the landscape; townships, villages and crossroads shops were closely spaced along the main roads. The railroad had reached Kapunda in 1860, and that erstwhile copper center was now the colony's largest wheat receiving station and had twice-daily service to and from Adelaide.[2] Surveys of the Northern Extension to the Burra, branching from the Kapunda line at Roseworthy, had been completed in 1868; construction was underway, and service to the south bank of the River Light had been opened in time for the harvest. From these railheads heavily traveled roads led northward.

The larger townships already had a degree of stability and range of facilities — shops, hotels, banks, churches — reflecting the rather full settlement of surrounding farm lands. Clare prided itself as being the "northern metropolis," a pretension at least locally justified. Numerous retail shops, four hotels, two banks, a flour mill, an agricultural machine shop, daily coach and mail service to Kapunda, and a telegraph line to Adelaide offered some measure of its functions and importance. For some years it had served both its own small but productive agricultural locale and the rich pastoral runs of the Broughton district. In 1869 its position clearly destined it to be the main portal to the incipient agricultural frontier to the north.

Some expansion of colonization was already underway on the plains west of this hill country. A special modification of land laws in 1867 had allowed long-term leases on selected areas in the mallee country, but clearing the scrub was a laborious and costly process.[3] There were, however, numerous small districts of more open country scattered along the eastern margins of the plains and these were attracting a considerable number of settlers. On the Blyth Plains such developments had not as yet proceeded far

[2] This sketch of conditions in 1869 is based upon *Statistical Register of South Australia, 1868* (Adelaide, 1868); *Official South Australian Gazetteer and Road Guide, Second Edition* (Adelaide, 1869); Josiah Boothby, *The Adelaide Almanack Town and Country Directory, and Guide to South Australia for 1869* (Adelaide, 1869); and the Parliamentary Papers to be cited.
[3] *S. A. Parl. Paper No. 172* (1868–69).

enough to support local townships, and the colonists remained tied to the string of communities along the Main North Road, especially Clare and Auburn. Farther south, colonization was more extensive. Two Wells was a thriving township with a flour mill, coach service to the Salisbury rail station, and prospects for a government wharf at Port Gawler. Mallala, with only a church and a school serving some 250 people in the vicinity, was in the earliest stage of emergence as a community. Here, too, there was much interest in the development of a local port. In all, there were about 15,000 people resident in this agricultural area north and west of the Kapunda rail line.

Beyond this farming frontier lay more than just a huge pastoral domain. Numerous developments had already taken place which would give attraction, direction, or assistance to the forward movement of colonists. Most conspicuous were the mining camps which stood as islands of population and diverse activities. The largest of these had already prompted roads, telegraph lines, and railroads to be built or surveyed; ports had been opened and shipping services established, and the numbers of people and working livestock were sufficient to induce both experimental local cultivation and cartage of truck crops, grain, and hay from the main farming region.

At the Burra the cluster of settlements (Kooringa, Redruth, and Aberdeen) had a population of 4,200 in 1868 (somewhat fewer than a few years before), the telegraph line was completed, the railroad was under construction, and although much of the land was held by mining companies or pastoralists, a few hundred acres were in cultivation. At the base of Yorke Peninsula the developments were considerably more impressive: the mines were highly productive, the Wallaroo smelter was the largest in the colonies, the port was busy, and the three centers of Kadina, Moonta, and Wallaroo were interconnected by a horse-powered tramway. A population of more than 8,000 and the flourishing state of the mines offered a considerable market. A small farming nucleus of a few hundred acres existed on Green's Plains a few miles to the east, but only hay was being grown, and connection with the main agricultural region was being actively sought. Some flour, feed, and produce were carted in from Clare, but it was a laborious two-days' haul, and a railway from Clare to Kadina for which the government had recently approved exploratory surveys was a topic of major interest.[4] Overland contact with Adelaide was via the telegraph and road which skirted the head of St. Vincent Gulf. A joint sea-land connection via Port Clinton, near the apex of the gulf, had not proved satisfactory.

Farther north mining had also had a noticeable though much smaller influence upon the settlement pattern. Port Augusta, at the head of Spencer Gulf, had been surveyed as a government township in 1856 to serve both the wool trade of the northern interior and the many small copper mines scattered far inland to the northeast, such as Blinman, Sliding Rock, Yudanamutana, and a dozen others of vaguely known location and irregular production and shipment. Melrose, the only other community in the northern country, owed its beginnings to a copper enterprise at Mt. Remarkable which soon failed.

The pastoralists had also undesignedly prepared a legacy of some importance to the future colonists: when their leases were terminated, roads, fences, and improved water holes remained. Likewise they had opened numerous coastal shipping points, which would later be developed into wheat ports. Port Pirie, Port Germein, Parara, and many others were initially minor wool ports. In 1869 the importance of this heritage was about to be demonstrated at Port Wakefield, originally developed to serve the Burra mines but later the most important wool port between Port Adelaide and Port Augusta.[5] The farmers of the Auburn and Clare district had looked upon it as a logical shipping outlet, and after two years of surveys and debate the government had authorized the construction of a tramway. The years of wool shipments had been an important pioneering phase during which navigation and lightering had been tested and numerous ship masters made fully familiar with its features.

[4] *S. A. Parl. Paper No. 141* (1867).

[5] Port Wakefield was used between 1849 and 1856 by the Patent Copper Company for the importation of coal and the export of Burra copper. When the railroad was extended such traffic was diverted first to Gawler and later to Kapunda; *S. A. Parl. Paper No. 62* (1866–67). Wool exports in 1868: Port Adelaide 18,845,487 lbs., Port Augusta 4,210,307 lbs., Port Wakefield 1,763,450 lbs.

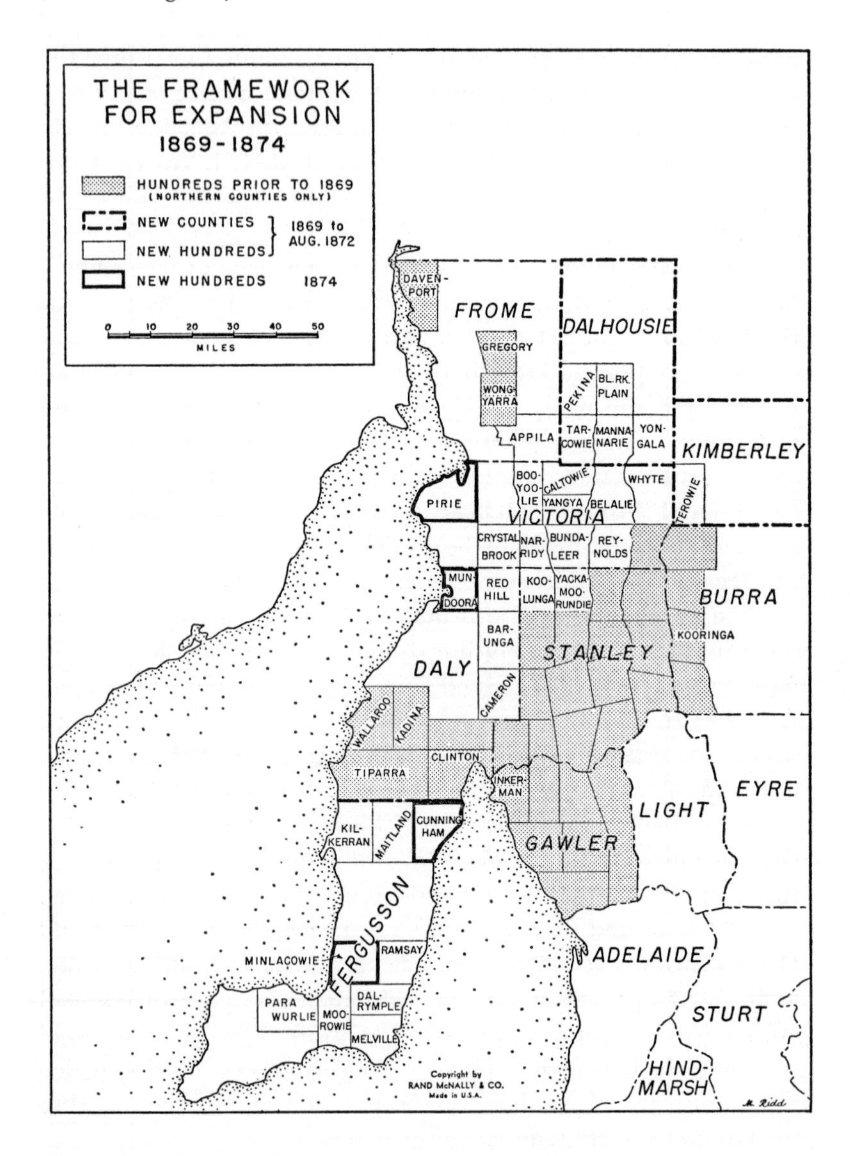
THE FRAMEWORK
FOR EXPANSION
1869-1874
HUNDREDS PRIOR TO 1869
(NORTHERN COUNTIES ONLY)
NEW COUNTIES
NEW HUNDREDS
1869 to
AUG. 1872
NEW HUNDREDS
1874
0
10
20
30
40
50
MILES
DAVEN-
PORT
FROME
GREGORY
WONG-
YARRA
DALHOUSIE
PEKINA
BL. RK.
PLAIN
APPILA
TAR-
COWIE
MANNA-
NARIE
YON-
GALA
KIMBERLEY
BOO-
YOO-
LIE
CALTOWIE
WHYTE
PIRIE
YANGYA
BELALIE
TEROWIE
VICTORIA
CRYSTAL
BROOK
NAR-
RIDY
BUNDA-
LEER
REY-
NOLDS
MUN-
DOORA
RED
HILL
KOO-
LUNGA
YACKA-
MOO-
RUNDIE
BURRA
BAR-
UNGA
KOORINGA
STANLEY
DALY
CAMERON
WALLAROO
KADINA
CLINTON
TIPARRA
INKER-
MAN
EYRE
LIGHT
KIL-
KERRAN
MAITLAND
CUNNING
HAM
GAWLER
FERGUSSON
RAMSAY
MINLACOWIE
ADELAIDE
PARA
WURLIE
MOO-
ROWIE
DAL-
RYMPLE
MELVILLE
STURT
HIND-
MARSH
Copyright by
RAND McNALLY & CO.
Made in U.S.A.
M. Ridd

Map 6

Some portions of the pastoral area had already been surveyed, an essential prerequisite to the sale of lands. Gawler, Stanley, Burra, Daly, Victoria, and Frome counties had been delimited, though only partially subdivided into hundreds (Map 6).[6] Several of these hundreds had been proclaimed only in order to allow townships to be developed and not in anticipation of any rural settlement. Such was the case with *Kadina, Wallaroo, Tiparra* (Moonta), *Clinton* (Port Clinton), *Inkerman* (Port Wakefield), *Davenport* (Port Augusta), and *Kooringa* (the Burra townships).[7] The anomalous "island" of *Wongyarra* and *Gregory* was the result of special surveys associated with the abortive Mt. Remarkable copper scheme. The remainder of the hundreds made up a considerable block of land just beyond the northern and western margins of the agricultural salient. These lands had been opened for sale in anticipation of further expansion of the farming frontier. However, westward colonization had been impeded by the dense mallee while in the much open and desirable lands north of Clare pastoralists had gotten control and established huge freehold estates (Map 5).[8]

Thus despite the considerable extent of lands already surveyed beyond the agricultural area of 1869, nearly all of it was either unavailable or unsuitable for any rapid and extensive farm colonization. It was necessary, therefore, to extend the surveys into the area of pastoral leases in order to create a fresh agricultural frontier. In 1869 nine new hundreds were proclaimed opening a continuous arc of land from Barunga Range northeastward through the middle Broughton district.[9] Three others were surveyed within the new county of Fergusson in a wholly new area directly across the gulf from Adelaide near the southern tip of Yorke Peninsula.[10] However, it was the new idea of credit sales

[6] Counties in South Australia are merely survey units rather than part of a functioning political hierarchy.
[7] In *Tiparra* and *Davenport* no rural lands had even been offered for sale. In order to make distinctions easier among the welter of local places, the names of hundreds are italicized in this study.
[8] Cf. *S. A. Parl. Debates,* Dec. 3, 1868, col. 1020.
[9] From southwest to northeast: *Cameron, Barunga, Redhill, Koolunga, Yackamoorundie, Bundaleer, Yangya, Reynolds, Whyte.*
[10] *Melville, Moorowie, Para Wurlie.*

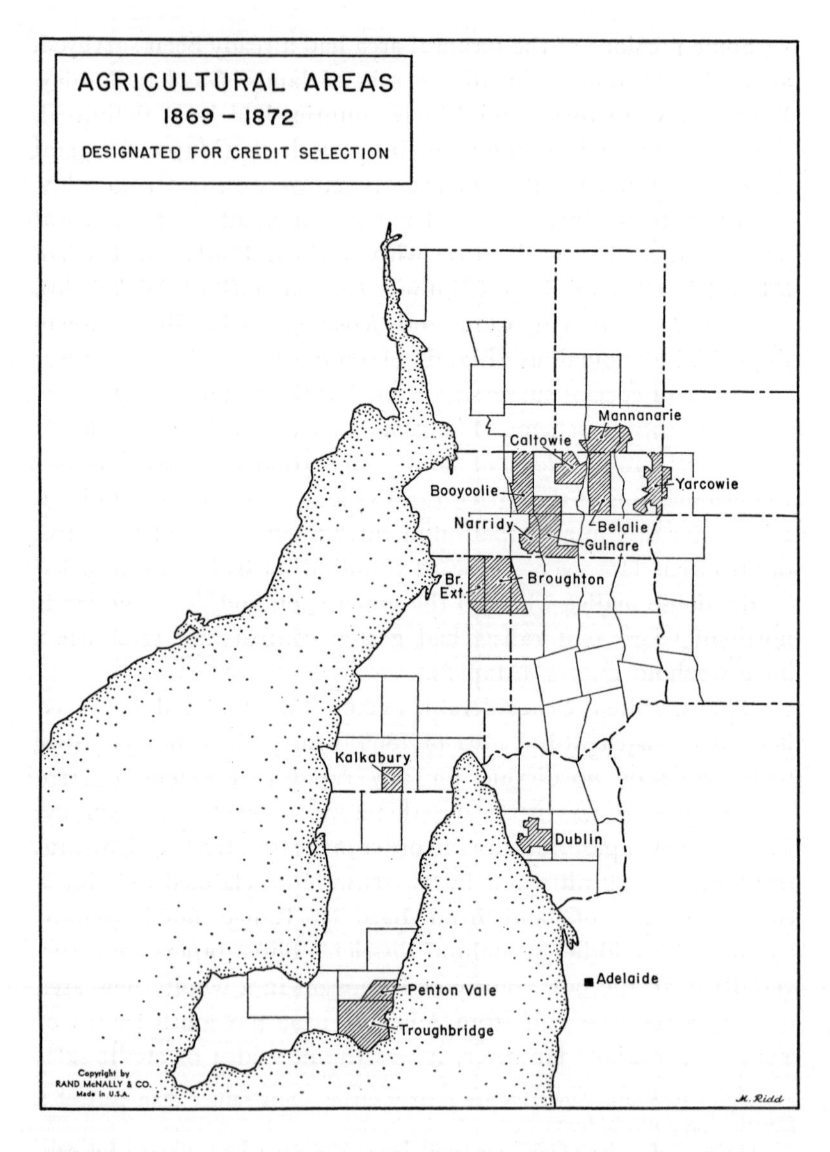
AGRICULTURAL AREAS
1869 – 1872
DESIGNATED FOR CREDIT SELECTION
Mannanarie
Caltowie
Yarcowie
Booyoolie
Narridy
Belalie
Gulnare
Br. Ext.
Broughton
Kalkabury
Dublin
Adelaide
Penton Vale
Troughbridge
Copyright by RAND McNALLY & CO. Made in U.S.A.
H. Ridd

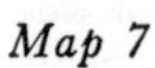
Map 7

within specially designated Agricultural Areas[11] which was the key feature designed to accelerate expansion, and initially only three of these were created: Gulnare and Broughton in the North, and Troughbridge, co-extensive with the hundred of *Melville,* in southern Yorke Peninsula (Map 7). Thus the initial influx of settlers would be channeled into but a few selected locales.

It took several months to survey these lands, but by mid-August, 1869, this new framework for expansion was completed, the farm blocks were put up for auction, and the new phase of colonization – experimental in legislation and in area – was underway.[12]

COLONIZATION DEVELOPMENTS, 1869–72

"There is a large quantity of agricultural land to the north of Clare; but it wants to be generally known," observed the editor of the local paper in the autumn of 1869.[13] But by mid-winter the Agricultural Areas were established, and soon he could report almost weekly on the farmers passing through to inspect those lands. It was immediately apparent that the effect of the new law was not to be wholly positive for the colony as a whole, for the migrants appeared to be mainly from the older districts where the crops had been light.[14] That they found these new lands to their liking is indicated by the fact that over 2,000 acres were broken out for cultivation in the first year and Victoria County entered the ranks of the wheat-producing counties.[15] It was certainly no great land "rush," but it seemed an optimistic beginning.

[11] Whenever the term "Agricultural Areas" is capitalized it refers specifically to those lands established under that name by the provisions of the Strangways Act of 1869 referred to in Chapter II.
[12] It should be noted that contemporary with the era of this study, efforts were being made to promote colonization in two other regions of the colony, in the South East (the Naracoorte–Mt. Gambier district) and on Eyre Peninsula. However, relatively little in the way of agricultural development was accomplished in either of these areas during this period.
[13] *The Northern Argus* (Clare), March 12, 1869.
[14] *Ibid.,* Oct. 29, 1869.
[15] Statistics specifically showing the status of land and productions within each Agricultural Area were not located, and the figures cited are in every case estimates derived from county statistics. In this instance, for example, Victoria is listed as having 1,085 acres in cultivation as of March 31, 1870, and it is assumed that nearly all of this is within the large Gulnare Agricultural Area. The Broughton A. A. which overlaps Daly and Stanley counties is assumed to have an approximately equal amount.

The selection of lands to be designated as Agricultural Areas was in the hands of Goyder, the Surveyor General. The legislation specifically stated that most of each Area should be suitable for agriculture. However, Goyder's reconnaissances during the great drought of 1864 were still fresh in his mind and he had serious doubts about the wisdom of fostering agricultural expansion northward. He could not block the intent of Parliament, but he could and did sound a warning. For example, when he established Belalie Agricultural Area in September, 1870, he described its potential with characteristic caution:

> The soil is generally good agricultural land, the ranges only being rough and stony; the whole is excellently grassed. Permanent water exists in several places, but great risks will be run by agriculturists from hot winds, which are frequent and cannot but have a destructive effect upon growing crops from October to December.[16]

But his opinions were no deterrent. Good soil, grass, and water could be seen, hot winds remained to be experienced, and there was a quick scramble for the best farms. Over five thousand acres were selected in two months, with from two to eleven simultaneous applications for each farm block.[17]

The harvest of 1870–71 was excellent; crops of 25 to 30 bushels per acre were reported in the Broughton country, with no market problems as the local demand for seed wheat by new colonists took most of the crop.[18] An acceleration of expansion caused by "glowing reports of abundance" was predicted and a cry for prompt opening of new Agricultural Areas voiced.[19] The government responded with surprising alacrity. In July, 1871, two new counties, Dalhousie and Kimberley, and a block of eleven new hundreds were declared, reaching north to the *Pekina* hills and east to *Terowie.* Three new Agricultural Areas, Narridy, Caltowie, and Booyoolie, were opened within that belt during the year, and were quickly taken up by credit selectors.[20] The success of the new legislation in stimulating developments in the North was now certain.

In the other regions progress was also apparent but the scale

[16] *S. A. Parl. Paper No. 89* (1870–71).
[17] *S. A. Parl. Paper No. 154* (1870–71).
[18] *The Northern Argus* (Clare), Feb. 17, 1871.
[19] *Ibid.,* Feb. 3, 1871.
[20] *Ibid.,* various issues, Sept.–Dec., 1871.

and over-all prospects were considerably smaller. The Clare paper in 1869 also called attention to the land north of the Burra as being "particularly adapted for agricultural purposes, and well worthy of the farmers' notice." The railroad which was under construction was an added inducement.[21] However, the crops of 1869–70 were very poor, four to five bushels to the acre, much of the land was locked up in pastoral estates, and the absence of any "credit lands" placed the area at a disadvantage in the competition for settlers. The designation of the Yarcowie Agricultural Area in 1872 was more an eastward extension of the main northern frontier than a northward advance from the Burra.

The westward advance in the plains north and south of the River Wakefield was also much slower than that of the Broughton district. There seemed no question that the land just below the hills was well suited for wheat, but the clearing costs remained high. Again, no credit lands were available at first, and when an Agricultural Area was proclaimed in August, 1871, it was located in *Dublin* hundred, on the very dense mallee and sandy soils near the coast. The most significant development in this region was the construction of the tramway east from Port Wakefield. Although originally designed to serve the older agricultural region, with Auburn, "a rising place and very centrally situated,"[22] as the tentative terminus, the high cost of construction into the hills prompted a change in plans and a decision to terminate on the plains.[23] After long delay, twenty-eight miles of nearly level line were opened as a horse-tramway just after harvest in 1870. It was by no means a great success that first year. The harvest was light, the facilities crude and unsubstantial, and two successive private lessees gave up after a few months' trial. The government took over operation in December and made extensive renovations so as to be ready for the next harvest. With seventeen horses, about one hundred tons daily were brought down during January–March, 1871, insufficient to keep ahead of the demand, but enough to prove the general usefulness of the line.[24] By August a total of

[21] *Ibid.*, April 2, 1869. The Burra line was opened on Aug. 29, 1870.
[22] *S. A. Parl. Paper No. 39* (1866–67).
[23] *Ibid.*
[24] *S. A. Parl. Paper No. 37* (1872), pp. 23–24. See also *The Northern Argus* (Clare), Feb. 3, 1871.

435,000 bushels had been moved down to Port Wakefield.[25] The town of Hoyleton was laid out at the terminus and eight months later had a retail shop, a butcher, a saddler-bootmaker-blacksmith, and a wine shanty.[26] It was a meagre development for such a seemingly advantageous site. No doubt the tentative nature of the terminus was partly responsible, for talk of a northward extension began even before the line was completed. But it also reflected the slow rate of farm colonization which gave it but a sparse local trade and made it principally a stopover for farmers carting from the hill lands to the east. The census figures of 1871 listed a total population in the hundreds adjacent to the line as 1,651, including 242 in Port Wakefield. Hoyleton with a population of 79, and Balaklava, midway along the tramway with but six houses and 24 persons, suggested that there had been no heavy influx into this region.

Still another portion of the new agricultural frontier was that in southern Yorke Peninsula. The official description of these lands was moderately favorable:

> undulating land and plain. The soil is generally of a light character, and water obtained at depths of a few feet to a hundred. The lands are partially sheltered from the hot winds by those of greater elevation to the north, which are mostly covered by a low dense scrub. There are available places for shipment in the several bays on the adjacent coast.[27]

But it was not an area familiar to agriculturists, it was more awkward to reach for most, and the lands had really not been tested at all. Consequently the response was only moderate at first. But the success of initial trials soon accelerated developments. By 1871 nearly seven thousand acres were in cultivation and in the following year two new hundreds, *Dalrymple* and *Ramsay,* and another Agricultural Area, Penton Vale, were opened just to the north. In addition, a new district was created when the Kalkabury Agricultural Area was set apart in *Tiparra* and when *Maitland* and *Kilkerran* hundreds were surveyed just to the south. Thus, if the tiny old nucleus on Green's Plains is included, agricultural colonization on Yorke Peninsula developed out of three separate districts, north, center and south.

[25] *The Northern Argus* (Clare), Aug. 11, 1871.
[26] *Ibid.,* Aug. 26, 1870.
[27] *S. A. Parl. Paper No. 161* (1868–69).

The crops of 1871–72 were a severe disappointment throughout the colony; yields of three to five bushels were reported over the new North. A few were quick to take a pessimistic view of the whole region, and even some supporters of expansion thought it a valuable demonstration of the need for changes:

> It is evident to all thinking people that the North is not so thoroughly adapted to wheat-growing as to guarantee a steady and reliable source of livelihood to farmers. Good crops for two years in succession are now seldom dreamt of, whilst consecutive seasons of bad crops are generally anticipated.

The writer went on to stress the need for better cultivation and diversification – "flax or olives seem the most feasible."[28] But such doubts and admonitions did little to stem the demand for land. Disgruntled farmers complained not of their lands but of the government and its cumbersome policies. The feeling seemed to be that if only the crippling restrictions on areas, acreages, and credit were removed all would be well – a poor year now and then was to be expected during this pioneer stage, but as cultivation progressed the seasons would likely "improve."

CRITICISM AND REVISION OF THE LAND ACT

The Strangways Act of 1869 had been mired in criticism from the beginning. The Clare editor probably expressed the common country sentiment when he grudgingly acknowledged that it was an improvement but "does not come up to the expectations and desires of some of our practical farmers."[29] The government indicated its own doubts by sending Goyder to Victoria to make a study of the operations of the more liberal laws of that colony and his report was a matter of lively public interest upon his return.[30] But the Surveyor General was never one to bend his ideas to fit the popular pattern, and in general he upheld the South Australian policies of restricted credit selection. He saw three serious dangers to throwing open all lands:

1. It would allow the "eyes of the country" to be picked out, and thereby "enrich a few individuals at the expense of

[28] *The Northern Argus* (Clare), April 19, 1872.
[29] *Ibid.*, Feb. 26, 1869.
[30] *Ibid.*, Feb. 25 and May 6, 1870.

the entire community and . . . reduce the value of adjacent lands much greater in extent."

2. It would offer "a premium to the exhaustion of the soil by giving new or virgin soil in exchange for worked out land."
3. It would sacrifice the benefits of closer settlement and induce a scattering which would have serious social consequences, especially in the lack of schools and churches. Uncontrolled pioneering might well produce "hardy men and women, brought up to a practical and laborious life," he noted, "but it is the development of muscle, without a proportionate expanse of mind."[31]

No aspect of the land law escaped popular criticism, but certainly the main grievance was the policy of restricting credit sales to the limited Agricultural Areas. Strangways, himself, anticipated the danger "that persons would be led to believe that all the land in them was well fitted for agriculture, whether it was so or not."[32] When put in operation, local complaints quickly justified his fears. Likewise, probably no area was opened during these years without prompting grumblings at the stupidity of the officials who couldn't tell good land from bad. Calling for the creation of new Agricultural Areas, the Clare editor admonished that they must include superior land "and not, as has been the case in several instances in the past, of such a quality as to be totally unfit for the agriculturist."[33] When the small Narridy Agricultural Area was proclaimed, public meetings of protest were held to point out that at the same time the larger, immediately adjacent, and "superior" hundred of *Booyoolie* was surveyed for cash sale, and therefore, so the speakers assumed, would be grabbed by the pastoralists who could afford to outbid the farmers.[34]

Such discontent soon brought results. The simplest solution to these kinds of complaints was to do away with the Agricultural Areas concept and allow any of the farm blocks to be purchased

[31] *S. A. Parl. Paper No. 23* (1870–71), pp. 6–8.
[32] *S. A. Parl. Debates,* Dec. 3, 1868, col. 1010.
[33] *The Northern Argus* (Clare), Feb. 3, 1871.
[34] *Ibid.,* July 7, 1871. It was apparently a successful meeting, for *Booyoolie* was withdrawn from sale and opened for credit selection in October.

on credit. Yielding to the popular clamor this is precisely what the government proposed to do in the autumn of 1872. A particular line would be drawn across the northern country, separating the area of pastoral leases from the new farming domain, all south of that line would be surveyed and open to credit selectors. Having thus swept away the principal controversial issue, the next few weeks were devoted to ironing out the lesser questions relating to the amount of initial deposit, payment schedules, and further means of protecting against sales to speculators and pastoralists. Ultimately the initial deposit was reduced to 10 per cent, and credit extended to six years. To ensure that the land was taken by *bona fide* farmers a cultivation requirement was included. Initially "cereal" cultivation was proposed and several members protested that "from the tone of the debate it appeared as if many members regarded farming as merely wheat-growing."[35] Unquestionably most did, but largely in deference to the interests of the South East, other crops were included. The final bill required cultivation of at least one-fifth of the land each year, defined as "ploughing, digging, or trenching and planting cereal, hemp, flax, pulse, or root crops." By mid-winter the new act was approved and came into force on August 15, 1872.[36]

Although the complex restrictive provisions of the older act were objects of bitter complaint, it was the general success of that act in stimulating a fresh surge of colonization which had built up the pressure for change. In the three years of the Strangways Act over a million acres had been sold in the colony, nearly 60 per cent of which had been on credit within twenty-four Agricultural Areas.[37] In the new lands north and west of the 1869 frontier three new counties and twenty-seven new hundreds had been proclaimed and approximately 160,000 acres brought under cultivation.[38] The fact that in the new law the designated line of separation between the agricultural and pastoral domains could be described in terms of the outer boundary of the existing

[35] *S. A. Parl. Debates,* May 9, 1872, col. 850.
[36] *S. A. Acts of Parliament, No. 18* (1872).
[37] A total of thirteen areas had been declared in the North, eight in the South East, and three on Eyre Peninsula.
[38] Acreage calculated on the increase between 1868–69 and 1871–72 in Gawler, Stanley, Burra, Victoria, Daly, and Fergusson counties.

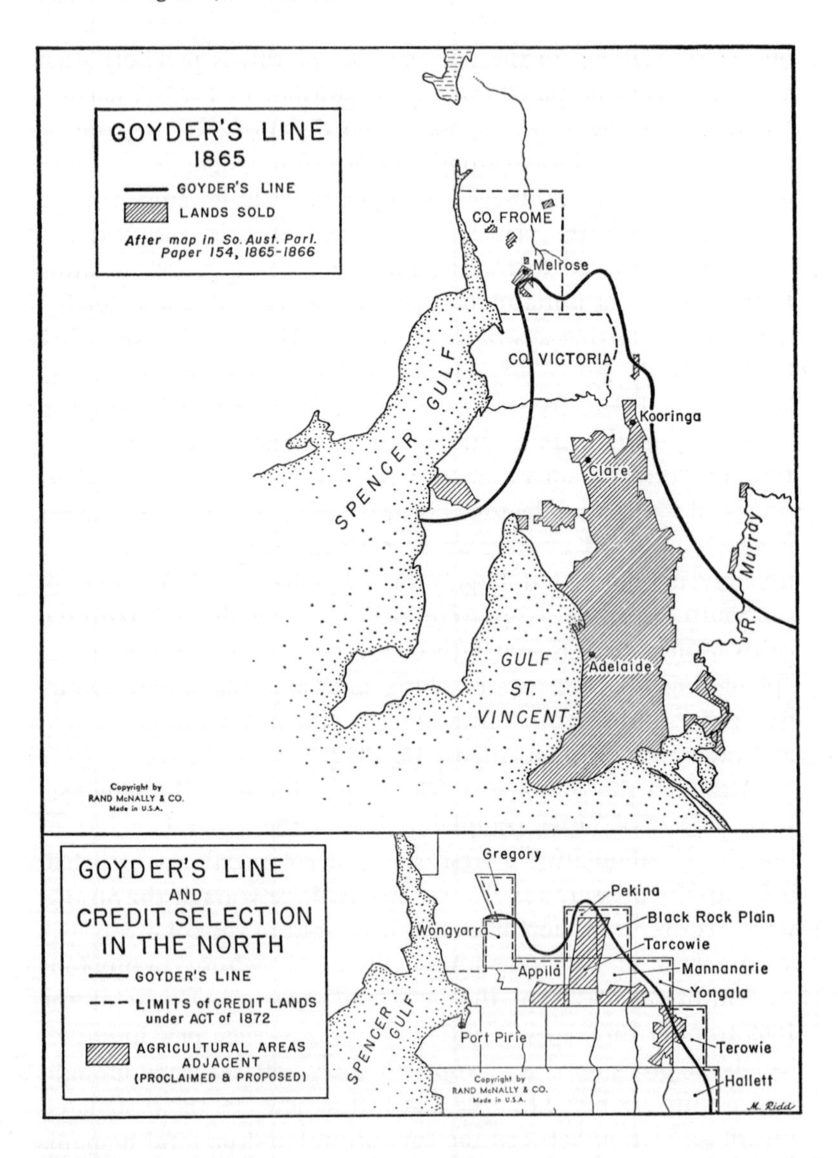
GOYDER'S LINE
1865
GOYDER'S LINE
LANDS SOLD
After map in So. Aust. Parl. Paper 154, 1865-1866
CO. FROME
Melrose
CO. VICTORIA
Kooringa
Clare
SPENCER GULF
R. Murray
GULF ST. VINCENT
Adelaide
Copyright by RAND McNALLY & CO. Made in U.S.A.
GOYDER'S LINE
AND
CREDIT SELECTION
IN THE NORTH
GOYDER'S LINE
LIMITS of CREDIT LANDS under ACT of 1872
AGRICULTURAL AREAS ADJACENT (PROCLAIMED & PROPOSED)
Gregory
Pekina
Black Rock Plain
Wongyarra
Tarcowie
Appila
Mannanarie
Yongala
SPENCER GULF
Port Pirie
Terowie
Hallett
M. Ridd

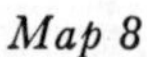

Map 8

block of hundreds showed that the immediate pressure for land could be met not by expanding the gross limits of the agricultural domain but merely by removing the sales discriminations applying within that region which had already been so greatly enlarged under the original act.

"GOYDER'S LINE"

That line of separation was not a simple arbitrary choice of the moment. Rather it was based upon a division laid down upon the map a few years before and which, in time, would become the most famous qualitative demarcation of areas in South Australia: Goyder's "Line of Rainfall." Its origin goes back to the spring of 1865 when Goyder was sent to examine the drought-stricken pastoral country. The Surveyor General was instructed to make such regional observations "as may enable you to determine and lay down on a map, as nearly as practicable, the line of demarcation between that portion of the country where the rainfall has extended, and that where the drought prevails."[39] A month later Goyder returned and produced his map showing the "line of demarcation," which extended "considerably further south" than he had anticipated (Map 8).[40] A program of relief relating to tenure and assessments of leases was then acted upon. It was not long, however, before some began to wonder if the immediately renowned "Goyder's Line" might not have broader implications. In 1867 Goyder was asked whether his Line might be regarded as separating the lands suitable for agriculture from those fit only for pastoral use. He replied:

> It does to a certain extent; but there is some portion of the country where, although the soil is eminently adapted for tillage, and will grow anything, the peculiar position of it, and its openness to hot winds, render it such as can only be safely continued as pastoral land. That is inside the line — and outside it, the whole of the land is only fit for pastoral purposes; that is as far as we know of growing cereals at present.[41]

[39] *S. A. Parl. Paper No. 62* (1865–66).
[40] *S. A. Parl. Paper No. 78* and *No. 154* ("Map of Northern Runs") (1865–66). See also F. J. R. O'Brien, "Goyder's Line," M.A. Thesis, Department of History, University of Adelaide, in which Goyder's notebooks have been drawn upon to document his knowledge of the North before and at the time, and which also examines in some detail subsequent variations and controversies related to the Line.
[41] *S. A. Parl. Paper No. 14* (1867), p. 113.

Soon, however, he began to regard his Line as being precisely this sort of separation. In his report on the land laws of Victoria in 1870 he strongly advocated government prohibition of settlement in areas unsuited to agriculture and pointed out that "in South Australia nature has clearly established a line of demarcation beyond which permanency of tenure may be given to the pastoral tenant, without detriment to the agriculturist."[42] Moreover, as Surveyor General, Goyder had principal control over the choice of land to be surveyed into hundreds and in the north had obviously shaped his selections to conform with his earlier demarcation (Map 8). It was sheer coincidence that *Wongyarra* and *Gregory*, which had been proclaimed many years before, very nearly conformed with the western promontory of his Line, but the outward boundaries of *Appila, Pekina, Black Rock Plain, Yongala,* and *Terowie* were clearly drawn to give a rectangular approximation of his curving line to the east. Further, his selection of Agricultural Areas reflects the same pattern. The Mannanarie and Yarcowie areas impinged closely upon the northeastern boundary, and just prior to the end of the old act two additional areas almost exactly conforming to the curve northward to Pekina Hill were already on the maps as future Agricultural Areas.[43]

Thus Goyder, himself, gave his "Line" a significance quite beyond its original intent, and a role which was to make it a persistent issue in South Australian colonization history. In 1872, however, it was not yet really a controversial matter. For the moment enough land was available south of the Line to relieve the pressure for farms, and it was employed in the new law as merely a convenient, well known boundary and no voices were raised in debate against it.

COLONIZATION DEVELOPMENTS, 1872–74

As if to confirm the wisdom of making the lands more readily available, the rains came in good time, the hot winds withheld their searing touch, the red rust was rarely seen, and the crops of 1872–73 were superb. Sixteen to twenty bushels per acre were

[42] *S. A. Parl. Paper No. 23* (1870–71), p. 8.
[43] See map attached to *S. A. Parl. Paper No. 40* (1872).

reaped all over the North and the Peninsula, and many localities surpassed this handsome average. A rash of complaints arose over the scarcity and cost of farm laborers, the shortage of rail trucks to the south, and the inadequate marketing facilities in the new areas. Optimism over the excellence of the frontier lands was reinforced and "the fame of the Areas spread like wildfire, and such a rush set in from the old district as taxed the whole surveying power of the Surveyor General to supply the demand."[44] The Clare editor abandoned his solemn caution of a few months before and hailed the results as "sufficient to prove the fertility of the Northern areas."[45] When the harvest of 1873 proved equally good, the scramble for farms was so great that a conservative Melbourne reporter traveling over the area could only describe it as a genuine "land panic." There were a dozen applicants for every good farm lot offered, and under the required auctions among simultaneous selectors land prices soared. When *Mannanarie* Hundred was opened just north of Jamestown competitive sales reached £7/10/0 per acre.[46]

Townships which had only recently been staked out on the dry plains suddenly blossomed under the forced growth of local demands as well as sheer speculation. Jamestown, Caltowie, Laura, and Georgetown, faced with an intense competition for tradesmen, loudly voiced their needs and advantages. Georgetown, plotted on a grand scale in the midst of the rich lower Broughton plains, certain of a natural destiny as the trade center of the North, boasted of three retail stores, two butchers, two blacksmiths, one baker, a hotel, a fine Roman Catholic chapel, and called for more.[47] In the spring of 1873 Port Pirie, surveyed on the bleak mud flats only a year before, claimed a population of 160 and contained two general-merchandise establishments, two butchers, a blacksmith, a baker, a bank, one hotel ("pub"), and four wheat stores.[48] Farther north new townships, Wirrabara, Appila, and Yatina, each laid out on ample dimensions, were soon to join in the rivalry. Complaints and suspicions over the government's

[44] *The Farmers' Weekly Messenger* (Adelaide), Dec. 11, 1874.
[45] *The Northern Argus* (Clare), April 18, 1873.
[46] *The Farmers' Weekly Messenger* (Adelaide), Dec. 11, 1874.
[47] *Ibid.*, May 9, 1873.
[48] *The Northern Argus* (Clare), Nov. 21, 1873.

township policies were numerous. *Crystal Brook* selectors vented their impatience at the delay in surveys, and the withdrawal from sale of the *Narridy* township and suburban lots was laid to plans for a railway which would increase their value and thereby yield a grasping government a higher return from auction sales.[49]

The North continued as the chief focus of interest, but the surprising success of the early selectors on Yorke Peninsula, where "the despised scrub land" was proving excellent for wheat, gave a sharp stimulus to expansion in that area also. The great need for some "cheap, simple, and efficient implement for grubbing," did little to stem the demand.[50] When a portion of the hundred of *Maitland* was offered in late 1872, 157 selectors competed for 36 sections with eight to twelve applicants for choice lots, driving the price to more than double the offering level.[51] Wherever surveys lagged protests were heard,[52] and when the lands were opened as often as not complaints against the harassed sheepmen followed: "the squatters have taken care to feed off every vestige of grass on all the roads traversed by land selectors."[53] But such actions were a minor deterrent and represented the last-ditch stand of the squatters whose leases were being terminated. The Peninsula was now a mosaic of little agricultural frontiers pushing out in all directions, diminishing, fragmenting, and ultimately destroying the great runs. In two years the acreage in wheat in Fergusson County increased more than fivefold.

Nearly 250,000 new acres in wheat was the chief statistical measure of the land boom in the years 1872–74, and the almost two million bushels reaped from those lands in 1874 were a crushing glut upon the meagre marketing facilities. The government was besieged with a proportionate glut of petitions from the frontiers calling for immediate attention to roads, tramways, railroads, jetties, channel improvements – every possible instrument that might help move the harvests. That it was properly a governmental duty was assumed, for such was part of their heritage. The Moonta editor undoubtedly spoke for nearly all the settlers,

[49] *Ibid.*, May 29, 1874, and Aug. 23, 1872.
[50] *The Farmers' Weekly Messenger* (Adelaide), Aug. 28, 1874.
[51] *The Yorke's Peninsula Advertiser and Miners' News* (Moonta), Oct. 18, 1872.
[52] *Ibid.*, May 27, 1873.
[53] *The Farmers' Weekly Messenger* (Adelaide), Aug. 28, 1874.

farmers and townsmen alike, when he noted that the government was "offering special facilities for settling the country with an agricultural population, and to be consistent with their own policy, we opine, they are bound to furnish the farmers with a means of communication with their markets."[54]

The demand was not new in type, only in magnitude, for with the first leap northward of the frontier, the question of transportation came alive. Within a few months of the enactment of the liberalized land laws "the chief topic of conversation" among the new settlers was "the making and extension of railways." In August, 1869, 225 petitioners in Stanley County called for an extension of the still uncompleted Port Wakefield tramway on through Blyth Plains to the Broughton River where "fresh land . . . is being rapidly brought under cultivation."[55] But it was easier for the Crown to open lands than to serve them with railways, and colonization persistently outran the facilities. As soon as an actual surplus of wheat was obtained, settlers loaded their wagons or bullock carts with the bagged grain and struck out, either long distances southward to rail terminals or westward to the muddy shores of Spencer Gulf. In 1871 trial shipments were made from Port Broughton with sufficient success to prompt petitions for a jetty.[56] A wharf of sorts was privately built for the next season, but by then wheat acreage inland had tripled and the appeal for help was intensified.[57] The road through the mallee was a long, dry haul, rainwater had to be obtained from a storekeeper's 30,000 gallon tank at 2*d.* per bucket, and the loading facilities were quite inadequate. Funds were appropriated to meet these needs, but by 1873, 45 coastal ketches and two larger vessels carried away 156,000 bushels, and a tramway and long jetty were now urgently demanded.[58]

Similarly, from the moment areas farther north were opened, an ever-mounting plea for facilities to and at Port Pirie began.

[54] *The Yorke's Peninsula Advertiser and Miners' News* (Moonta), April 22, 1873.
[55] *The Northern Argus* (Clare), Aug. 27, 1869, and *S. A. Parl. Paper No. 74* (1869–70).
[56] *The Northern Argus* (Clare), June 23, 1871, and *S. A. Parl. Paper No. 48* (1871).
[57] *S. A. Parl. Paper No. 67* (1872).
[58] *S. A. Parl. Debates,* June 19 and July 3, 1872, cols. 1299–1300, 1441–42; *S. A. Parl. Paper No. 141* (1873), pp. 21–22.

Again the settlers were forced to take the initiative, a few loads were sent out in 1872 and private stores and wharves were constructed. By 1873 hundreds were signing petitions calling attention to "impassable" roads, "insufficient" water, and exorbitant cartage rates (9*d*. per bushel for 25 miles). Moreover, as settlement broadened and the government began to consider a railway, arguments over the specific route became a matter of keen controversy. Petitions were followed by counterpetitions arguing the "obvious" advantages of rival routes, and the government compounded it all by showing belated doubts about the feasibility of sinking money into the desolate mud flats at Port Pirie at all and undertaking investigations of nearby Mt. Ferguson as a more worthy site.[59]

The rash of demands pushed the Crown into comprehensive study of the whole railroad question. An intricate web of surveys was made, the practicabilities of various ports studied, and scheduled programs of construction were laid out. Such planning was a rational approach to the problem, but necessarily a time-consuming one, and could not but heighten the impatience of the farmers. In 1874 the average haul of wheat to Port Pirie and Port Broughton was 35 miles, but the new settlers in *Pekina* and *Black Rock Plain* were carting 60 miles over extremely difficult roads. As the farmers were busy preparing ground as soon as the harvest was over, hired bullock teams hauled a large share of the traffic. At Port Broughton four shipping merchants had "commodious" warehouses, the government jetty extended out about twenty chains into eight feet of water, from where the wheat was lightered out nine miles to large vessels. Port Pirie had five wharves and a flour mill, but not enough space, lighters, or vessels to clear the heavy congestion, and the shortage of water for vessels, townsmen, and teams was critical.[60]

On Yorke Peninsula a similar agitation was growing. Nearly the whole of Green's Plains was in cultivation by 1874 and a railway either to Port Wakefield or to Kadina to connect with the

[59] *S. A. Parl. Paper No. 40* (1872), *Nos. 57, 60, 66, 107, 117, 133* (1873), and *No. 206* (1874).
[60] *The Farmers' Weekly Messenger* (Adelaide), Dec. 11, 1874, and *The Northern Argus* (Clare), Feb. 13, 1874.

Fig. 4 Quorn, *c.* 1880. Transcontinental Hotel and flour mill in left background; railway line toward Pichi Richi Pass over the Flinders Range to Port Augusta in the right background. (S. A. Archives)

Fig. 5 Wheat stacks at Crystal Brook, on the newly-opened railway to Port Pirie, *c.* 1876. (S. A. Archives)

Figs. 6 and 7 Two views at Port Pirie, *c.* 1876. (S. A. Archives)

private mining tramway to Wallaroo was sought.[61] To the south, after the first year of cropping *Maitland* settlers began talk of a tramway angled across the peninsula from Moonta to Parara. The Moonta paper thought "they were perhaps looking a little ahead to the time when they will require a market for their produce,"[62] but it took little foresight. By the next season a public meeting was called to discuss the "urgent" need for a tramway and a jetty at Ardrossan, the new government township surveyed at Clay Gully, just north of the old wool shipping beach at Parara.[63] Down the coast the cry was the same: Oyster Bay (Stansbury) needed a jetty, Edithburgh, which now had regular steamer service to Adelaide and coaches into Yorketown, forwarded the plea of 170 petitioners for improved facilities to meet the "great and growing trade."[64]

Again the intensity of complaints was but a measure of the success of a new surge forward which seemed to confirm all the sanguine hopes and smother the slightest doubts of previous years. "Every day," wrote the Clare editor as he watched the harvest of 1874 roll in, "brings with it additional proof that South Australia is destined to become one of the finest agricultural colonies in the world.[65] "Such a golden flood ought to convince the most bigoted as to the capabilities of the North for producing wheat. All the supposed difficulties and failures have given way to a practical test, and what was regarded as a barren waste is now the granary of the colony. . . . The primitive roads of the North are giving way to railways and a career of commerce has begun."[66] Given such railroads, a Melbourne observer agreed that it would be a promising career, for the North "could grow wheat to pay against the world, not excepting California."[67]

[61] *S. A. Parl. Paper No. 141* (1873).
[62] *The Yorke's Peninsula Advertiser and Miners' News* (Moonta), April 22, 1875.
[63] *The Farmers' Weekly Messenger* (Adelaide), Aug. 28, 1874. See also *S. A. Parl. Paper No. 22* (1875), pp. 118–21, on the preference for Ardrossan over Parara: "There is heavy sand at Parara, and you have to take the loading into the sea to get it to the boats. There are bad places in the sea, and you might smother the horses."
[64] *The Farmers' Weekly Messenger* (Adelaide), July 3 and July 10, 1874; *S. A. Parl. Paper No. 95* (1874).
[65] *The Northern Argus* (Clare), Feb. 13, 1874.
[66] *Ibid.*, May 22, 1874.
[67] *The Farmers' Weekly Messenger* (Adelaide), Dec. 11, 1874.

FURTHER CRITICISM AND REVISION OF THE LAND ACT

Such a transformation of the North was an exhilarating spectacle – and need it end: "must all this terminate at Goyder's boundary line?"[68] And again the paradox had appeared: the very success of a new land act brought it almost immediately into disrepute. The gross liberalization of credit sales, opening all south of Goyder's Line, had soon merely converted that boundary into a galling restriction. The very first harvest after the new law (1872–73), though entirely gathered south of the Line, was translated to mean a complete refutation of such a limitation upon agriculture: that "theory . . . is now exploded"; "Goyder's Line of rainfall was all nonsense."[69] And it was already a matter of immediate concern; "upwards of 1,000 persons" were reported tramping over the country around *Pekina* and *Black Rock Plain* during the winter of 1873 in search of selections, only to find that the remaining land available was "utterly worthless" while beyond lay "fertile plains."[70] By the next autumn the campaign to remove this "imaginary line" was well underway. Meetings were held, petitions were signed, and the visions of almost unlimited possibilities for expansion quickly took shape. At Melrose a meeting was convened to discuss a plea to have the settlement boundary shifted forty miles north to open the attractive lands of Beautiful Valley (in the vicinity of the township of Wilmington, to be established later). So modest was the request that the farm editor reporting felt compelled to point out that "Beautiful Valley is by no means the limit of available land, and before long Port Augusta will be busy with the shipment of wheat grown even north of its own latitude."[71] More typical was the proposal at Laura "that Mr. Goyder's rainfall [line] be shifted out of the colony."[72] Far to the north, eighty-three residents of Sliding Rock and Blinman concurred, pointing out the "large tracts of country suitable for agricultural purposes" which lay between them and the restrictive line.[73] Even from the east on the

[68] *The Northern Argus* (Clare), May 22, 1874.
[69] *Ibid.*, May 16, 1873 (editorial), and June 20, 1873 (report of a local speaker).
[70] *Ibid.*, Aug. 29, 1873.
[71] *The Farmers' Weekly Messenger* (Kapunda), April 17, 1874.
[72] *The Northern Argus* (Clare), March 29, 1874.
[73] *S. A. Parl. Paper No. 104* (1874).

relatively minor frontier beyond the Burra came a plea for the immediate opening of a new tier of hundreds east of *Kooringa, Kingston,* and *Hallett.*[74]

The very idea of a "line of rainfall" was an obvious invitation to ridicule:

> I came into a store at Pekina, on the other side of the "rainfall," on Tuesday, May 4, about 9 o'clock in the forenoon, wet to the skin, and it rained steady all that day and night and part of the next day, and I defy Mr. Goyder or any other man to say at which side of the hedge the most rain fell.[75]

That the gentleman who would thus defy Mr. Goyder had never before been north of Clare was quite unimportant; all that mattered was that he, like many others, had seen the country and noted its "excellent" soil and "abundance of water."[76]

Undoubtedly a more telling and reasonable argument was that stated succinctly by the Burra petitioners:

> The question of the suitability or otherwise of this land for agriculture should not rest on the dictum of one individual; it being notorious that much of the land now under culture and growing good crops, has been formerly pronounced totally unsuitable for that purpose by people apparently well qualified to form an opinion.[77]

The point was incontrovertible. It was common knowledge that South Australian agriculture had from the very beginning advanced only by cautious experimentation in the face of heavy doubts. A whole succession of boundaries beyond which farming could not possibly succeed — the River Para, the Gawler, the Wakefield, the hills of Clare, the Burra — had been set up by pessimistic, and usually majority, opinion only to be demolished by the harvests obtained. It was a devastating precedent which expansionists rarely failed to cite to confound those who defended the restricting lines. Inevitably as the magnitude of successful colonization grew so did the visions of the potential; if a few years

[74] *S. A. Parl. Paper No. 34* (1874). Interestingly, *The Farmers' Weekly Messenger,* normally a strong advocate of expansion, opposed this idea because of the lack of water, poor land, and inevitable ruination of the pastoral interests; see issue of Sept. 25, 1874.

[75] *The Farmers' Weekly Messenger* (Adelaide), May 22, 1874.

[76] Cf. *The Northern Argus* (Clare), June 2, 1874.

[77] *S. A. Parl. Paper No. 34* (1874).

ago "it was thought to be of no use to go north of Gawler," they would soon be going "as far as Blinman."[78]

And so a new land bill was brought before Parliament just two years after the seemingly very liberal amendment of 1872. In July, 1874, the Chief Secretary (Honorable A. Blyth) stated the arguments in favor of abolishing the restriction of Goyder's Line and opening the entire province to credit selection. His list of points was familiar for most had been cited time and again at the country meetings:

1. The Line had been "laid down on the map entirely in connection with the question of pastoral leases" and "not for the purpose of agricultural settlement. . . ."
2. "He was old enough a colonist to know the time when it was asserted that the land north of the Para was not fit for cultivation."
3. When the last act was passed no one thought it would be an "exceedingly crippling" restriction, but such had now proved to be the case.
4. One had only to look "at the configuration of Frome and Dalhousie and the Hundred of Gregory" to see "how unsuited this line of rainfall had been for determining what land was fit for agricultural purposes."
5. "He had always held that it was no use for the Government to say, 'This land is suitable and that land is not,' but the duty of the government was to survey the land and let the people select the land which would be suitable for their purposes."[79]

To the pastoralists such a law brought a spectre of ruin. One of their spokesmen insisted that "some limit must exist in the interest of both parties between the lands occupied for pastoral and agricultural purposes, or neither could be successful."[80] Goyder, years before, had put forth the same logic. Any selector who invaded the lands unsuitable for cultivation must have one of two objects in view, he argued, "either to settle and cultivate the soil, which

[78] *The Northern Argus* (Clare), June 20, 1873, quoting a resident of Blyth Plains.
[79] *S. A. Parl. Debates,* July 14, 1874, cols. 905–6.
[80] *Ibid.,* col. 910.

will not repay his labor in that locality, and thereby shows that it is a mistake to allow the selection; or he wishes to harass the holder of the run, and to be bribed to go off; and, in such case, the squatter is entitled to protection, whilst the other deserves punishment."[81] But in the view of the selectors, such an argument would only prove that Goyder was in league with the pastoralists. "Break through Goyder's boundary," cried a country spokesman, "the most absurd thing known in squatters' ingenuity."[82] Furthermore, argument over the need for some kind of boundary between the two occupiers of land was overwhelmed by the simple but insatiable desire to break down the particular line in question. The settlers had reached the line, they wanted more land, and that beyond seemed "as good if not better."[83] It was Goyder's judgment of what was and was not suitable land that was under attack. Called to report upon the agricultural land available in the colony, the Surveyor General never wavered in his position:

> Beyond the limit of the First Schedule [Goyder's Line], from Melrose northward and north-easterly the land, except in the ranges is mostly good agricultural soil; its extent is very great, but the rainfall, hitherto, has not been reliable — the result of farming is therefore doubtful.[84]

But his opinions had lost their power. When this same paragraph was read before Parliament by the Commissioner of Crown Lands it was ridiculed with jeers and laughter.[85] As the debates dragged on, the Chief Secretary, whose original statement had been quite temperate and fair, became increasingly sensitive to the popular clamor and impatient at the delay, and called for a "doing away with Goyder's absurd line of rainfall – a line prepared for another object and not having anything to do with the matter under present circumstances."[86] The legislature complied: on November 6, 1874, yet another Waste Lands Amendment Act came into force opening for credit selection, under basically the same conditions as before, all unappropriated lands "situated south of

[81] *S. A. Parl. Paper No. 23* (1870–71).
[82] *The Northern Argus* (Clare), May 22, 1874.
[83] The fear of Victorian competition for settlers was again raised: "At Horsham [western Victoria] it is nearly all Adelaide people that have settled there, and plenty more are going." *S. A. Parl. Debates,* Nov. 5, 1874, col. 2236.
[84] *S. A. Parl. Paper No. 239* (1874).
[85] *S. A. Parl. Debates,* Oct. 27, 1874, col. 2161.
[86] *Ibid.,* Nov. 5, 1874, col. 2235.

the twenty-sixth parallel of south latitude" — the whole of South Australia.[87]

Thus within a span of five years South Australia had abandoned a major part of her complex tradition of intricate control over colonization. Land still had to be surveyed before sold, and it could be purchased only in the farm blocks as surveyed, but all the careful devices to insure the principle of concentrated settlement, the optimum balance of land and labor, the relationship between colonization and emigration were jettisoned. All pretense of regulating an orderly advance of the agricultural frontier upon the pastoral domain was gone. And, step by step, from the abolition of Agricultural Areas to the elimination of Goyder's Line, the Crown had withdrawn from being the supreme judge of land and no longer presumed to separate the good land from the poor.

The settlers were on their own. How far would they go? The answer was quite simple: they would advance just "so long as experience shows that a profitable crop of wheat can be grown."[88]

[87] *S. A. Acts of Parliament No. 22* (1874). The twenty-sixth parallel was the boundary separating South Australia from Northern Territory which was at the time under its administration.
[88] *The Northern Argus* (Clare), Feb. 3, 1871.

IV.

Settlement Expansion: 1875 – 1880

> Who'd have thought it? . . . wheat will grow even beyond Wonoka . . . . Seventy miles north of Port Augusta!
>
> — WONOKA CORRESPONDENT
> *The Areas' Express and Farmers' Journal* (Gladstone), Nov. 13, 1878

COLONIZATION DEVELOPMENTS, 1875–76

The wheat growing thick, heavy, and unblighted over all the North and West through that spring of 1874 must have provided a forceful argument for the expansionists. And in the summer hardly had the votes on the new Land Bill been counted than the harvest reports seemed to underscore all the optimism and confirm the wisdom of Parliament. The yields were fat; from southern Yorke Peninsula to the Broughton and east to the Burra whole hundreds averaged twelve to sixteen bushels to the acre, and ten bushels from the fresh land of *Pekina* seemed certain proof of the absurdity of the "rainfall line."

The government hastened its surveys on every front to enable the settlers to advance. In part, it was a completion of the framework within the old limits, in part an extension beyond. Two months after the new law, all remaining area south of Goyder's Line, excepting only the remote tip of Yorke Peninsula, was blocked out into hundreds, and most of the land in surrounding sections which had been held off the market was opened for selection (Map 9). By this action the way was cleared for the coalescence of the three farming nuclei on Yorke Peninsula: Green's Plains, Maitland-Ardrossan, and the lands back of Edith-

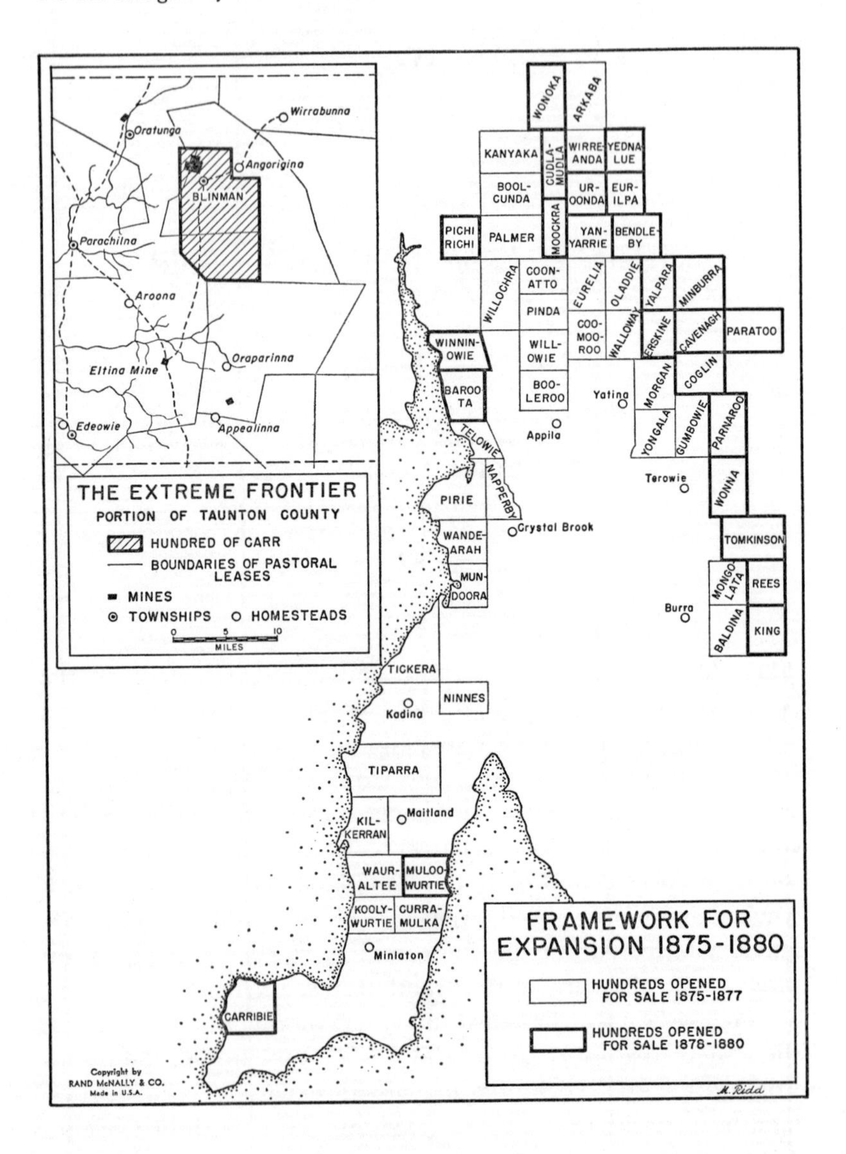
THE EXTREME FRONTIER
PORTION OF TAUNTON COUNTY
HUNDRED OF CARR
BOUNDARIES OF PASTORAL LEASES
MINES
TOWNSHIPS
HOMESTEADS
0 5 10
MILES
Wirrabunna
Oratunga
Angorigina
BLINMAN
Parachilna
Aroona
Oraparinna
Eltina Mine
Edeowie
Appealinna
FRAMEWORK FOR EXPANSION 1875-1880
HUNDREDS OPENED FOR SALE 1875-1877
HUNDREDS OPENED FOR SALE 1878-1880
WONOKA
ARKABA
KANYAKA
CUDLA-MUDLA
WIRRE-ANDA
YEDNA-LUE
BOOL-CUNDA
UR-OONDA
EUR-ILPA
PICHI RICHI
PALMER
MOOCKRA
YAN-YARRIE
BENDLE-BY
WILLOCHRA
COON-ATTO
EURELIA
OLADDIE
YALPARA
MINBURRA
PINDA
COO-MOO-ROO
WALLOWAY
ERSKINE
CAVENAGH
PARATOO
WINNIN-OWIE
WILL-OWIE
MORGAN
COGLIN
BAROO TA
BOO-LEROO
Yatina
YONGALA
GUMBOWIE
PARNAROO
Appila
TELOWIE
NAPPERBY
Terowie
WONNA
PIRIE
Crystal Brook
WANDE-ARAH
TOMKINSON
MUN-DOORA
MONGO LATA
REES
Burra
BALDINA
KING
TICKERA
NINNES
Kadina
TIPARRA
KIL-KERRAN
Maitland
WAUR-ALTEE
MULOO-WURTIE
KOOLY-WURTIE
CURRA-MULKA
Minlaton
CARRIBIE
M. Ridd

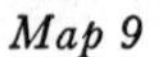
Copyright by
RAND McNALLY & CO.
Made in U.S.A.

Map 9

burgh in the far south. Northward along Spencer Gulf, west of the Barunga Range, the land, covered with dense mallee and without surface water, was not yet in demand, but the hundreds were marked off in preparation for subdivision and sale at a later date.[1] The surveyors then shifted to the areas north and east to pave the way for the surge beyond the discredited "line of rainfall." In mid-winter the lands most eagerly sought, just north and east of Melrose, were opened for sale, momentarily easing the pressure, and another broad strip lying just beyond the old limit was rapidly surveyed to keep ahead of the demand.

As the harvest got underway in late 1875, heavy rains came, flattening some of the standing grain and threatening to damage that reaped but unthreshed. It was an unusual kind of climate hazard. "A change of season seems to have been established," reported a farm editor, and as for worrying about droughts "it looks as though the tune will have to be changed." True, they might require some new adaptations in farm practices, but summer rains were better than the hot winds; after all, "South Australia can do better with floods than droughts."[2] As it turned out the damage in this case was slight. But the belief that "a change of season" was taking place now rapidly gained in favor. As colonization reached and then passed beyond Goyder's Line the old folk-idea that "the rain follows the plough," latent since the early years of settlement when the seemingly dry Adelaide Plains had yielded surprisingly good crops, was revived as a topic of general interest and belief. Once again harvests were being reaped in areas regarded by prominent authorities as too arid for agriculture. Some explanation was necessary; the rains did appear to be heavier, and it seemed reasonable to many persons that the "breaking up of the soil," resulting in the absorption of more moisture and thence its evaporation into the atmosphere, was responsible. The rural press propounded this doctrine, the Minister of Agriculture endorsed it in 1875, and from

[1] *Tickera, Ninnes, Wiltunga, Wokurna, Wandearah,* and *Telowie* were proclaimed in December, 1874. *Pirie* and *Mundoora* (Port Broughton), established earlier in order to survey townships at the ports, were not yet opened for farm selection.

[2] *The Farmers' Weekly Messenger* (Adelaide), Dec. 31, 1875.

that time on it became a prominent ingredient in the surging optimism of the times.[3]

The harvest of 1875 was again excellent. With this crop South Australia reached a new pinnacle of development: wheat production for the first time exceeded ten million bushels. Local spokesmen again launched into their seasonal cycle of praising the results, scoffing at past doubts, and predicting an even greater future.

The excellent crops on Yorke Peninsula were hailed as exposing "the impudently asserted fallacy" that the area was unsuited for farming. Indeed, it now seemed "marvellous" that such a notion could have been "so successfully maintained" for so long.[4] A new belt of hundreds had been surveyed, and mostly opened for sale, which would soon unite the southern nucleus with that around Maitland.[5]

In the North new symbols of progress appeared. Port Pirie, after having served as a shipping point for three years, was finally formally surveyed as a township, ending the threat that the government might bypass it in favor of Mt. Ferguson. Early in 1876 *The Port Pirie Gazette and Areas News* was launched to chart and promote the development of the "Liverpool of South Australia." It was a particularly auspicious moment for the first issue could report a happy event: the trial run of the newly-landed locomotive three miles inland to the end of track, from where the graders were shaping the roadbed eastward into the rich Broughton country. Upon its return it was halted in front of Howe's Hotel and a proposal was made "to 'christen' the locomotive and toast the new line of railway; champagne having been provided, 'Success to the Port Pirie and Gladstone Railway' was enthusiastically drunk."[6] Such enthusiasm was well grounded

[3] The first mention of this idea during this era was made in a statement about the settlement possibilities of Beautiful Valley, beyond Melrose, the first locality north of Goyder's Line to be colonized; *ibid.*, May 15, 1874. For the Minister's statement see the issue of Sept. 3, 1875, of this same paper. See also *ibid.*, Dec. 4, 1874; *The Northern Argus* (Clare), Dec. 4, 1874, and Aug. 13, 1875; and *The Port Pirie Gazette and Areas News*, Feb. 4, 1876.

[4] *The Farmers' Weekly Messenger* (Adelaide), Jan. 21, 1876.

[5] *Tiparra, Kilkerran, Wauraltee,* and *Koolywurtie* were put on the market in 1875, *Curramulka* in 1876.

[6] *The Port Pirie Gazette and Areas News*, Feb. 4, 1876.

upon the prospects of the railroad when completed, for its construction was far behind the demand. Long lines of wagons were trailing into Port Pirie from as far away as Jamestown. As many as 150 a day unloaded at the wharves and the shipping facilities were heavily congested. During a typical week fifteen ketches (45–80 tons), one brigantine (99 tons), two barques (200–700 tons), and five ships (700–1700 tons) were loading grain.[7] Over a million and a quarter bushels of wheat and 2,687 tons of flour were exported in that year.[8]

Such traffic – and the much greater potential – prompted a sharp rivalry among the northern outports. Port Broughton interests had put up a strong campaign to become the terminus of the railroad serving the inland Broughton district. Losing to Port Pirie, they were given a meagre consolation prize: a horse-powered tramway ten miles inland. Completed in March, 1876, it was little more than a bridge across the strip of dry mallee country to connect with a small area of colonization at the base of the Barunga Range. Though much poorer in waterfront facilities and hinterland than its nearby rival, over a quarter of a million bushels were exported from Port Broughton in 1876.[9] Port Wakefield also sought to tap that newly productive interior. In March, 1875, its tramway was extended from Hoyleton ten miles northward to the heart of Blyth Plains, and the press of traffic was sufficient to warrant refitting the line for locomotives, which were placed in operation in August.[10] Adding the nearly 800,000 bushels of wheat and 615 tons of flour from Wakefield, the total shipments of the three northern outports amounted to 2,322,000 bushels and 3,302 tons of flour.[11]

The surveyors continued to be hard pressed to keep ahead of the demands. A million acres were marked off in 1876, and it was planned to increase the rate by half again as much in the following year. Twelve parties worked along the northern margins. Over 250,000 acres were selected almost as soon as the lands

[7] *Ibid.*, Feb. 25, 1876.
[8] *S. A. Parl. Paper No. 117* (1876).
[9] *Ibid.*, and *S. A. Parl. Paper No. 232* (1876).
[10] *S. A. Parl. Paper No. 66* (1877).
[11] *S. A. Parl. Paper No. 117* (1876).

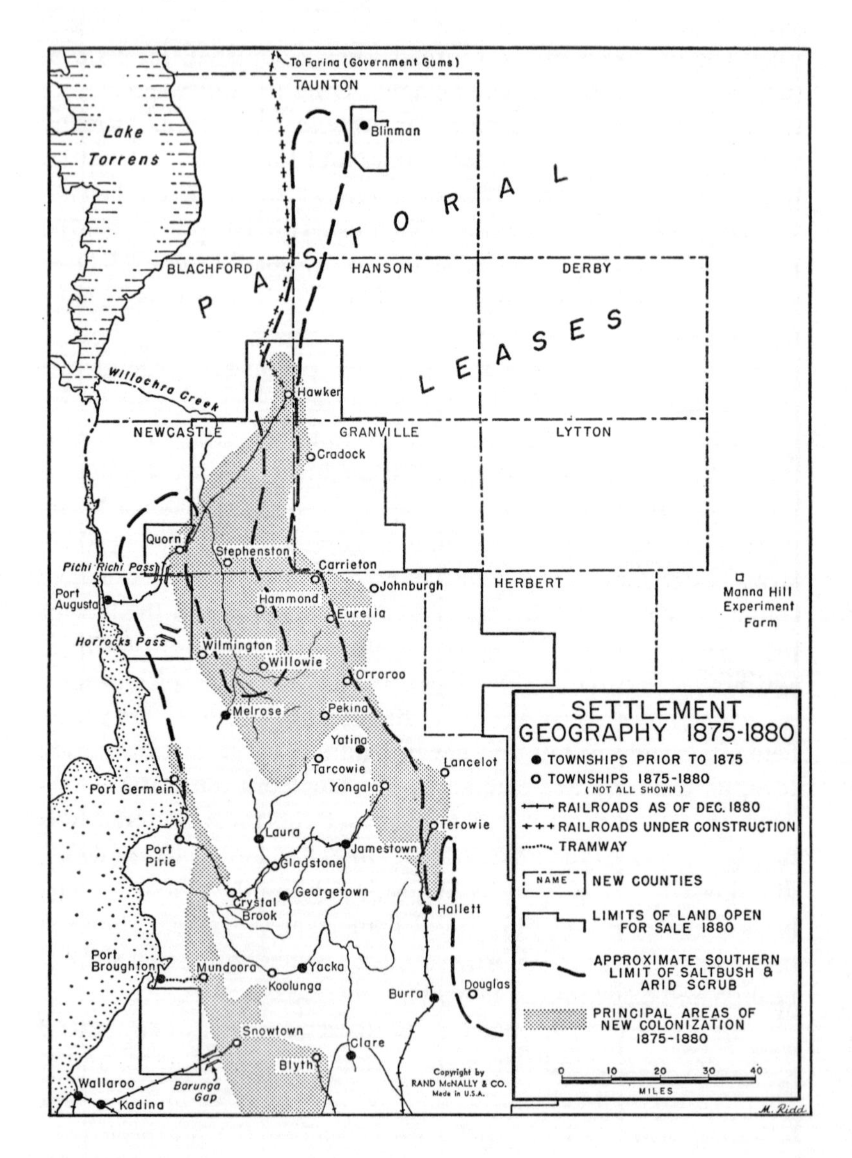
To Farina (Government Gums)
TAUNTON
Blinman
Lake Torrens
PASTORAL LEASES
BLACHFORD
HANSON
DERBY
Willochra Creek
Hawker
NEWCASTLE
GRANVILLE
LYTTON
Cradock
Quorn
Stephenston
Carrieton
Pichi Richi Pass
Port Augusta
Hammond
Johnburgh
HERBERT
Manna Hill Experiment Farm
Eurelia
Horrocks Pass
Wilmington
Willowie
Orroroo
Melrose
Pekina
Yatina
Tarcowie
Lancelot
Port Germein
Yongala
Terowie
Laura
Jamestown
Port Pirie
Gladstone
Georgetown
Crystal Brook
Hallett
Port Broughton
Mundoora
Yacka
Koolunga
Burra
Douglas
Snowtown
Clare
Blyth
Wallaroo
Kadina
Barunga Gap
SETTLEMENT GEOGRAPHY 1875-1880
TOWNSHIPS PRIOR TO 1875
TOWNSHIPS 1875-1880 (NOT ALL SHOWN)
RAILROADS AS OF DEC. 1880
RAILROADS UNDER CONSTRUCTION
TRAMWAY
NAME
NEW COUNTIES
LIMITS OF LAND OPEN FOR SALE 1880
APPROXIMATE SOUTHERN LIMIT OF SALTBUSH & ARID SCRUB
PRINCIPAL AREAS OF NEW COLONIZATION 1875-1880
0 10 20 30 40
MILES
Copyright by RAND McNALLY & CO. Made in U.S.A.
M. Ridd

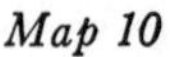

Map 10

were opened in the Willochra Plains and the hill country north of *Pekina*. In June, Newcastle and Granville counties were set out to prepare the framework for a further surge north. Even a poor crop could not stem the tide. The harvest of 1876–77 was little more than half that of the previous year, less than six million bushels, yet it caused hardly a murmur of caution from the country spokesmen. Indeed, anyone who talked of crop "failures" was viewed with suspicion, for it was firmly believed by some that a certain Adelaide paper and a few members of Parliament actually hoped for failure in order to halt the agricultural advance and protect the pastoralists.[12]

Certainly there was little evidence of shaken confidence on the part of the selectors. Fifteen new hundreds were opened for sale in 1877. These were in three quite separate districts: the dry and dense mallee lands along the northeast shore of Spencer Gulf, *Mongolata,* just northeast of Burra, and nine in various sectors of the north.[13] The last was by far the most important area of expansion. Land seekers now moved in upon the whole of the Willochra Plains, far north in the hill country to *Arkaba,* fifty miles beyond the lands available the previous year, and northeast upon the widening plains of *Oladdie* where their horizon lay far out into the seemingly limitless expanse of the interior basins (Maps 9 and 10).[14] And the government which but a few seasons back had so cautiously stemmed and steered the farmers into carefully selected areas, now in a seemingly frantic effort to outrun even the most sanguine popular optimism proclaimed six new counties in January, 1877: Blachford, Hanson, Taunton, Herbert, Lytton and Derby.[15] With these the

[12] *The Farmers' Weekly Messenger* (Adelaide), Nov. 17, 1876, made this accusation.

[13] The Spencer Gulf hundreds were: *Tickera, Mundoora, Wandearah, Pirie, Telowie;* those in the North: *Coonatto, Palmer, Boolcunda, Kanyaka, Yanyarrie, Wirreanda, Arkaba, Oladdie, Gumbowie.*

[14] For example, *The Areas' Express and Farmers' Journal* (Booyoolie) [Gladstone], Oct. 27, 1877, reporting selections in *Kanyaka* and *Arkaba.*

[15] The reason for establishing so many counties at once was because a new law required three years' notice be given to pastoralists of the resumption of leases. The demand for land was heavy and therefore a large area was set aside in order that enough would be available for sale a few years later. *S. A. Parl. Paper No. 28* (1888), p. 72.

framework of selected and potential lands *north* of Goyder's Line was nearly *twice* as great as the entire frontier area south of the Line settled since 1869.[16] And with this action the "official frontier" was shoved far to the north halfway along the dismal salt bed of Lake Torrens and northeast over one hundred miles beyond the present settled limits. It was a perfect mockery of Goyder's Line – such ideas about the limitations on wheat cultivation were "mere theoretical baubles."[17]

GOYDER'S WARNING

Ironically this frenzy of activity which was to most persons a symbol of magnificent progress was viewed by the man in charge as a dangerous mistake, for Goyder was still Surveyor General. His predictions of chaos if the agricultural frontier was allowed to advance freely into the pastoral domain had proved true. The Lands Department had been refusing to renew leases and resumed some pastoral runs on such short notice that the sheepmen had to sell their flocks at great loss; in some instances it was claimed they had not even had a chance to shear before vacating.[18] Belatedly this situation was ameliorated by the law requiring the government to give notice of resumption three years in advance. More important, Goyder was completely unmoved by all the signs and talk of farming success in these new lands and steadfastly upheld his earlier views. His concise descriptions of land quality, which were published routinely as each new hundred was proclaimed, always concluded with the same refrain: "rainfall unreliable."

In the first years of expansion into the Broughton country that theme was perhaps but a mild caution. As the settlers moved on north into the Willochra Plains and northeast to the Oladdie, however, Goyder made it clear that he was not merely suggesting caution, he was sounding a dire warning. For in these areas the mallee gave way to a much more open landscape covered with

[16] Calculated on the basis of blocks of hundreds, the area within counties north of Goyder's Line was about 14,500 square miles, that south of the Line and north of the 1869 frontier, excluding eastern Burra County, 8,200 square miles.
[17] *The Areas' Express and Farmers' Journal* (Booyoolie), Nov. 3, 1877.
[18] *S. A. Parl. Paper No. 145* (1876).

low shrubs and sparse grass. For the first time, the settlers were encountering a country quite different from any heretofore: the saltbush plains. While the general public joined in an ever-strengthening chorus of optimism over the prospects for agricultural expansion, Goyder drew upon his own experiences to give a vivid portrayal of the capricious realities of the North:

> During the last twenty years I have crossed and recrossed the country in question during all seasons of the year, and have seen the surface in good seasons like a hayfield, teeming with rich, rank, and luxurious vegetation; and during drought destitute of grass and herbage, the surface soil dried by the intense heat, in places broken and pulverized by the passage of stock, and formed by the action of the wind into miniature hummocks, surrounding the closely-cropped stumps of salt-bushes, &c., and the soil blown away in places to a depth of several inches, the drift covering the fences of yards, troughs, &c., and so denuded of feed as to be altogether useless for stock of any description. Had the soil been ploughed at that time the whole of the depth of the furrow must inevitably have blown away.[19]

He strongly urged that surveys be halted until experiments could be made to determine whether such country would in fact prove reliable farm land or not. If so, an orderly advance of settlers could be aided with confidence, but if not it would save the ruination of pastoralists and farmers alike. Was it not folly to drive the sheepman off his lease, sacrificing all of his improvements, in order to replace him with a score of would-be farmers, who, after destroying the natural pasture, might never succeed in reaping a harvest?

But such a view found little support from either the farmers or the government. To be at all reliable such experiments would need several years, and it was now politically impossible to dam up the tide of expansion to await the results. Once the government had relaxed its control over colonization it could not re-establish it without contradicting itself as well as the great majority of the public. If the land needed testing the farmers were quite willing to do it.

Though unwilling to block the sale of lands in the area already surveyed, the government did authorize the establishment of an experimental farm out beyond those limits. In the autumn of 1877 Goyder chose the site, two square miles of shallow reddish

[19] *Ibid.*, p. 2.

loam covered with saltbush at Manna Hill Well, far out on the track to the Barrier Range, nearly one hundred miles northeast of Terowie, the current margin of settlement (Map 10). It was a desolate country, as one visitor noted, "the name would suggest that it is somewhere in juxtaposition to the Garden of Eden, but before the late rains the appearance of the surrounding country bore nearer analogy to the wilderness through which the Children of Israel passed."[20] But it was a daring experiment with exciting possibilities, for if such a locale would grow wheat "an immense area will be thrown open for agriculture which has hitherto been thought only good for sheep."[21] The first harvest, in late 1877, was considered "satisfactory"; five acres of wheat yielded twelve bushels per acre, and smaller plots of other grains did as well or better.[22] It was a minute but hopeful beginning.

COLONIZATION DEVELOPMENTS, 1877–79

In 1877 the northward probing agricultural frontier entered and quickly spurred development of a whole new sub-region. From the first leap forward into the Broughton in 1869 until this time the northern margin had been developing into a sub-region oriented along the Port Pirie–Gladstone–Jamestown axis, a line firmly anchored by the completion of the railroad to Gladstone in 1876 (Map 10). But now, as the Willochra Plains were reached a new pattern of trade began. In November, 1877, a farmer of *Pinda,* the first selector in that locality northeast of Melrose, forwarded a load of wheat to Port Augusta, and a few weeks later the first shipment (199 bags) of grain was sent out of that port.[23] By January the harvest was reported pouring into Wilmington, a flour mill was under construction at Melrose, and the bullock teams which for decades had hauled the wool down to the sea, now were carting wheat. It was a "strange" sight:

> It was only a few years ago when the idea of wheat being shipped at Port Augusta in any quantities would have been scoffed at as the chimera

[20] *The Farmers' Weekly Messenger* (Adelaide), May 4, 1877.
[21] *Ibid.,* April 27, 1877.
[22] *Port Augusta Dispatch,* Jan 1, 1878; *S. A. Parl. Paper No. 146* (1878).
[23] *The Farmers' Weekly Messenger* (Adelaide), Nov. 8, 1877; *Port Augusta Dispatch,* Dec. 15, 1877.

of an over-sanguine brain, but this season will surely convince the most skeptical.[24]

In that same month the first sod was turned on the railway to be built deep into the outback to Government Gums. In anticipation of that festive ceremony the editor of the *Port Augusta Dispatch,* who had established his paper but a few months before as a harbinger of the new age, envisioned "long trains of trucks . . . following each other down the line, laden with the hundreds of tons of wool, copper, wheat, and other produce." Originally projected to serve the copper and pastoral interests far inland, the final survey had been shifted through Pichi Richi Pass to tap the new agricultural areas along the northern Willochra Plains, but this was now by no means the limit and the editor confidently predicted that "agriculture will spread farther north than many of us in the present generation are able to realize."[25]

The frontier advanced so rapidly and successfully as to make such visions but modest projections of the present (Map 11). Never had the seasons opened so favorably as in 1878. Climatic change seemed to be "running ahead" of the plough rather than "following." Tremendous rains spread over the lands east of the Flinders and far out to the north and east. The creeks were in flood, and miles of waving grass covered all the ground still to be broken by the plough.[26] It was a powerful attraction, for "where grass grows wheat will grow,"[27] and even beyond the grassy margins the land lay damp and fertile and local spokesmen set to work to demolish the last restraint by arguing against the "unfounded prejudice against Salt Bush Country"[28] (Map 10).

Many selectors responded to the lure, the frontier moved forward with quickened pace and local enthusiasts happily charted the progress: "The numbers coming north to take up their sections since the flood, has been quite a sight," reported a Willochra correspondent;[29] from Orroroo came descriptions of many teams

[24] *Port Augusta Dispatch,* Jan. 19, 1878.
[25] *Ibid.,* Jan. 12, 1878. See also *The Farmers' Weekly Messenger* (Adelaide), Jan. 18, 1878.
[26] *Port Augusta Dispatch,* March 16 and May 11, 1878.
[27] *The Areas' Express and Farmers' Journal* (Gladstone), Oct. 9, 1878.
[28] *Port Augusta Dispatch,* April 20, 1878.
[29] *Ibid.,* March 30, 1878.

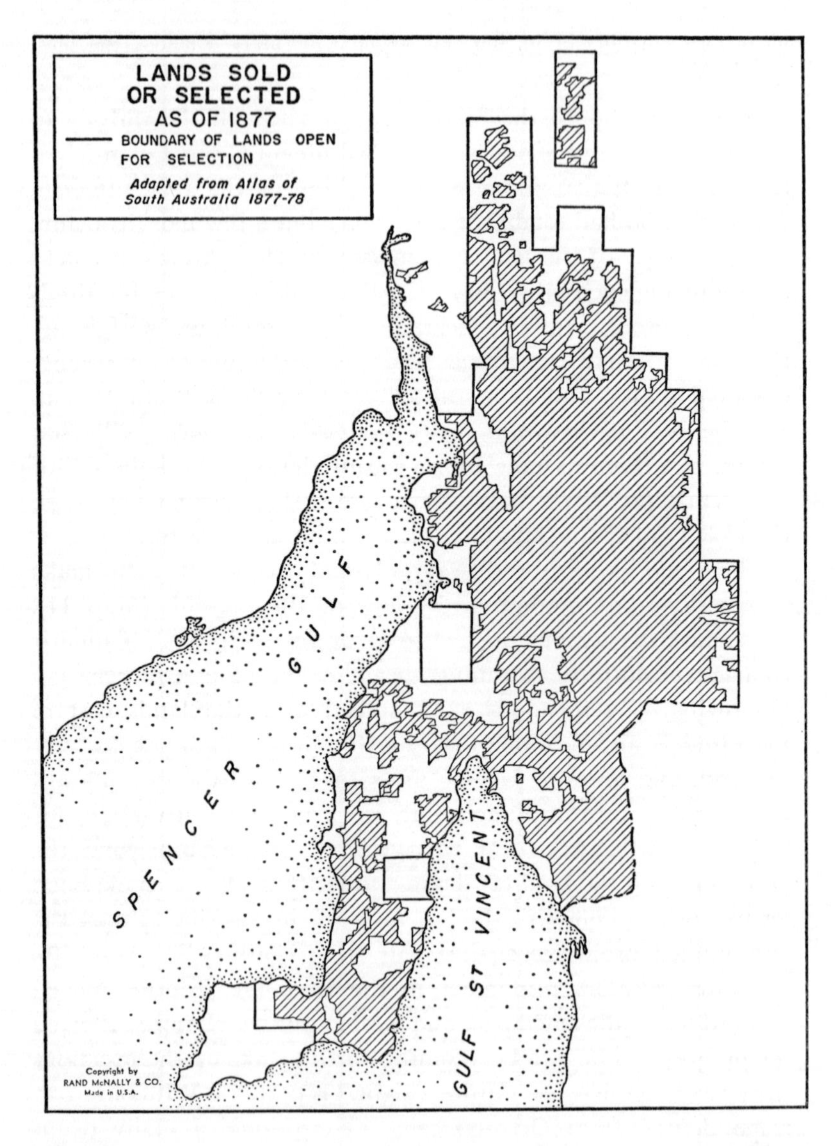
LANDS SOLD
OR SELECTED
AS OF 1877
BOUNDARY OF LANDS OPEN
FOR SELECTION
Adapted from Atlas of
South Australia 1877-78
SPENCER GULF
GULF ST VINCENT

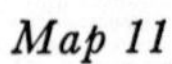
Copyright by
RAND McNALLY & CO.
Made in U.S.A.

Map 11

now passing through to *Walloway* and *Oladdie,* "it being proved that wheat of good quality and in payable quantity can be grown on these plains."[30] All through the year the advance continued: "the rapid march of agricultural settlement . . . , and the grand influx or the 'mad rush' of settlers into the remote northern hundreds seems not to be abating."[31] In that year, 300,000 acres were selected, and half of it broken out for cultivation in this fresh pioneer region north of Goyder's Line.

And once more the harvest served only to compound the optimism. The entire Willochra Plain averaged over ten bushels per acre and fields of thirty bushels were reported. New land in *Eurelia* and *Coomooroo,* in fact all along the northeastern fringe from Yongala to Carrieton, gave similar returns, and an average of more than thirteen bushels from the initial crop on 1500 acres in *Arkaba* seemed to suggest that the land might even get better farther out.[32] Some certainly must have thought so, for in early 1879 colonization took a giant stride clear into the middle of Taunton County, just west of Lake Frome (Map 9, inset, and Map 10). Hardly had the hundred of *Carr* been opened for sale when an enterprising farmer from Wonoka arrived with a load of wheat which he sold at a handsome price to selectors anxious to get in a crop.[33] A month later a Blinman correspondent reported that

> the farmers are still drawing North. About 2,000 acres were taken out last week in this Hundred [*Carr*] and I believe that every acre open for selection will be applied for in a very short time.[34]

To be sure, this detached nucleus was in a locality next to the high ranges presumed to be especially favorable. Even Goyder, when the area adjacent to the mining township of Blinman was surveyed three years before, had stated that "the greater portion of the land is fit for tillage, and with sufficient rain for general agricultural purposes."[35] But there were others who would not

[30] *The Jamestown Review,* March 14, 1878.
[31] *The Areas' Express and Farmers' Journal* (Gladstone), Oct. 2, 1878.
[32] *Ibid.,* Dec. 4, 1878, and Jan. 1, 1879; *Port Augusta Dispatch,* Jan. 17, 1879, and official statistics.
[33] *Port Augusta Dispatch,* March 7, 1879.
[34] *Ibid.,* April 11, 1879.
[35] *S. A. Parl. Paper No. 203* (1876).

limit the prospects so narrowly. When the name of "Government Gums," the terminus of the railroad under construction 200 miles north from Port Augusta, was changed to "Farina," it was "facetiously proposed that the next two townships should be called . . . Bran and Pollard." But even the Beltana correspondent who reported the jest, implied that, in time, such labels might not be inappropriate:

> More land ought to be surveyed and sold soon, both at Farina and Beltana. The latter requires suburban allotments only, whilst the former requires both kinds. I think the suburban allotments would go a long way in the useful direction of experimenting in cultivation and agriculture. Gardens and farms might eventually be not uncommon in the Far North, . . . who knows but that new agricultural areas might succeed such small attempts?[36]

Such courageous optimism was especially congenial to the editor who reported them, for Port Augusta was an obvious beneficiary of all such developments. The prospects seemed almost boundless:

> Our children may see the present narrow belt of cultivation extended far into the interior, and thousands of thriving homesteads and busy towns, where now not even sheep can live, except in winter time.[37]

If a change in climate was necessary, the means seemed to be at hand. Not only would "the breaking up of the soil" help to "equalize" the climate (more even distribution of rainfall through the year), but the planting of trees would certainly increase the annual rainfall. The editor thought that trees would be more effective instruments than the plough, and he thereby became an ardent propagandist of a second "rainfall theory" which received wide publicity during these years of rapid northward expansion.

Unlike the "plough theory" the "influence of trees upon rainfall" was more of a scientific than a folk idea, and it was a topic of world-wide interest at the time.[38] Its most eminent local advo-

[36] *Port Augusta Dispatch,* May 4, 1878.

[37] *Ibid.,* Nov. 3, 1877.

[38] C. W. Thornthwaite notes the persistence and importance of such theories in "Modification of Rural Microclimates," in William L. Thomas, Jr., ed., *Man's Role in Changing the Face of the Earth* (Chicago: University of Chicago Press, 1956), pp. 567–83. For an examination of these and other "rainfall theories" prevalent in an area colonized at about the same time as South

cate was Dr. Richard Schomburgk, the distinguished Director of the Botanic Garden in Adelaide. A few years before Schomburgk had become alarmed at the extensive clearing of trees, which was an inevitable accompaniment of colonization, and he was a major force in getting several forest reserves established. The practical needs of fuel, building material, and fencing were probably the decisive facts for such Parliamentary action, but the Director put great emphasis upon the deterimental climatic effects of such denudation of the land.[39] As the colonists pushed farther inward to drier and more open country, the emphasis was shifted to the need for extensive plantings as a necessary security against drought. The rural press of the North quickly took up the theme[40] and in 1878 the new Conservator of Forests, John Ednie Brown, gave the theory an importance equalled only by the most vociferous of local lay enthusiasts. Indeed, Brown elevated trees from a mere "influence" into an almost complete "control" over climate, and explained the aridity of interior Australia simply by the absence of trees.[41]

Such views, however, seemed to have been largely ignored by the farmers. Perhaps this was in part because although the "tree theory" promised an ultimate amelioration, it clearly emphasized the unpleasant idea that the saltbush country *at present* was a dangerously dry region for farmers. Thus Schomburgk, Brown, and others were really supporting Goyder's evaluation of such lands, although, quite unlike him, they were certain they held a cure. On the other hand, the country editors in general blithely ignored the contradiction inherent in the concurrent praise of the

Australia see Donald W. Meinig, "The Evolution of Understanding and Environment: Climate and Wheat Culture in the Columbia Plateau," *Yearbook of the Association of Pacific Coast Geographers,* XVI (1954), 25–34.

[39] The materials related to this topic are extensive. Schomburgk's first major statement was "Influence of Forests on Climate" (Aug. 9, 1870) in *Papers Read Before the Philosophical Society and the Chamber of Manufactures* (Adelaide, 1873), pp. 1–7; for his principal official report see *S. A. Parl. Paper No. 26* (1873). An ardent Parliamentary spokesman of the theory was F. E. H. W. Krichauff, whose lengthy paper "Forest Conservancy and Timber Supply" was published in *South Australian Industries and Manufactures, Papers Read Before the Chamber of Manufactures* (Adelaide, 1875), pp. 255–79.

[40] For example, *The Northern Argus* (Clare), March 21, 1873, Feb. 13 and Sept. 15, 1874, and Jan. 19, 1875; *The Port Pirie Gazette and Areas News,* Feb. 4, 1876; the *Port Augusta Dispatch,* Nov. 3, 1877.

[41] *S. A. Parl. Paper No. 83* (1879) and *No. 139* (1880).

immediate agricultural potential of such lands and advocacy of tree planting to improve the climate.[42]

Whatever the implications of such theories the scramble for lands on easy credit terms continued unabated. Nor were farms the only lure. A dozen and a half new townships were surveyed by the government in this new northern area. Under the auction system lot prices soared. When Port Germein was put up for sale, over 200 township lots were immediately purchased at prices ranging up to £153. Many such lots were taken purely on speculation in hopes of rapid town development. In November, 1878, for example, the prospectus of the "Northern Areas Land and Investment Company, Limited" appeared in several local papers. The promoters were all from Jamestown, Belalie, and Orroroo, and the object was to purchase and hold for resale the available allotments in and around the new townships "which are now so rapidly increasing in the North." To illustrate the possibilities it was stated that whole acres which had been sold by the government in Jamestown for £4 were now worth £10 per foot, and in Orroroo prices had risen from £7 per half acre to as much as £3–5 per foot.[43] Scattered over the frontier lands six to twenty miles apart, these little towns were in feverish competition, "pushing, scrambling, holding meetings, and forming deputations,"[44] seeking roads, railroads, flour mills, water supplies, and domination over an extensive hinterland. A few, because of rich lands adjacent or advantageous traffic sites, almost immediately showed signs of solid development, such as Orroroo, the gateway to the Oladdie Plains, and Wilmington, serving Beautiful Valley and all the traffic across Horrocks Pass to the Gulf (Map 10). Quorn, gateway to the Willochra Plain at the foot of Pichi Richi Pass, and on a definitely-located railroad route, enjoyed the most certain position of all and its development reflected these advantages. Surveyed in May and June of 1878, by December it had several shops, two hotels, and a substantial stone flour mill (Fig. 4).[45] Other towns, such as

[42] However, the Port Augusta editor recognized the contradiction in the two "rainfall theories" and did note that the farmers ought to destroy fewer trees, for while they were "unconsciously doing good" by ploughing, they were "neutralizing its effect" by cutting the forests. *Port Augusta Dispatch,* April 4, 1879.
[43] *The Areas' Express and Farmers' Journal* (Gladstone), Nov. 2, 1878.
[44] *Ibid.,* Oct. 2, 1878.
[45] *Port Augusta Dispatch,* May 25 and Dec. 21, 1878.

Willowie, Amyton, Hammond, Stephenston, Carrieton, Eurelia, Johnburgh, and Cradock, had no such assurances of success and could only hope for an expanding agriculture, future rail lines, and the possibility of getting an edge on their nearest rivals in the number of shops and services in hopes of drawing from an ever-widening region.

DEVELOPMENTS IN THE OLDER FRONTIER

Behind this new frontier zone developments were steadily underway which if less dramatic were even more important in firmly establishing South Australia as a major wheat producer and exporter. It was a period of rapid consolidation and elaboration of agriculture and of service facilities. The land was nearly all in private control, but acreages and productions continued to mount as selectors worked to get all their holdings into crop. By 1876 Victoria County took the lead in wheat acreage and in the following year in actual production. Over a million and a half bushels after but six to seven years of settlement was a proud local achievement. The Port Pirie–Gladstone line was extended on to Jamestown in 1878 and surveys were being run further inland. At the moment a line north to Yatina appeared probable and township speculations at Mannanarie and the proposed terminus were brisk.[46] Along the existing line the towns were growing rapidly; reports from Jamestown, Caltowie, Gladstone, and Crystal Brook charted the progress in new shops, hotels, schools, institutes, and, each harvest, of the tremendous inflow of grain awaiting shipment (Fig. 5). Port Pirie continued to reflect this growth in its hinterland and to ridicule any threat of encroachment upon that rich trade area by advocates of Port Broughton or the new aspiring Port Germein, which was established and sent out its first wheat in 1879.[47] A local census in early 1879 gave Pirie a population of 1,330.[48] At the harbor thirteen wharves served the heavy seasonal traffic, and a large flour mill (thirty-five pairs of stone) handled a thousand tons of wheat a week. (Figs. 6 and 7).[49]

Railroads continued to be the greatest topic and specific routes the greatest controversy throughout the entire wheat domain. The

[46] *The Farmers' Weekly Messenger* (Adelaide), Nov. 9, 1877.
[47] *The Port Pirie Gazette and Areas News,* Jan. 24, 1879, and Jan. 30, 1880.
[48] *Ibid.,* May 16, 1879.
[49] *Ibid.,* Aug. 24 and Oct. 19, 1877.

most complicated issue was the tapping of the rich area of western Stanley County centered around Yacka and Koolunga. Four outports were in contention: Pirie, Broughton, Wallaroo, and Wakefield. Although extension of the Blyth Plains line on the north appeared logical on the map (Map 10), the heavy disadvantages of shipping at Port Wakefield were a strong argument against it. Port Broughton suffered from a similar defect. The superior deep water harbor at Wallaroo finally won a partial victory. The Barunga Gap line was begun in 1879 and opened for traffic the following March, prompting a heavy demand for lots at the newly-surveyed terminous at Snowtown.[50]

As usual on the North East, frontier developments were smaller and slower paced. In the Burra itself the great mineral period was over, the mines closed down in September, 1877, and the community braced itself for the difficult transition to a new role as only an agricultural-pastoral trade center.[51] The local newspaper had earlier tried to cheer its readers with the fact that the town would become "the focus of a vast extent of corn and wool-growing country to the north, east and west."[52] But progress continued to be relatively slow because of the competition of more promising areas in the main North. The crop of 1876–77 was nearly a failure, and yields were consistently somewhat lower than the general average elsewhere. The rabbit problem was more severe.[53] The Kapunda-Burra-Hallett area was the main portal of entry into the South Australian wheatlands of this plague as it spread out from its Victorian source, and the menace was already calling forth those superlatives of description which were later to become commonplace: the truth of the situation, it was stated, would be received "with incredulity and astonishment" by those who had

[50] *The Areas' Express and Farmers' Journal* (Gladstone), Jan. 22, 1879.
[51] *Burra News and Northern Mail,* Sept. 28, 1877.
[52] *The Northern Mail* (Kooringa), June 30, 1876.
[53] The introduction of rabbits from Europe into Australia is probably the most famous example of man, quite unwittingly, drastically upsetting an ecological balance. Loosed, perhaps accidentally, in Victoria in the 1860's upon a continent with a mild climate, ample forage, and almost no natural enemies, they quickly multiplied to astronomical figures and became a chronic menace to the pastoral and agricultural industries. For a brief account and a sketch map of the historic pattern of their spread see Griffith Taylor, *Australia, A Study of Warm Environments and Their Effect on British Settlement* (5th ed.; London: Methuen, 1949), pp. 317–19.

not witnessed it.[54] The railroad was extended north to Hallett in 1878, but there was little of the intense speculation in farm and town lands so characteristic of neighboring areas. Sales of government lots at Douglas in *Baldina* and Lancelot in *Gumbowie,* for example, were not very successful.[55] To some extent the trials at the Manna Hill Experimental Farm held the whole future in balance: if they were successful a huge intervening tract would undoubtedly be quickly selected; if not a more cautious probing would continue. But, for the time being, many evidently were content to let the government take the initial risks.

The reports of the second year at Manna Hill were not at all encouraging. It was a drier season, wheat yielded but four bushels per acre (acreage not given) from unploughed fallow, barley did better, but the lucerne crop was a near failure, and most of the fruit trees died. The annual report of the director was necessarily tempered by these results, though he was by no means ready to dismiss the possibilities of agriculture:

> If the theory of the rainfall following the plough be correct, Manna Hill may yet do, but I cannot presume to give an opinion on that point. I do not think, taking a series of years, that there has been much change in this district. The experiment in the North-East is an important one, and in the interests of all concerned I would strongly advise the continuance of the same sufficiently long to place the question of wheat-growing beyond doubt before inducing the agriculturist to settle in that quarter. It is my impression that when the country is cut up . . . the blocks will need to be large, so that the farmer may partake somewhat of the character of the squatter.[56]

Considering the general attitudes of the times, it was a remarkably modest and sensible statement.

On Yorke Peninsula special difficulties likewise hindered expansion, but it continued to be a lively frontier. Between 1875 and 1878 the increase in land in cultivation averaged about 26,000 acres annually, despite serious problems in developing local water

[54] *The Garden and the Field* (Adelaide), September, 1878. See also *S. A. Parl. Debates,* June 13, 1878, col. 132, for a geographical description of the infestation. The huge pastoral freeholds just beyond Clare were claimed to be major local sources of rabbits. For an earlier complaint see *S. A. Parl. Paper No. 74* (1873), a petition from the Kapunda-Eudunda-Burra districts for governmental action on the problem.

[55] *The Northern Mail* (Burra), July 6, 1877, and *The Areas' Express and Farmers' Journal* (Gladstone), Jan. 22, 1879.

[56] *S. A. Parl. Paper No. 31A* (1879).

supplies and in clearing the dense scrub. The invention of a curious "stump-jump" plough by Mr. R. B. Smith of Kalkabury was hailed by some as the final answer to the mallee problem for it was was designed to plough land in which the heavy, shallow roots still remained.[57] It was shown at the Moonta Agricultural Show in late 1876 but was not as yet in wide enough use to be certain of its real success.[58]

A railroad from Yorke Valley to Ardrossan continued locally to be an object of keen interest,[59] but most agitation was naturally focused upon jetties and navigation improvements. And a whole series of local ports had sprung into existence. By 1878 jetties had been constructed at Stansbury, Point Turton, Minlacowie, and Port Victoria, and the older ports at Ardrossan and Edithburgh continued to increase their shipments. Inland, Maitland, Minlaton, and Yorketown, spaced down the peninsula, reported rapid town growth. The construction of a good causeway across Moorowie Swamp ended the winter isolation of the far south, the farmers were burning off the black grass and getting excellent crops, and Warooka quickly became a thriving little community.[60]

Moving forward through the latter 1870's, not steadily nor evenly, punctuated by seasonal and local variations – sudden advances, temporary retardations – but always, cumulatively, forward, the agricultural progress of all these sub-regions momentarily coalesced at the close of the decade in an unprecedented harmony of success which shattered all previous records: fourteen million bushels of wheat, nearly five million more than ever before. Curiously, in many localities the harvest of 1879–80 did not equal the very best of some previous years, and a few crop failures were reported in scattered points along the extreme frontier, but, generally, for the first time really good crops were reaped in all major areas in the same year. Roads, railways, jetties and shipping were swamped by the demands. In six months the rail lines north of Adelaide moved six million bushels to port, exports from Port Augusta quadrupled, Pirie sent out two and a

[57] The nature and importance of this invention is described in Chapter VI.
[58] *The Farmers' Weekly Messenger* (Adelaide), Nov. 17, 1876.
[59] *S. A. Parl. Paper No. 46* (1879).
[60] *The Farmers' Weekly Messenger* (Adelaide), May 11, Nov. 30, and Dec. 8, 1877.

quarter million bushels[61] and suddenly became one of the major wheat ports of the world, and a dozen smaller outlets contributed to the outflow to English, African, and Australasian markets.

Just ten years after South Australia had firmly put her faith in wheat as the single great medium of economic progress all the prophets of success seemed to be vindicated, every major section had passed the practical test and every costly facility had been pressed into maximum use. It was the perfect reward for having focused nearly the entire interest, action, and resources of the colony into the creation of a huge new agricultural domain. And the frontier was still pushed forward: eleven new hundreds were opened for sale, and selectors moved on north into the hills of *Wonoka* and northeast well out upon the broadening saltbush plains.

[61] *S. A. Parl. Paper No. 27* (1881), p. 135.

V.

Drought and Retreat: 1881 – 1884

Goyder's ghost seems to hover about.
— Friedrich Kuttler
Winninowie farmer[1]

THE DROUGHTS OF 1880–82

The autumn and winter of 1880 were unusually busy seasons. The heavy harvest had to be hauled to rail sidings or ports and, as soon as the rains began, much larger acreages were prepared for the next crop. In the North the wheatland was expanded by 170,000 acres, on the extreme fringe in Newcastle and Granville counties total cropland was doubled, and the first plantings were made in Herbert. In the North East new selectors broke up land in *Parnaroo, Wonna,* and *King,* and another 26,000 acres were added by the farmers on Yorke Peninsula.

The season opened with good rains in late April and early May, but the next several weeks were unusually dry. As the winter lengthened, the crop conditions worsened and in the Far North, June, July, and August rainfalls were less than half that of recent years. Heavy rains fell briefly in September, after the drought had taken a heavy toll, but they were followed by an extremely dry and hot season. The red rust extensively infected the wheat, and as the meagre crops shriveled in the fields the locusts swarmed in upon many localities. By November complete crop failures were reported widely throughout the North and near failures over much of the province. Hope continued that early estimates might, as in

[1] Cited in *S. A. Parl. Debates,* June 22, 1882, col. 171.

years past, prove unreliable, but as the harvest got underway the worst fears were confirmed. Along the frontier margins there was simply little or nothing to harvest. The Willochra, the northernmost hills, and the northeast plains of *Oladdie* and *Minburra* averaged less than two bushels per acre. The sandy, dry lands west of the Flinders were similarly stricken. In *Baroota,* between Port Pirie and Port Augusta, 12,000 acres yielded but a thousand bags, and the selectors petitioned for an extension of credit payments. Farther south in the lower Broughton and Barunga area, and in the entire scrub land region on through Balaklava to the Gawler Plains, few fields were abandoned but the average yield fell below five bushels; Yorke Peninsula was only slightly better. Only in the central hill country from Clare to Caltowie were the crops near to an average yield (Map 12).[2]

It was a heavy shock after the tremendous over-all production of the previous season. The total dropped by nearly six million bushels and was even a million less than that of six years before when the acreage had been less than half that of 1880. Predictions that "this season will crush many in the north"[3] might have seemed at first an exaggeration, for a single bad season ought not to have proved disastrous. But it was soon apparent that the general success of the previous year had tended to obscure the fact that all along the northern fringe only marginal crops had been obtained. Many selectors after two or three seasons had yet to harvest a paying crop. In *Arkaba,* the northern salient of settlement, thirteen bushels to the acre had been reaped in 1878–79, but from a total of only 1500 acres; in the following year 10,000 acres averaged but three bushels, and now 20,000 acres yielded almost nothing. Similarly, the Willochra Plains had averaged six bushels in 1879–80, but many selectors had obtained less and this year nearly the entire crop was abandoned. West of the Flinders, in *Telowie* and *Baroota,* after three years of trial, farmers had yet to obtain a profitable crop. Thus, locally in the North, the drought of 1880–81 was not, as elsewhere, an abrupt setback, it was a harsh prolongation of defeat:

[2] The details on acreages, productions, and yields in this chapter are based upon *S. A. Parl. Paper No. 76* (1883–84).
[3] *Port Augusta Dispatch,* Dec. 3, 1880.

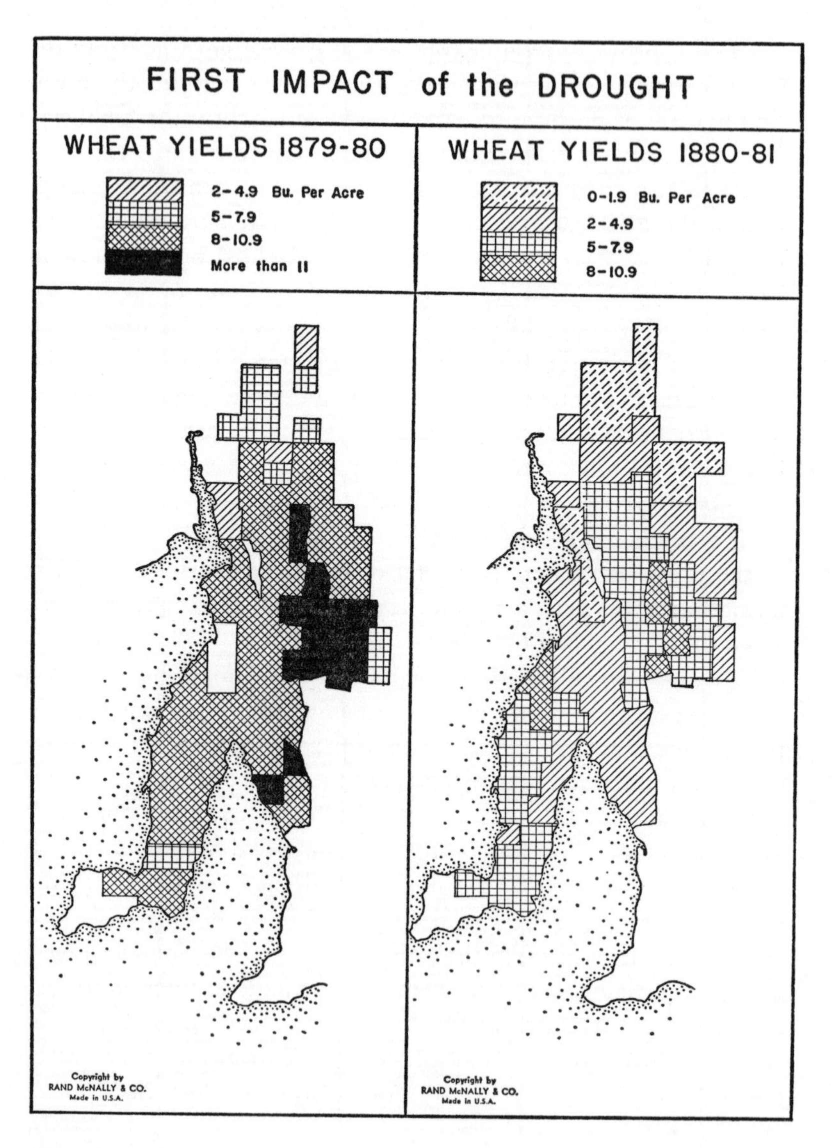
FIRST IMPACT of the DROUGHT
WHEAT YIELDS 1879-80
2-4.9 Bu. Per Acre
5-7.9
8-10.9
More than 11
WHEAT YIELDS 1880-81
0-1.9 Bu. Per Acre
2-4.9
5-7.9
8-10.9
Copyright by RAND McNALLY & CO. Made in U.S.A.
Copyright by RAND McNALLY & CO. Made in U.S.A.

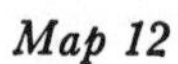

Map 12

Such a beggardly yield following upon the small returns for 1879-80 may well in the minds of the most enthusiastic advocates for the extension of agricultural settlement, give rise to a doubt as to whether farming will pay in the remoter districts of the North.

An over-all slowing of expansion was clearly apparent; north of Victoria County the increase in wheat acreage in 1881 was but 42,000 as compared with 170,000 the year before, and reductions of acreage in older areas brought a net increase of only 35,000 for the entire colony, in contrast to 275,000 which had followed the great crop of 1879–80. And yet even such reduced figures proved that the frontier advance was far from stalled. The Commissioner of Crown Lands reported that land sales were continuing surprisingly well:

the people seemed to have sufficient faith in the land, and the earth-hunger was sufficiently strong to induce them to select to the same extent as in more prosperous times.[5]

Nearly 20,000 acres were put in wheat in those newly-opened areas. The railroad under construction from Terowie to Orroroo and Quorn, skirting the margin of the saltbush country, offered some incentive by at least promising to reduce marketing costs – if anything could be raised to send. Only in the extreme North East was settlement at a standstill. The Manna Hill Experimental Farm had failed, and no crops had been obtained in *King, Mongolata,* or *Parnaroo;* "selection was stopped and the Government had discontinued surveying."[6]

A change of outlook began to be noticeable. "Wheat growing in South Australia is to say the least of it a precarious occupation," wrote the usually optimistic editor in Port Augusta; though acknowledging the drought he went on to emphasize the ravages of wheat rust, a widespread problem, and thus tempered any criticism of the North as a peculiarly precarious area.[7] In the Assembly the difficulties of the wheat-growers were discussed, but no major program of amelioration was passed.

[4] *The Register* (Adelaide), quoted in *S. A. Parl. Debates,* Aug. 11, 1881, col. 564.
[5] *Ibid.,* June 14, 1881, col. 79.
[6] *Ibid.,* col. 80.
[7] *Port Augusta Dispatch,* Dec. 3, 1880.

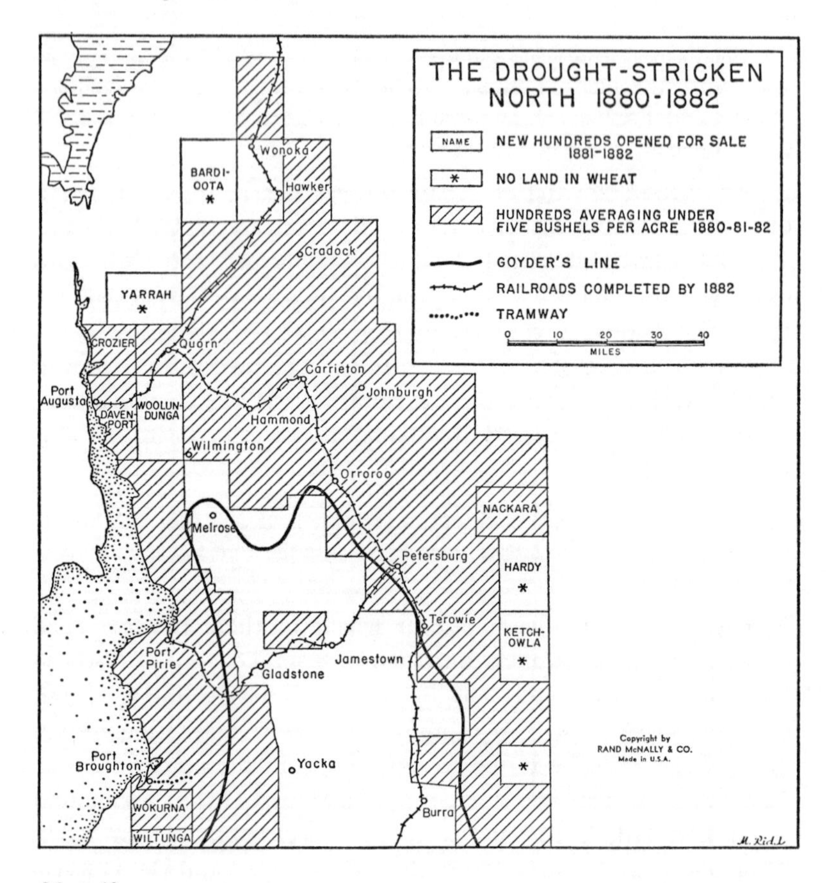

Map 13

Thus the drought of 1880–81 produced only a modest slackening of expansion and tempering of confidence. But the seasons of 1881 proved even worse than the year before. The early rains were less, those of winter sporadic, and the spring disastrously dry. Despite the greater acreage, total production dropped further by a half million bushels. The Northern fringe was again hardest hit, complete failures were even more extensive than before, and Port Augusta exports declined to barely 100,000 bushels, less than a fifth of two years before.[8] The cry of distress was now widespread and urgent. Petitioners from the Willochra asked for cessation of interest payments and government mortgages on their selections

[8] *Port Augusta Dispatch,* Jan. 13, 1883.

as the only hope of continuance. At Johnburgh selectors of *Oladdie, Walloway, Yalpara,* and *Minburra* documented their petition with some examples of typical yields — such as 35 bags from 600 acres, 28 bags from 300, or 3 bags from 200 — to support their plea for the government to supply seed wheat to forestall abandonment.[9] All over the North, at Winninowie, Port Pirie, Cradock, similar meetings were held, the disastrous facts set down, and urgent petitions forwarded.

In response, the Crown sent an inspector to tour the areas and assess conditions. His findings fully confirmed the local reports: everywhere on the plains from the Willochra to the Oladdie Plains there had been an almost total failure (Map 13); the average yield of the entire frontier was one and a half bushels per acre; heavy locust infestations had again coincided to complete the ruination. Yet he also found the farmers anxious to hang on, confident of success. Nine-tenths of the selectors were ready to plant again, citing the yields of 1878–79 and 1879–80 as proof of the potential. As for relief, the inspector suggested that the best help would be the development of local water supplies, to end a genuine hardship very widely felt.[10]

Badly as water was needed, such a suggestion fell far short of the desires of the selectors. The most immediate problem was to obtain seed to put in the next crop. Despite strong appeals the government refused to subsidize the farmers with seed wheat, quite realistically pointing out that it would have set a dangerous precedent and the pastoralists could as rightfully ask the Crown to restock their runs after every drought.[11] But if the government could reject such a request as a "vicious principle" the need nevertheless was there, and the Farmers' Mutual Association set up a program to distribute voluntarily-contributed seed wheat on loan. Applications quickly poured in from all over the North and from a few as far south as Balaklava. Ultimately enough seed was ob-

[9] *Ibid.,* Jan. 11, 1882.
[10] *Ibid.,* Feb. 24, 1882: "To add to their trouble a great many of these selectors are obliged to keep a man with a horse team constantly running to distant wells for water." *The Garden and the Field* (Adelaide), April, 1882, pp. 160–61. The problem was widespread, water was being shipped by rail from Gawler to the Kadina area; *S. A. Parl. Paper No. 71* (1882).
[11] *S. A. Parl. Debates,* June 22, 1882, cols. 163–64.

tained to meet about a third of the requests.[12] In general, the farmers scraped up enough to put in about the same acreage as before, somewhat less in some areas, a bit more in others. Curiously, the hundreds of greatest failure showed the greatest increase, for many selectors still had much new land and their only chance of success was to get it into cultivation and hope for a decent harvest.

Those who thought they had a cure for droughts were now put to the test. Brown, the Conservator of Forests, was directed to survey the Willochra Plains to see if the planting of trees might be successfully undertaken with a view of modifying the dry conditions. To his credit Brown's faith and enthusiasm did not falter in face of the challenge. He made a hurried reconnaissance, returned convinced that "the dearth of forest land in the district is undoubtedly the chief cause of the uncertain rainfall," and recommended an emergency program to protect all existing trees and set aside extensive reserves for immediate planting.[13] The proposal was approved and Brown began work on some experimental blocks along the railroad beyond Quorn.

REACTION AND CONTROVERSY

But the general agricultural prospect had been profoundly changed and the general confidence in the frontier regions severely shaken. "While we ourselves do not for a moment believe it will be found necessary to abandon agricultural settlement in the distressed districts," wrote the Terowie editor, "we think . . . it will be well not to survey nor offer for selection any fresh land in the far north for the present; nor until it has been decided whether the attempts already made are likely to prove successful."[14] It was a remarkably subdued outlook for a local booster, but the stark facts were all about, and far out on the plains the Manna Hill experiment, the great hope of his own sector, was written off as a failure.[15] Even those who proclaimed their faith in the North acknowledged that "there are perhaps lessons to be learned from past experiences" and urged "those who are pursuing this pre-

[12] *Port Augusta Dispatch,* April 7, 14, and 21, 1882.
[13] *S. A. Parl. Paper No. 109* (1882), pp. 20–21.
[14] *The North-Eastern Times and Terowie News,* April 21, 1882.
[15] *S. A. Parl. Paper No. 142* (1881).

carious profession of agriculture . . . to devote attention to arboriculture, the conservation of water, and a more thorough and systematic method of cultivation than has hitherto existed, as a means of inducing a 'dependable and more regular rainfall.' "[16]

Inevitably, the answer to the question of where to place the blame for this melancholy situation was pursued with bitter zeal. The first cry for broad governmental assistance brought an unusually stern answer. The Commissioner for Crown Lands gave little hope of the colony assuming mortgages on these lands and placed the blame squarely upon the selectors:

> This northern country was urgently asked for on the representation of practical men, who ought to know what amount of rainfall were [sic] necessary for the successful cultivation of wheat. After considerable pressure this land was resumed from the squatter, and placed on the market for selection. It was not fair then to charge the Government for mistakes the men themselves had made with their eyes wide open.[17]

The *Port Augusta Dispatch* retorted that it was "absurd" to blame the farmer: "The Government knew that the survey of the 'saltbush' land would inevitably result in the complete ruin of hundreds of families, and yet they consented to work this ruin in order to meet a popular cry."[18] But this was a marvellously lame reply, for few had done more to sustain the "popular cry" than that paper. Moreover, the editor compounded the irony by going on to castigate the Crown for not insisting upon Goyder's Line – in the same newspaper which just two years before had scoffed at the very mention of that demarcation: "Goyder's Line of rainfall has been abolished by the Farmers' Mutual Association."[19]

But the issue was not entirely clear-cut. Certainly it would be unreal to have expected any democratic government to ignore the demand for land over these past years; such a government would have soon been out of office. Yet, viewed in perspective, the Crown inadvertently brought some blame upon itself by having for years set itself up as the benevolent judge of what was and what was not agricultural land. Through controlled surveys, "Agri-

[16] *Port Augusta Dispatch,* Dec. 30, 1881.
[17] *Ibid.,* Dec. 30, 1881.
[18] *Ibid.,* Feb. 3, 1882.
[19] *Ibid.,* Feb. 27, 1880. Whether it was the same man writing in each instance is not certain.

cultural Areas," and, finally, Goyder's Line the government had built up a tradition of guidance. A particular administration could abandon such policies, but it could not so easily abandon the tradition, and the very act of surveying and offering land for selection, even though done at the insistence of selectors, could not but carry with it some measure of implicit governmental approval and responsibility for the colonization of such land. Moreover, the persistent concern of some members of the government to maximize the revenues from land sales also brought the inevitable accusation of having crassly lured people to ruin for the sake of increased sales.

On the other hand, the farmers could hardly be blamed for having selected such lands for trial for they had successfully broken through a whole succession of presumed limits to agriculture:

> if they had gone a little too fast they were sustained in their action by the knowledge of the fact that the farmers had again and again gone where they were told ruin would attend their operations, but instead of ruin they had found fortunes.[20]

And they had not only profited themselves, they had greatly enlarged the resources, development, and wealth of the entire colony. If their most recent trials proved that the limits of successful agriculture had at last been reached, or rather overstepped, then, again, they had made an important contribution and perhaps deserved some measure of governmental relief as compensation for a painful but valuable service to the colony.

The issue of who was to blame was naturally a popular one but really not fundamental at all. The real question was: what did these recent experiences along the frontier prove? Had they demonstrated beyond doubt that farming was and would always be a failure in these areas? The very petitions for relief certainly gave little suggestion that the farmers thought so, for the main pleas were for greater security of tenure and subsidization of further crops. Certainly the most widespread local view was that the farmers themselves were the best judges of whether such lands had been adequately tested or not, and if they were willing to keep trying the government ought to help.[21]

Despite the obvious severity of the drought, the hope for cli-

[20] *S. A. Parl. Debates,* June 29, 1882, col. 227. See also June 15, 1882, col. 133.
[21] *Port Augusta Dispatch,* March 10, 1882.

matic change was by no means destroyed. Although some members in Parliament pointed out that quite evidently the rain had not followed the plough in South Australia, and contrary to all the talk about world-wide evidence in support of the theory it had not done so in similar areas such as California either, the proponents of the rainfall theories were not yet ready to admit defeat.[22] To some supporters of the "influence of trees on rainfall" the situation was merely proof that the devastation of forests had already gone too far.[23] Those who supported the "plough theory" could blame the inadequate, shallow tillage.[24] "Whether the rain follows the plow or not is still a moot matter," wrote the Terowie editor,[25] and many people, farmers, editors, and officials, agreed. That many had taken to the idea a bit too enthusiastically and had been "buoyed up by a delusive hope of an entire change in climate," was admitted, but in time, with more cultivation, tree-planting, tanks and reservoirs, some definite amelioration of aridity was surely possible.[26] In short, few were as candid as the

[22] *S. A. Parl. Debates,* June 15, 1882, col. 133, and June 22, 1882, cols. 164–65. The Great Central Valley in California had suffered several extremely dry seasons beginning in 1864. It should be emphasized that this era of settlement expansion in South Australia was not coincident with any extended "wet cycle." The years 1871 through 1875 can now, measured against the cumulative records to the present, be seen as "average" rainfall years. The next year was distinctly dry, as was well recognized at the time. Only in 1878 and 1879 was rainfall above average in the most northern agricultural area, which was, to be sure, the period of most rapid penetration in that direction. But comprehensive statistics were not available at the time, nor were those few that were given much publicity. Impressions were more important than scientific measure; a few heavy rains spaced through the growing season would likely prompt belief in an increase even though the season total was no more, or even less, than previously. Most important, the simple fact that crops were being reaped in areas considered to be dry was quite enough to give substantiation to popular beliefs in rainfall theories. Precipitation data for these years are available in "Results of Rainfall Observations Made in South Australia and the Northern Territory 1839–1950," Bureau of Meteorology, Commonwealth of Australia (n.d.). The relevant months for wheat-growing are April through November. See E. A. Cornish, "Yield Trends in the Wheat Belt of South Australia During 1896–1941," *Australian Journal of Scientific Research, Series B, Biological Sciences,* II (February, 1949), 83–136.

[23] *City and Country* (Adelaide), Sept. 22, 1882, reprint of an article "On the Influence of Forests on Climate and Rainfall," from *Rural Australian.*

[24] *The Agriculturist and Review* (Jamestown), Jan. 4, 1882.

[25] *The North-Eastern Times and Terowie News,* April 21, 1882.

[26] *Port Augusta Dispatch,* Jan. 17, 1882. See also the issues of April 28 and May 5, 1882, for editorial comment and reprint of Dr. Schomburgk's latest "Botanic Garden Report" which still strongly supported the possibility of change through tree plantings. See also *S. A. Parl. Debates,* June 29, 1882, col. 227.

farmer of *Winninowie:* "like so many others, I thought that rain follows the plough, and I paid dear for my folly."[27]

Acknowledging most of these considerations on behalf of the farmers, the government was prepared to offer some kind of help. The questions of what kind and for whom, however, were controversial in the extreme. As an introductory statement in support of a bill, the Commissioner of Crown Lands outlined the serious nature of the situation and offered specific examples in illustration, among them the plight of Mr. Orchard of *Baroota:*

> he had been led to give £6/6/8*d.* an acre for his selection, because when visiting the spot before bidding for the land there was water in the creek two and three feet deep; there was green grass on the flats eight to nine inches long, and everything about the place looked promising. The first year he got 125 bags of wheat from sixty acres, in the second 800 bags from 450 acres, in the third sixty-three bags from 550 acres, and this year he expected to get one bag to the acre from 750 acres. His prospects were so bad that unless something was done for him he would have to leave his selection, and he did not want to do this, because he had built a house, fenced-in his selection, planted a nice garden, and altogether made a substantial farm.[28]

It was not an entirely convincing example; if to some this was testimony of the hardy perseverance of Northern settlers, to others it was equal proof of obstinate foolishness: "why should the whole colony be taxed simply to make a present of a few hundred pounds to Mr. Orchard?" asked a legislator. He had indeed made substantial improvements, "yet it would have been better for the colony and for Mr. Orchard himself if he cast his money into the Gulf instead of spending it on the land there and thus destroying the native bushes, which were the only possible means of support for stock in that country."[29] Everyone admitted that the farmers had often paid ridiculously high prices for land in unproved districts, but was this the fault of the selectors or of a government which insisted upon auction sales and gloated over mounting revenues? And so the debate raged on all through the winter of 1882.

[27] *S. A. Parl. Debates,* June 22, 1882, col. 171.
[28] *Ibid.,* June 15, 1882, cols. 134–35.
[29] *Ibid.,* June 22, 1882, cols. 172–73. See also *The Garden and the Field* (Adelaide), March, 1882, pp. 145–56, which called those farmers who wanted to stay on the land "simply madmen."

Inevitably, arguments over governmental assistance included arguments over the extent and severity of the drought – and, inevitably, Goyder's Line, "that buried demon of settlement,"[30] was resurrected into central prominence. Goyder himself must have derived some sad satisfaction from this harsh confirmation of his views, though no evidence was found that he in any way gave public expression of his vindication. He could well remain content in the knowledge that he had warned of the dangers of all this Northern country and that he had specifically stated his lack of faith in any of the theories of climatic improvement. As Chairman of the Forest Board he had opposed Brown's scheme for emergency planting in the North as a certain costly failure.[31] Actually, local spokesmen throughout the North were quick to take the lead in reviving that "line of rainfall" which they had so recently scorned. Although rarely making any explicit retraction of their earlier views, they now quite readily admitted that the demarcation had some significance. Usually there was no suggestion that settlement north of the line was a mistake, only that it was more precarious and therefore deserving of special consideration. The government's original bill accurately reflected such views by proposing to differentiate between selectors north and south of the line in the type and degree of assistance, and in support, offered comparisons of yields over the past three years of adjacent hundreds on opposite sides of the line[32] (Map 13). Such figures made a rather convincing case for the general accuracy of Goyder's demarcation in the North, yet they did not account for the drought zone which extended southward, west of the hill country, as far as Gawler. And so the debate dragged on further between those who were

[30] *Ibid.*, July 4, 1882, col. 243.

[31] Goyder's Memorandum of opposition was not included in the Parliamentary Paper, but it was reprinted, together with Brown's report, in the *Port Augusta Dispatch,* Jan. 24, 1882, and in *The Agriculturist and Review* (Jamestown), Jan. 25, 1882. Goyder explicitly denied the "plough theory" in testimony during a railroad hearing regarding the settlement prospects in the Orroroo district, just before the full impact of the drought was apparent. In that same hearing nearly every farmer interviewed expressed faith in some degree of climatic change. *S. A. Parl. Paper No. 127* (1881), p. 5.

[32] *S. A. Parl. Debates,* June 22, 1882, cols. 165–66. The following comparisons were made: *Apoinga* with *Baldina* and *Mongolata, Mannanarie* with *Walloway, Appila,* with *Terowie,* and *Wongyarra* (though mistakenly called *"Yangyarra"* in the record) with *Baroota.* County comparisons were also made.

prepared to accept the line, those who insisted upon some modification, and those who wanted no geographical discrimination at all. Several members quite sensibly pointed out that there really was no drought *line* but a *zone*. As Mr. Hawker put it:

> it was absurd to say it was a fixed line, and he would rather call it a strip of debatable ground, where in some seasons the rains gushed out further than it did at other times. During the very favourable seasons this kind of ground might be successfully occupied, but in unfavourable seasons it would give nothing. Outside this belt of forty or fifty miles in width the settler got beyond the influence of coast rains; and the rainfall then was so thoroughly unreliable that no one would depend in the slightest degree on successfully cultivating the ground.[33]

With this the concept of "marginal lands" was beginning to emerge.

Ultimately, however, it proved to be politically inexpedient to make any area division, and relief measures were allocated according to the degree of crop failure, wherever the selector might reside. A harvest of six bushels per acre as an average of the past three seasons was established as the minimum profitable crop; those who received less were allowed a remission of interest payments, graduated according to how far below the minimum their results had been. More important were provisions allowing the selectors to surrender their holdings and not only re-select but to transfer the amount of their original purchase money and value of improvements as part payment on the cost of the new selection. In part, this allowed a subsidized retreat from the most hopeless areas, but its principal function was to reduce the debt of those who stayed, for a farmer was allowed to surrender and re-select his own land at a reduced offering price. The auction system still prevailed, but not only had the drought quelled the competitive clamor for land, for the most part there was a sort of tacit understanding which allowed a selector to bid on his own land unopposed.[34]

[33] *Ibid.*, July 11, 1882, col. 303.
[34] *S. A. Acts of Parliament No. 275* (1882). On the operation of the law see Goyder's testimony, *S. A. Parl. Paper No. 28* (1888).

END OF AN ERA

The frontier advance was now very nearly stalled. Here and there some new land was ploughed, but considerable areas, especially in the North East, were abandoned, and for the first time since the beginnings of the surge north in 1869 the total acreage in wheat in the colony declined. "Splendid" rains in May brought hope that the 1882–83 season would return to "normal," but as the months passed the drought renewed its grip. The earliest harvest reports suggested at least some crops had been obtained, but by the end of the year the general picture was once more a nearly complete failure. Total production dropped another three-quarters of a million bushels, and the average yield for the entire colony was 4.2 bushels, the lowest in history. With this an era had ended. Through 1883 and 1884 forfeits and surrenders of selections totaled nearly 600,000 acres. In 1884 an entirely new departure in land legislation was begun by which selectors were allowed to convert their holdings from credit purchases into long-term leases. Essentially, it marked the end of the purely agricultural advance and the beginning of the readjustment of the frontier into a broad agricultural-pastoral zone. By 1885 so rapidly had selections been forfeited or surrendered for conversion that total purchased land in all the counties beyond Stanley declined by nearly one and a half million acres. Brown's experimental plantings in the Willochra, though marked by extensive failures of several species, did prove to him at least that some trees would grow and he continued to press for a more extensive forestry program. Yet, though he continued to maintain the probable climatic benefits to be obtained, he no longer laid major stress upon that aspect and the government now showed little interest in the program.[35]

Proof that the boom had ended could be found in the general reaction to the brief break in the drought in 1883 and 1884. Provincial production rebounded to fourteen million bushels, the over-all average climbed to more than seven bushels per acre, and

[35] *S. A. Parl. Papers No. 73* (1884) and *No. 63* (1885).

even the Far North reaped marginally-profitable crops for two successive seasons. Inevitably a few began to talk of a change of outlook, but they found little support. Even a most ardent optimist of the past quickly warned against such views:

> The unusually good harvest which is now being reaped may naturally be expected to revive the glowing anticipations with which the selectors in the North first took up their holdings. . . . It is, however, sincerely to be hoped that such sanguine views with regard to the future will not be extensively indulged in. It may now be regarded as an established fact that wheat cultivation by itself, except in very favorable seasons, is not a remunerative pursuit in the dry areas of the North.[36]

But the warning was not really needed, for the experience of past seasons had taught the lesson quite effectively. Goyder's Line was now firmly established as a sort of base line for the evaluation of land. For thirty years the wheat acreage of the entire province remained nearly stationary, and though the actual Northern frontier of production fluctuated from season to season, it did so within very narrow limits and never in any significant way advanced beyond the margin of this boom period.

That great northward stream of settlers could now be likened unto one of those real, erratic, perplexing Australian streams that flowed into the outback: fed by the wet fertile districts, swollen by the good seasons, gathering momentum as it ran swiftly among the ranges, fanning out broadly and thinly onto the saltbush plains, transforming all that it touched with an illusion of goodness and then, as the seasons changed, slowing, ebbing, dying, leaving as far as the outermost margins of its reach the scars of its momentary presence.

[36] *Port Augusta Dispatch,* Dec. 15, 1884.

VI.

Domesticating the Land

> . . . the same monotonous wheat field after wheat field continues, fenced with, as a rule, three wires; hardly any stock is to be seen in any direction; the farm houses built of the white soft kind of stone prevalent in the district, and standing at wide intervals apart in naked loneliness. No garden, no stacks, no barns. . .
>
> — MELBOURNE REPORTER
> "Agriculture in South Australia,"
> *The Farmers' Weekly Messenger*
> (Adelaide), Nov. 13, 1874

CONTINUITY AND CHANGE

The distinctiveness of these dozen years of expansion into the new wheatlands of South Australia is displayed in many ways. The most obvious feature was the sheer pace and magnitude of expansion as compared with that of the years immediately before and after – a marked pulsation in the colonization history of the colony. And the era was distinguished by more than such external dimensions; internally in both phenomena and processes there were new features also and these together with the more obvious geographical and historical movements combine to characterize a distinct phase in the development of the colony.

And yet while there was much that was new, such changes were an evolution rather than an abrupt departure from the old. This was particularly apparent in the whole process of "domesticating the land" – of settling, organizing, and establishing a workable relationship with the basic conditions in the new areas.

Certainly the thirty years of earlier pioneering in South Australia were an essential prelude to the rapidity and success of the agricultural expansion of the 1870's. The general peculiarities of the physical environment were by that time well recognized, and new modes of life and work had been evolved. And the general peculiarities of pioneer conditions, of starting life anew with little capital, labor, or equipment, of evolving a working economy out of a narrow range of opportunities, a small population, primitive transport, and limited uncertain markets, had become commonplace. In that solid core of settlement which had been established well before the late 1860's, much of the raw, harsh conditions of pioneer life had been overcome. The expansion into the new wheatlands grew directly out of that older nucleus. The colonists, especially in the first years of expansion, were not naïve immigrants but locally-experienced hands; many were not farmers, but even these could not be ignorant of the general nature of farming life in the colony. If, therefore, as the new areas were entered there was necessarily a brief reversion to difficult, primitive conditions, these were largely a repetition of a familiar context; the basic problems had been faced before and experience had shown the way to meet them. That the colonization of the North was initiated by South Australians, not by untried overseas immigrants, underlies all that happened on that frontier.

But as we review what happened it becomes clear that it was by no means a mere repetition. The general process was familiar enough but the settlers now encountered new kinds of lands which had to be dealt with in somewhat different ways and for somewhat different purposes. It is important therefore not only to examine the processes involved and the results obtained but to sort out what was old and what was new.

ORGANIZING THE LAND

Before any sale of land and permanent settlement could take place the surveyors had to set the framework. This initial process of "organizing the land" was itself an indicator of the differences between the older area and the new: the basic structure and procedures remained the same, but with numerous significant differences in detail.

Surveys proceeded, as before, through the successive levels of the hierarchy of counties, hundreds, and farm blocks, with normally at least one township also laid out within each hundred. One new feature readily apparent upon the evolving map of the colony was the almost complete adherence to rectangular boundaries for counties and hundreds in the new Agricultural Areas, in contrast with the predominant use of streams and terrain features in the gross subdivisions of the older area (Map 14A). This use of the more simple geometric procedure was perhaps the most reasonable for those extensive areas of the new frontier which had few streams or conspicuous landscape irregularities, but even the rugged Flinders Range was not allowed to disrupt the pattern.[1] Very likely the sheer haste of the surveys made necessary by the rapidly mounting pressures for land is a sufficient explanation for this change in practice. Despite the use of rectangular divisions the result was not a uniform gridiron, for commonly both counties and hundreds were of varied size, though neither were significantly different in scale from those in the older districts. The hundreds in the post-1869 area ranged in area from 66 square miles *(Telowie)* to 268 *(Tiparra)* but both of these extremes were quite anomalous and the great majority were between 90 and 130 square miles.

A much more significant difference was apparent in the scale and procedures of farm block surveys. By the time colonization was initiated in the new areas the farmers were "alive to the necessity of carrying on their operations on a more extensive scale."[2] The legislators concurred and therefore the eighty-acre section was abandoned as the general standard.[3] The 1869 land act allowed 640 acres as a maximum credit selection, but few as yet viewed that amount as necessary and units of a quarter to half that size were most commonly surveyed. The internal pattern was thereby enlarged but it was also significantly altered in type. Paradoxically,

[1] Except at its southernmost extension just west of Port Pirie where a narrow sliver of useless mountain was left unsurveyed until 1891 (the hundreds of *Darling* and *Howe*).

[2] "Agricultural and Livestock Statistics," in *Statistical Register of South Australia, 1870–71* (Adelaide, 1871), p. iv.

[3] "Section" and "farm block" both refer to the ultimate cadastral survey unit, the individual lot or allotment.

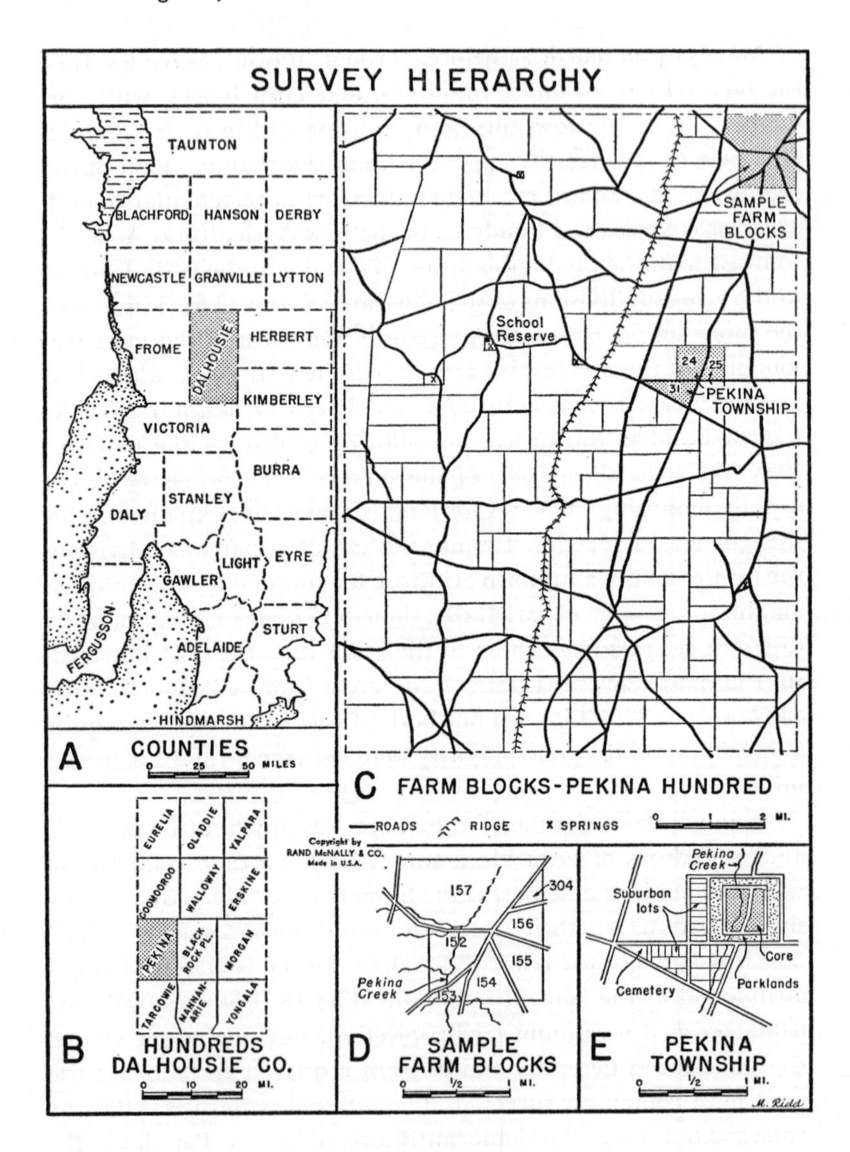
SURVEY HIERARCHY
TAUNTON
BLACHFORD
HANSON
DERBY
NEWCASTLE
GRANVILLE
LYTTON
HERBERT
FROME
DALHOUSIE
KIMBERLEY
VICTORIA
BURRA
STANLEY
DALY
LIGHT
EYRE
GAWLER
STURT
FERGUSSON
ADELAIDE
HINDMARSH
A
COUNTIES
0 25 50 MILES
SAMPLE FARM BLOCKS
School Reserve
24
25
31
PEKINA TOWNSHIP
C
FARM BLOCKS-PEKINA HUNDRED
ROADS
RIDGE
X SPRINGS
0 1 2 MI.
EURELIA
OLADDIE
YALPARA
COOMOOROO
WALLOWAY
ERSKINE
PEKINA
BLACK ROCK PL.
MORGAN
TARCOWIE
HANNAN-ARIE
YONGALA
B
HUNDREDS
DALHOUSIE CO.
0 10 20 MI.
Copyright by
RAND McNALLY & CO.
Made in U.S.A.
157
304
156
152
155
154
153
Pekina Creek
D
SAMPLE FARM BLOCKS
0 1/2 1 MI.
Pekina Creek
Suburban lots
Core
Cemetery
Parklands
E
PEKINA TOWNSHIP
0 1/2 1 MI.
M. Ridd

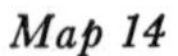
Map 14

at this level of the hierarchy the change was opposite to that affecting the larger frameworks: a lessened rather than a greater use of rectangular subdivision.

In the older area the smaller units necessitated so dense a system of survey lines that it appears that a simple formula was temptingly advantageous. Thus a uniform grid pattern of eighty-acre sections was very common, though no hundred was completely subdivided in this manner and the irregular boundaries of the hundreds themselves further disrupted the whole into a complex patchwork. The density of land units in such districts had necessitated a proportionate density of access roads and together with the rectangular propensity of the surveyors had resulted in a relatively rigid alignment of roads in utter disregard of local terrain. As these older districts were nearly all in very hilly country such a procedure brought many complaints. "We have only to look around us to see evidence of the folly of such a course," wrote the Clare editor. "The most formidable barriers exist in very many places, the roads leading over hills and rocks most unsuited for public thoroughfares."[4] Certainly the hundred of *Clare* was a good exhibit of such imposed difficulties. However, such criticisms were an old refrain and had already been effective, for he went on to note that "of late years the survey department have [sic] acted on a different principle, by first defining the roads so that the country to be traversed may be as even as possible, and capable of being constructed at the lowest possible cost." An examination of the internal patterns of the new hundreds proves this observation to be correct and it was this change in procedure which caused the farm blocks of the North to be much more varied in shape and size despite the much greater rectangularity of the encompassing frameworks of hundreds and counties.

The county of Dalhousie and its hundred of *Pekina,* surveyed in 1871, are good examples of these new survey patterns (Map 14A and B). Dalhousie is an elongated rectangle of 1,230 square miles, subdivided into 12 hundreds. All of the latter, with slight exceptions in the southernmost tier, are also rectangular units, but vary in size from 85 to 119 square miles. *Pekina* (99 square miles) was

[4] *The Northern Argus* (Clare), June 19, 1874.

further subdivided into 231 rural land units, and three of these were further resurveyed into the township of Pekina and its suburban lands (Map 14C).

The land of *Pekina* is quite varied. Much of the eastern part is a nearly level plain, the western half is hilly and these two portions are separated by a narrow longitudinal ridge bisecting the whole hundred. Three small creek systems drain in divergent directions: west, northeast, and south. Despite this complexity of terrain features, the bisecting ridge was the only one used directly to demark farm units. Indirectly, however, a much more comprehensive concordance was established. As in all these new hundreds, *Pekina* had been occupied for some years by pastoral lessees. Their waterholes, holding paddocks, shearing yards, and herders' huts are noted on the original survey maps. A much more extensive and important imprint was the dense network of cart roads and sheep trails. By their very nature these were likely to be intimately adapted to the most local details of the terrain and thereby they existed as a ready answer to the surveyors' search for the most serviceable road pattern. It is quite evident that the surveyors recognized this fact and that their roads, therefore, were largely only a formalization of these pre-existing tracings upon the land.[5]

Once the road pattern had been marked upon the map, the intervening lands were parceled into farm blocks. In *Pekina* such boundaries were, with slight exception (most notably along the ridge), straight lines oriented to the cardinal points. There was no attempt to delimit farm blocks in uniform size. Parcels varied from nearly a square mile (640 acres) to well under a hundred acres. There was a noticeable tendency to create larger units in the rougher country west of the ridge. The road framework was rigidly adhered to – only two farm unit boundaries crossed a road – and this had certain special consequences. For one thing,

[5] There are few detailed maps available of such areas prior to survey and subdivision, but there are enough to give more than a hint at this kind of continuity. Field reconnaissance confirms the close adaptations of roads to terrain, and little more than a glance at a map of these hundreds is needed to convince one that no surveyor would ever have laid out such devious patterns entirely on his own; they bear the indisputable mark of the informal routeways of pastoral occupation.

the only straight roads are the few stubs added *after* subdivision to give access to isolated farm units.[6] For another, it resulted in numerous sharp-angled and oddly-shaped fragments, especially around complex road junctions (Map 14D).

A striking illustration of these special survey policies was the curious form of the Pekina township and suburban area (Map 14E). The sequence of surveys was roads – farm blocks – township; thus the core of the latter was created out of two already delimited farm blocks (Nos. 24 and 25, Map 14C) which faced one another along the still earlier determined road. Within these two farm parcels the standardized South Australian country township pattern of business core, parkland belt, and suburban lots was laid out.[7] Then to enlarge the suburban area another farm block (No. 31) was selected and subdivided into small lots. This particular block was an acute triangle and lay quite eccentric to the rest of the design. The over-all result is an oddly-shaped plan.

The reserve of major springs for community use, and of sites for rural schools were common features in most of these hundreds. In some, particularly those near the border of lands still under pastoral leases, special stock routes, roads of twenty chains (one-fourth mile) or wider, were surveyed through the farm country to allow sheep to be driven to a railroad station. When the patterns of either or both pastoral operations and railroads changed and such strips were no longer needed they were segmented and made available for sale to adjacent farmers.

As were so many other features of this colonization movement, these survey procedures were creative adaptations peculiar to South Australia. The most distinctive imprint of the land survey on this frontier – the terrain-adapted road pattern as the basic framework for local subdivision of land – was really the unwitting creation of sheepherders and, as much, of the very sheep themselves. In a real sense, they were the first "organizers of the land."

[6] A close scrutiny of insert C of Map 14 will reveal three units untouched by a road. Each of these carries the same number as an adjacent unit but is designated as an "East" subdivision. I do not know just what this indicates as to survey procedures.

[7] See Chapter VIII for further discussion and illustration of such township designs.

SOME PIONEER NECESSITIES: HOUSING AND FENCING

The first need of the pioneer as he moved out upon his selection was a house. Compared with his contemporaries who were colonizing the broad plains of North America the South Australian had a distinct advantage. The widespread scrub forests and shallow soils may have been agricultural liabilities, but at least in many instances they allowed the settler to build his own home with his own hands from the materials of his own farm. Crude wattle and daub structures, constructed "basket-fashion" of vertical posts interwoven with slender poles and covered with a clay plaster, were a common makeshift.[8] Though presumably temporary, some were used for many years, to the despair of progressive-minded citizens who were appalled at "the miserable hovels" with which so many farmers seemed content. But others began with and most turned to more permanent materials. Exposed stone was available in every district and the intense faulting and folding of this geological "shatter belt" had provided a great variety of potential materials: limestones, sandstones, granites (and even marble in the Mt. Lofty Ranges). Stone houses, varied according to the colors and textures of local "country" rock – from dull whites to tans and deep reddish browns, often distinctively mottled or streaked – were dotted over hills, valleys, and plains as a distinguishing feature of the South Australian landscape.[9]

Often a small rectangular hut with a sloping roof of corrugated iron sheets was first erected, to which later an enlarged, more carefully constructed addition might be made at the front, or which might be relegated to an outbuilding of a new residence, erected

[8] The first houses in the colony were of this sort and they long remained a common feature. See, for example, the 1840 description of agricultural laborers' huts in Clark, *op. cit., infra.,* Vol. 1, p. 211.

[9] The 1881 Census returns listed over 60 per cent of the permanent houses as stone and only 18 per cent wood. The continued emphasis upon stone in South Australia and the contrasts among the several states today in housing materials is explored in A. J. Rose, "Regional Variations in the Use of Building Materials in Australia" (mimeographed), paper read at A.N.Z.A.A.S. Congress, Adelaide, 1958. Rose demonstrates how the pattern of stone dwellings coincides with the South Australia–Victoria boundary excepting only for one district in the latter state which was colonized by South Australians.

nearby.[10] But improved buildings could not easily be added immediately and the starkly primitive appearance of farmstead facilities remained for years:

> Any one travelling in the Northern agricultural districts must be struck with the wretched and altogether insufficient building accommodation on many farms. The occupier and his household, beside those employed by him, are obliged to dwell in apartments of the most limited dimensions, destitute of that comfort and privacy essential to the proper training of children. . . . Stable accommodation is very defective on the majority of farms. A sort of breakwind is erected, and the horses are permitted to run loose, and frequently there is but a poor makeshift for stalls — the hay is trampled under foot and much is actually wasted. . . . The absence of barns is also very noticeable in the areas. On most farms a quantity of land is under wheat, and yet no provision has been made to protect the grain when reaped from wet. . . . We believe scarcity of labor is the principal drawback in the construction of barns, but if stone buildings cannot be put up it would be better to construct temporary iron houses. . . .[11]

Scarcity of labor was undoubtedly a factor, but it was by no means the only one. A reasonably mild climate made solid warm structures less essential for either man or beast; certainly the tradition of building fine barns was not strong and the whole context of this particular pioneering phase fostered an even greater neglect and indifference to such matters.

Fencing was another essential for which the minimum initial requirement could usually be obtained from the land itself. In dense scrub areas a mere stacking of tree trunks and brush as it was cleared from the land might form a temporary barrier. A next step, more orderly but still lavish in its use of timber, might be a "zig-zag" or "snake" rail fence – stacks of long poles piled one upon the other with each panel bound in angled connection with the next. More common of the purely wooden fences was the slotted post and rail, much more economical of both timber and ground, but, as with all of these wooden fences, so laborious to build that they were mainly confined to the immediate farm yard area. Many locales, however, were not heavily encumbered with forest and even post and rail fences might be beyond the resources of the farm itself. Cartage of timber for any distance was expen-

[10] *The Farmers' Weekly Messenger* (Adelaide), Dec. 11, 1874.
[11] *The Northern Argus* (Clare), May 28, 1875.

sive, and concern over the fencing problem was soon a topic of general interest. The initial and much of the continued debates over forest legislation sprang from this need. Some called for reservation of belts of timber in each hundred as it was opened as a prudent policy,[12] others directed attention to the establishment of large reserves in the best timbered areas where both controlled cutting and reforestation could be fostered. Yet still others opposed any government restrictions on the ground that the need was so acute and immediate that no hindrance ought to be placed in the farmer's way:

> It would take every tree in the forest reserve . . . to fence the land already taken up. . . . And if the landholders were not allowed to cut it the Government might as well burn the Agricultural Areas Act for all the use it would be.[13]

Some argued that already timber was so scarce that the cost of fencing was greater than the cost of the land itself. Inevitably with colonists of British heritage, there was an early interest in "live fences" – thorn hedges of some sort. A wide variety of plants were suggested but none were really satisfactory. Such fences were laborious to plant, gave no protection until mature and often insufficient protection when they were. Many of the plants were ill-suited to the long, dry summers, while others were so well adapted that they soon became a menace. The prickly pear was favored by some but already its rapidly spreading tendencies had brought petitions for prohibitive legislation.[14]

The real solution was already at hand: wooden posts and smooth iron wire. Wire was already common in the older areas; it was rare in the frontier because of its expense and the tradition and continued hope of fencing with free local materials. But as soon as wood became scarce and costly and live fences, after a brief flurry of interest, proved unsuitable, wire was seen no longer as a luxury but as the most reasonable material. Fences of closely-spaced drilled posts and three wires became the common style on farms, and as the selectors moved north enveloping the pastoral

[12] *The Farmers' Weekly Messenger* (Adelaide), Feb. 19, 1875.
[13] *S. A. Parl. Debates,* May 3, 1872, col. 770. The debate was over the proposed Booyoolie Forest Reserve.
[14] *S. A. Parl. Paper No. 221* (1872) and *The Northern Argus* (Clare), July 2, 1869.

freeholds, the sheepmen began to enclose their runs with the same material. Thus wire became one of the many new industrial tools essential to pioneering in this newly-opened frontier.[15]

SPECIAL PROBLEMS IN THE MALLEE

There was one area where the fence problem did not exist: the dense mallee lands covering much of the plains bordering Gulf St. Vincent and Yorke Peninsula. Here it was not fencing but clearing which was apt to cost more than the land itself. The Scrub Lands Act of 1866 was designed to foster the colonization of such country by allowing 640 acres on lease at a very small rental with the right to purchase at £1 per acre after 21 years. Only one-twentieth of the land was to be cleared each year but initially the costs were averaging nearly £2 per acre and it was slow and extremely heavy work.[16] Cutting down the trees was not enough, for the mallee roots vigorously "suckered"; repeated intensive burnings could eventually check this but the problem of stumps and roots remained. "The great want is that of a cheap, simple, and efficient implement for grubbing," wrote the Moonta editor,[17] and it was a want that persisted for years. A great many types of stump pullers were tried, some used manpower, some horses, but none were wholly satisfactory: they were too light for the work, or too heavy and cumbersome, or they broke the stump without extracting the root. In 1878 the government offered a bonus of £200 for a really efficient implement. Many different designs were tried in contests held near Gawler, but while several were fairly satisfactory, on at least one of these occasions three skilled axemen cleared more ground than any of the machines.[18]

Interest in such equipment continued but was overshadowed by an entirely different approach to the problem. In 1868 a settler named Mullens, at Wasleys north of Gawler, had cut the mallee

[15] Not a single reference was found in any of the contemporary source materials through 1884 of Bessemer steel barbed wire, the famous American solution to the fence problem which was invented in 1873 and quickly produced in enormous quantities.

[16] *S. A. Parl. Paper No. 172* (1867).

[17] *The Farmers' Weekly Messenger* (Adelaide), Aug. 28, 1874, a reprint of an article from the *Yorke's Peninsula Advertiser*.

[18] *Ibid.*, Sept. 6, 1878, and *The Garden and the Field* (Adelaide), Nov. 1, 1878. See A. R. Callaghan and A. J. Millington, *op. cit.*, p. 318, for illustrations of some of these machines.

on a portion of his farm to sell as fuel to the nearby railway which was then being built to Burra. He then devised a spiked log which could be dragged over the surface, which was still studded with shallow roots and low stumps, in order to open the ground for seed and cover it after broadcast sowing. The success of the crop prompted him to experiment with a cheaper means of initial clearing. He found that the slender, brittle mallee trunks which branched from the surface root could be quite easily knocked down by a heavy roller (his first was built from an old steam boiler). After drying through the summer the trunks and trash and exposed roots were then burned and a crop of wheat scratched in with the spiked log. After harvest the stubble was burned which killed the new mallee shoots and those roots which had been scraped up by the tillage. A few years of this completely killed the mallee and left a relatively clean surface, although many roots remained. This technique, which became known as "mullenizing," was soon adapted widely in the mallee lands.[19]

Mullenizing was an excellent pioneer expedient, allowing a crop with a minimum of effort and delay, but the problem of roots and larger stumps remained to hinder the use of equipment for proper cultivation. The invention of the "stump-jump" plough in 1876 met this problem. This decisive innovation was devised by R. B. Smith, a former agricultural machinery apprentice who had a farm at Kalkabury just north of Maitland on Yorke Peninsula. Smith's original design was a three-furrow plough in which the arm holding each mould-board was hinged to allow any of the shares to rise out of the ground upon striking an obstruction; a weighted beam was attached to each arm to pressure the share back into the ground as soon as it had passed over the obstacle. Such an implement allowed a proper seed bed to be prepared despite the underground remains of the mallee; in time, successive ploughings and burnings would get rid of roots and stumps.[20]

Smith also developed a single-furrow plough using the same device. When this was first exhibited at the Moonta agricultural show in November, 1876, one farm editor quickly saw that it

[19] See Callaghan and Millington, *op. cit.,* pp. 319–20, and photographs on pp. 150–51. See also Dunsdorfs, *op. cit.,* pp. 155–57.

[20] A fine illustrated account of early developments of stump-jump ploughs and scarifiers is in Callaghan and Millington, *op. cit.,* pp. 320–24.

would, "if adopted by agriculturists, cause a complete revolution in tilling uncleared land," and grubbing would be a thing of the past.[21] And apparently it was one of those rare inventions which in its initial design so successfully solved a common, oppressive problem that, at least locally, it was eagerly adopted by all. There was of course some delay in quantity manufacture, but several country machine shops were soon turning out a variety of ploughs based upon the original principle.[22]

An important corollary of this invention was a revision of the Scrub Lands Act in 1877 which greatly enlarged the acreage that could be leased, reduced the amount of annual clearing required to one-fortieth, and allowed purchase at £1 per acre at the end of eleven years. The need for innovations to deal with this kind of country was clearly revealed by the experiences of the first nine years under the old Act, wherein over two-thirds of the land leased had been forfeited because clearing was too slow and costly. Within a very few years, however, the situation was altogether changed. In 1881 it was reported that "so much headway has been made that in some of the scrub lands of the Peninsula people have become thoroughly settled down to the use of the stump-jumper."[23] In that same year the new plough was credited with having caused "a scramble" for scrub selections.[24] And the statistics supported this impression: in the years 1876–81 just over 600,000 acres were selected under the special scrub lands laws and less than 5 per cent had so far been forfeited.[25] By 1882 stump-jump ploughs of single-, two-, three-, and four-furrow design were being manufactured, and stump-jump scarifiers (which in principle were but a mechanical imitation of the spiked log) were also being tried.[26]

[21] *The Farmers' Weekly Messenger* (Adelaide), Nov. 17, 1876.
[22] In Morris, Hayter & Barry, *The Commercial and Trades Directory of South Australia, 1882–83* (Adelaide, 1882), implement makers in Curramulka, Edithburgh, Kadina, Maitland, Minlaton, Moonta, Port Wakefield, Snowtown, and Yorketown all advertised that they produced the "celebrated stump-jumping ploughs." Smith eventually established a large plant at Ardrossan.
[23] *City and Country* (Adelaide), Oct. 30, 1881.
[24] *The Garden and the Field* (Adelaide), October, 1881, pp. 66–67.
[25] *Ibid.*, February, 1882, pp. 130–31, for these and previously mentioned statistics on the Scrub Lands Acts.
[26] The scarifier has tines with cultivator shoes attached so that the ground is broken and opened but not raised and overturned as with a plough.

Though rapidly adopted in the mallee lands this whole technique of farming was, understandably, a strange and doubtful sight to others. A traveling reporter who visited the Balaklava area and observed this "*mullenised* system" commented:

> How this will pay remains to be seen. At present the shoots from the stumps are nearly as high as the crops and the reaping machine looks like a ship in a storm, as it rocks about going over the stumps.[27]

And the very localized origin of this system of farming is revealed by the reports of demonstrations held in the Willochra district in 1883. Many there were skeptical of the possibility of clearing with a roller and had never seen the stump-jump plough in action, but after witnessing a trial, hailed both as great inventions. Scrub land was much less extensive in that area, but the plough proved to be as well adapted to stony ground as to mallee, and this insured its widespread acceptance in the North.[28]

EXPERIMENTS WITH NEW HARVESTERS

If improvements in the techniques of mallee farming developed out of very localized interests, improvements in harvesting equipment were just as logically of very widespread concern. The Ridley stripper, South Australia's proudest contribution to agricultural progress, and the small stationary winnower were used by nearly every farmer (Fig. 8). These machines were well described by their names. The stripper did not use a cutter-bar but literally stripped the heads from the stalks by means of a comb, then employed beaters to loosen the kernels from the head, collecting the resultant mixture of chaff and grain in a large box. This product was dumped in a pile at the edge of the field where it was then shoveled into the winnower which separated the grain from the chaff.[29] Dissatisfaction centered chiefly upon the winnowers, which were of small capacity, did only a mediocre job of separation and cleaning, and required a great deal of hard labor to thresh a crop. If

[27] *The North-Eastern Times and Terowie News,* Dec. 16, 1881.

[28] See *Port Augusta Dispatch,* July 21 and Sept. 1, 1883, for reports of demonstrations at Wilson and Quorn.

[29] It may be noted that this system, wholly a South Australian development, was suited only to an area where there was little danger of rain during the harvest season. See Callaghan and Millington, *op. cit.,* pp. 337–43, for descriptions and photos of strippers and winnowers.

the two operations of reaping and threshing could be done by a single machine there would obviously be an enormous saving in time, cost, and energy, and the possibility was sufficiently clear to attract the interest of many persons.

In 1875 William Bowmans of Finniss constructed a combined harvester which was tried on a crop near Kensington, just east of Adelaide, the following January and reported to be a success.[30] However, it was evidently not sufficiently so to be accepted and initiate manufacture. It, and probably other experimental designs, did heighten interest in the idea and by 1878 there was discussion of the colony's offering a handsome bonus for the invention of a fully successful machine.[31] A sum of £4,000 was finally approved and trials were scheduled to be held near Gawler on December 17, 1879. It was an occasion of enormous interest. A large crowd attended, twenty-nine entries had been received although only fourteen machines were actually on hand and fit for trial. Two were from Victoria, one from Oregon, and eleven from South Australia. The sources of the latter entries showed clearly how the agricultural innovations of the time came directly out of the farming region itself, rather than from large metropolitan factories: there were three from Adelaide, two from Gawler, and one each from Middleton, Auburn, Waltham, Laura, Wirrabara, and Yongala. The actual trials (a second was held the following week) were rather chaotic; nearly every machine was plagued with breakdowns, several were obviously too cumbersome, and most cleaned poorly and wasted much of the wheat. No machine was fully approved, although some partial awards were made to the best.[32]

Although everyone concerned with farming was interested in the idea, opinion was still very much divided as to both the feasibility and the desirability of a combined harvester. The Port Augusta editor probably expressed well the doubts of many:

It appears to us . . . that in endeavouring to combine the reaper,

[30] *The Farmers' Weekly Messenger* (Adelaide), June 25, 1875, and Jan. 21, 1876. The term "combine" refers to a seed-drill-cultivator in Australia rather than to a harvester as in America.
[31] *The Garden and the Field* (Adelaide), October, 1878. Offer of a cash prize for agricultural inventions was a common practice in South Australia.
[32] *The South Australian Advertiser* (Adelaide), Dec. 18 and 24, 1879.

thrasher, and winnower in one machine we are trying to do too much, and so inviting failure.

Such a machine would be too heavy, cumbersome, and complicated, and a breakdown would halt the entire harvesting process; the important thing in South Australia, so he argued, was to reap before the onset of the hot winds caused shriveling and shattering; the winnowing could be delayed without disadvantage.[33] Undoubtedly there was also a good deal of inertia involved. It was stated that the Ridley stripper was so uniquely associated with South Australian farming and so completely accepted that, until recently, "it would have been looked upon as little short of treason to place any other harvesting machinery in serious competition."[34] And many who watched the Gawler demonstrations must have gone away quite content with their old familiar strippers and winnowers. But general interest did not wane, the inventors went back to the machine shops and continued to tinker and improve upon their designs. In January, 1882, two harvesters competed again near Gawler and it was claimed that the one of James Martin & Co., a prominent local agricultural machinery manufacturer, successfully reaped and cleaned the wheat.[35]

The honor of having invented the first fully successful combined harvester in Australia is usually given to Hugh Victor McKay of Victoria. McKay's machine was built in 1883, demonstrated publicly in 1885, and after considerable delay became the standard harvester of the whole continent.[36] But the South Australian evidence shows clearly that the evolution of such machinery was a diffuse process in which many hands and minds throughout the wheat country were working simultaneously toward the same objective. There were many harvesters before McKay's; recognition of his machine as the "first" obviously hinges upon the definition of what constituted a "successful" harvester.

There is another interesting aspect of this development. The Australian harvester was entirely a local innovation but all the

[33] *Port Augusta Dispatch,* Jan. 9, 1880. See also *The Garden and the Field* (Adelaide), January, 1880, pp. 113–14, for an evaluation of the Gawler trials and an unfavorable opinion of the objective.
[34] *The Areas' Express and Farmers' Journal* (Gladstone), Jan. 18, 1879, quoting *The South Australian Advertiser* (Adelaide).
[35] *The Garden and the Field* (Adelaide), January, 1882, p. 115.
[36] Callaghan and Millington, *op. cit.* pp. 343–45.

while there was an awareness that similar developments were taking place in America and this knowledge was an important spur to local progress. Even those who had doubts about the feasibility of a harvester agreed that Australian machinery must be constantly improved, "for we have a very powerful rival in America, and it is our duty to use every scientific means within our power to compete successfully . . . in the wheat emporium of the nations."[37] And in fact the scale and efficiency of American grain farming, and especially that of the great Pacific competitor, California, was a matter of persistent concern to the Australian farm press. The country papers and farm journals are thick with articles describing American machinery and systems of agriculture and editorials advocating their trial or imitation.[38] During this period principal attention was given to the California header system of harvesting.[39] But that system differed more in machine design and scale than in basic principle from the stripper-winnower method and apparently aroused no efforts at imitation.[40] Great interest was aroused by American combined harvesters. The Oregon machine which competed in the Gawler trials astonished Australians by its size: it required six horses and had a cutter-bar of eleven feet. Even more remarkable was the Houser, a California machine which was one of the first really successful harvesters. It was drawn by fourteen horses, cut a swath of fourteen feet, and required five men to operate. One was shipped to South Australia for trial in 1884 and performed in excellent fashion. Yet one farm reporter expressed his sorrow that the manufacturer had been so deluded as to send such a "monstrosity" across the Pacific. Local machines stripping a five-foot swath, drawn by three horses, and operated by two men were considered far superior.[41] The fact that the American machine would cost

[37] *The Areas' Express and Farmers' Journal* (Gladstone), Jan. 18, 1879.

[38] An excellent example is the article, reprinted from the Melbourne *Leader*, in *The Farmers' Weekly Messenger* (Adelaide), March 12, 1875, which describes California wheat-farming equipment.

[39] For example, *ibid.*, Feb. 26, 1875, and Feb. 4, 1876. See also *Port Augusta Dispatch*, Oct. 29, 1880.

[40] In 1875 a California header with a 14′8″ cut was demonstrated somewhere in Australia and the result was hailed by one farm editor as "sufficient proof that in the way of agricultural machinery the Americans are still far ahead." *The Farmers' Weekly Messenger* (Adelaide), Feb. 26, 1875.

[41] *The Garden and the Field* (Adelaide), February, 1884, p. 137. The Houser

£530 in South Australia as compared with £80 for local harvesters was an obvious mark against it, but the important feature was the great contrast in the size and elaborateness of the implements of the two countries. Although inventors in both were aiming toward the same general objectives, each worked within a separate distinct tradition. In South Australia the stripper, with its comb of four to five feet, drawn by three or four horses, set the scale which shaped the evolution of small light-weight winnowers and harvesters. In California the trend was toward ever-larger, heavier machines. Thus, despite plenty of publicity and the persistent urging of imitation there was virtually no trans-Pacific borrowing: each country successfully solved its own problems in its own way.[42]

THE NEW SCALE AND MODE OF FARMING

The stump-jump plough and the harvester were but the most notable items to come from the vigorous, progressive inventiveness which characterized this period of Northern expansion. Improvements in nearly every kind of equipment were made, and they were directly related to the needs of this new frontier. The days of wheat farming on an eighty-acre plot, with a team of horses and a meagre array of simple tools were rapidly fading. Some indication of the scale and variety of implements necessary for wheat-growing in the new manner may be obtained from the following examples (see also Fig. 9).[43]

A

Location:	*Booleroo* Hundred (near Melrose)

Harvester had been called to the attention of South Australians some years before. See *Port Augusta Dispatch*, Dec. 10, 1880.

[42] This difference in scale was apparent in lesser degree in most other machinery. Some American equipment was used, however, especially the Osborne and McCormick wire binders. The stripper principle, using a comb instead of a cutting-bar, was never used on American machines, and this may be one factor in the differences in scale, as the comb would cause an excessive drag if it were greatly lengthened on these early, light, horse-drawn machines. According to Callaghan and Millington, *op. cit.*, pp. 345–46, the cutter-bar was not used on Australian harvesters until 1910, more than forty years after it became common on California headers.

[43] Taken from the descriptive lists of farm auction sale notices in *City and Country* (Adelaide), Sept. 23, 1881. The "reapers" were undoubtedly "strippers." Both farms at that time were a long distance from a railway and the bullocks were probably used to haul the grain to a port or rail siding as well as for clearing the scrub.

Size of Farm:	514 acres (230 acres in crop)
Working Livestock:	22 draft horses, 2 teams of bullocks.
Equipment:	2 English wagons, tip dray, reaper winnower, chaffcutter, 2 double-ploughs, single-plough, set of 6 harrows, scarifier, horse rake, land roller.

B

Location:	*Pinda* Hundred (near Hammond)
Size of Farm:	1,389 acres (600 acres in wheat)
Working Livestock:	20 heavy draft horses, 10 saddle and light harness horses, 1 first-class buggy team, 4 teams (of 8 each) working bullocks.
Equipment:	4 wagons, 2 reapers, winnower, 2 scarifiers, 3 sets of 4 harrows, spring dray, express buggy.

Obviously the time had arrived when more than a strong back, willingness to work, and a handful of coins was sufficient to start up farming. Pioneering in this new wheat frontier required investment; the day of the farmer as capitalist had dawned. But few selectors had capital and, as the state offered land on credit, so the banks and merchants offered credit and the one was as important to this colonization as the other. Many thought the whole system was extravagant and deplorable:

> They need not know the difference between a plough and a wheelbarrow, and yet the State will set them up, upon credit, as thoroughly qualified farmers. They may get their fencing done on credit, buy implements and seed upon credit; the storekeeper gives them credit; the blacksmith hopes to be paid within two or three years' time; and the machinist supplies a machine — perhaps two or three — in the expectation that he will get some of his money when the crop is reaped.[44]

[44] *The Garden and the Field* (Adelaide), May, 1881, p. 178.

There were undoubtedly many evils to these practices, but without some such facilities the whole colonization process would surely have been greatly slowed.

This enlarged system of farming was directly associated with this colonization period. It was prompted by two factors: the need for a more efficient scale of operations to keep production costs competitive with rival wheat export countries; and, as drier country was reached, the need to compensate for the lower yields per acre. The land legislation reflected the successive appearance of these two needs. The original credit legislation of 1869 established 640 acres as a maximum block, and an act of 1877 allowed up to 1,000 acres. Actually most of the land was surveyed into considerably smaller units and most initial selections were well below the maximum. Larger farms could of course be acquired by purchase and the great instability of farm settlement during this period fostered the amalgamation of adjacent blocks. But the land laws, competition for land, and insufficient capital did not allow really huge farming estates to be created at this time. To be sure, a few such operations did exist but these were in the big pastoral freeholds which had been purchased before this new era of land legislation and had since been converted at least partially into agricultural holdings. The most notable of these was the Hill River Estate east of Clare, a domain of 60,000 acres which in 1874 had some 6,000 acres in cultivation (Fig. 10).[45] Such holdings were anomalous, few farms exceeded 1,500 acres and most were but a few hundred acres, but even so the contrast with the older settlement core was clearly marked.

Certainly another distinguishing mark of this era and area was concern over the seeming inefficiency of the common mode of farming. Farm editors were appalled at what they saw, constantly heaped abuse upon the farmers, warned of dire consequences unless they changed their ways, and offered an endless stream of advice toward improvement and salvation. Typical of the type

[45] William Harcus, *South Australia: Its History, Resources, and Productions* (London, 1876), Chapter 13. *The Farmers' Weekly Messenger* (Adelaide), Nov. 27, 1874, also has a detailed description of this estate. The scale of operations was prodigious for the time: e.g., 34 teams with double-ploughs, 27 strippers to harvest the crop.

and tone of the evaluations of the time was the following comment:

> A more slovenly farmer than the South Australian wheat grower it would be difficult to find . . . , his Ridley stripper . . . takes the grain off cheaply, but with great waste and foul effects on the ground. . . . There is no attempt at living from the farm through the year by the cultivation of other crops, dairying, or sheep-keeping. Nothing but wheat, the burning of the stubble, and wheat again. Of course this must have a rapidly deteriorating effect on the soil, notwithstanding its richness.[46]

Criticism was directed principally at the following features: shallow ploughing, insufficient fallowing, failure to keep livestock, disinterest in growing produce for the home, and an almost complete concentration on wheat to the exclusion of any other field crop. It is certain that all of these were features common to this South Australian wheat frontier, but it is also clear that there were reasons behind each, and only when these are explained can any fair judgment be made.

The controversy over seedbed preparation illustrates the degree to which the adaptation of wheat farming to South Australian conditions was still an experimental problem. All the self-styled experts of the time constantly hammered at the importance of deep ploughing and were sharply critical of the "bungling, slovenly" tillage which was everywhere apparent.[47] Shallow ploughing of four to six inches and a light harrowing were the common practices; fallowed ground was often seeded without reploughing. Critics scornfully referred to such a system as "scratch farming" or "skimming." But in many districts deeper tillage was impossible either because of thin stony soils or because of roots and stumps. Also, in the first years of settlement many selectors undoubtedly lacked enough equipment to work large areas thoroughly and had to "skim" in order to get an adequate acreage into crop. But there was a much more important reason: some

[46] *Ibid.,* Feb. 19, 1875, from a reprint of a series of articles in a Melbourne paper. They were also reprinted in *The Northern Argus* (Clare), Feb. 26, 1875, and were accompanied by an editorial castigating the farmer for his sloppy methods.

[47] For example, *The Northern Argus* (Clare), June 25, 1869, and in nearly every comment upon farming practices in every country paper and farm journal of this era.

farmers in the North had come to believe that shallow ploughing was actually better. Experience seemed to suggest that the yields were greater from "scratching" than from deep ploughing and that it was "best to break up as little of the surface as possible."[48] This belief had become strong enough to prompt the manager of the Manna Hill Experimental Farm to propose tests of both "deep and shallow ploughing, and cropping by scarifying and harrowing only, and in some instances by harrowing alone."[49] But such ideas were regarded as traitorous to real farming by the agricultural press and only served to intensify their criticisms and campaigns.[50] Even the remarkable innovations which alone made it possible to cultivate some sections with any efficiency were deplored: "stump-jumping and mullenizing cannot by any stretch of the language be called farming."[51]

And of course it was an impossible "stretch of the language" for those whose concepts of farming were still shaped by the memory of deeply, carefully tilled fields of the British countryside where the heavy plough cleaved and turned a perfect furrow of loamy moist soil. But a whole new rhythm of seasons had already forced the South Australian farmer to shed much of that heritage, and as he worked with the shallow, gritty red-earths of the North he began to rid himself further of the old ideas. These soils have been divided by modern scientists into two broad groups: the red-brown soils of the northerly hill country and the mallee soils of the gulf plains.[52] The two are similar in general characteristics: shallow productive horizons, a relatively sandy texture, and low organic content. The mallee soils are more extreme in all these features than the somewhat more humid red-brown earths. Both represent a degree of change from the deeper, more loamy soils

[48] *The Garden and the Field* (Adelaide), August, 1879, p. 40. The editor, characteristically, noted that it would merely take a few poor harvests to convince them of their error. See also *S. A. Parl. Debates,* June 27, 1882, col. 191.

[49] *The Farmers' Weekly Messenger* (Adelaide), April 27, 1877. See also *S. A. Parl. Paper No. 31A* (1879).

[50] See *The Garden and the Field* (Adelaide), July, 1883, pp. 25–26, in which the editor scathingly ridicules a Gawler newspaper which had the temerity to suggest that shallow ploughing was best.

[51] *Ibid.,* October, 1881, pp. 66–67.

[52] Callaghan and Millington, *op. cit.,* pp. 50–53, 58–61.

Fig. 8 Stripping near Hammond, December, 1883. A typical pioneer homestead in the background: stone house with corrugated iron roof, small iron shed, straw-covered animal shelter. (S. A. Archives)

Fig. 9 "General View of Implements and Stock on the Farm of Mr. John Riggs, Gawler Plains." From William Harcus, *South Australia: Its History, Resources, and Productions* (London, 1876).

Fig. 10 Farming operations, Hill River Estate, *c.* 1875. From top to bottom: seeding, stripping, winnowing, hauling. (S. A. Archives)

Fig. 11 Horse car, Port Broughton tramway. This photograph was taken about 1909, but the car is similar to (perhaps even the same as) those used on such tramways in the 1870's. (S. A. Archives)

of the older hill country settlement region, and all, of course, are markedly different from anything found in Britain. But the agricultural science of the time was wholly a product of the homeland and the divergence of opinion between the "experts" and the farmers was to persist for years. The first professors of agriculture tended to support the merits of deep ploughing; gradually, however, the experiments of soil scientists and agronomists proved that under the special conditions of this particular wheat belt deep ploughing and repeated fine tillage were highly detrimental to soil moisture and structure.[53] This is not to suggest that the pioneer farmers had quickly evolved an "ideal tilth" but they were working in that direction and it was not the only instance in which empirical folk-knowledge was in advance of the science of its time.

DIVERSIFICATION CONTROVERSY

A much more important general feature of this agriculture was its emphasis upon wheat to the exclusion of all other crops or activities. Critics viewed this as nothing less than an ignorant, irrational obsession which promised certain ruin. Certainly much of the area was cropped year after year in a ravenous exploitation of the virgin fertility. Acreages in fallow gradually increased, but it was by no means a widespread practice, and even where it was, its full potential value was probably rarely attained because of inadequate weed control and improper tillage.[54] The wheat straw and stubble were looked upon by some as the key toward diversification; the straw and chaff which were often burned as a useless residue ought to be fed to livestock. Those who strongly advocated the value of this fodder often saw the continued use of the stripper as an evil and urged the adoption of the binder:

> Then the steam thrashing-engine will become an institution, and the valuable food contained in the straw of wheat and barley and oats will be utilized in the feeding of cattle and sheep; thus being turned into

[53] See Callaghan and Millington, *op. cit.*, pp. 121–24, 322–23.

[54] Fallowing fluctuated between 20 and 30 per cent of the total wheat acreage in the state as a whole during these years, but it was undoubtedly less in the frontier region. See Dunsdorfs, *op. cit.*, p. 371.

substantial meat instead of being offered up in the form of smoke as a burnt sacrifice to waste and extravagance.[55]

It was recognized, however, that this could only be a partial solution; the livestock manure could be used on the wheat fields, but what was really needed was a sound rotation crop which would not only provide fodder much superior to mere straw, but directly restore fertility to the soil. In 1877 one farm editor was urging lucerne as the key to combining "meat growing with wheat growing," and in the following year hailed the success of a *Kulpara* farmer in raising field peas from a plot which had been in wheat for six successive years as pointing the way toward a long overdue revolution in South Australian farming. He foresaw a fourfold succession of rape, wheat, peas, wheat as the ideal rotation.[56] Undoubtedly numerous other plants were being tried, prompted by curiosity or concern for the future. On the model farm at the Hill River Estate, plots of maize, millet, and sorghum were tested,[57] but certainly most farmers were as yet indifferent to the question. It is apparent that most of those who did talk of a wheat-sheep combination had in mind a system of large holdings which would combine cropping areas and natural pasture rather than a system of wheat-fodder rotations.

Propaganda urging diversification was by no means limited to the question of livestock. A wide variety of crops was urged upon the wheat farmer. Probably the olive was the most commonly advocated; some pointed out its suitability for fencerows and windbreaks, other had visions of vast acreages covering the rolling hills of the North. The government tried to encourage such plantings by recognizing one acre of olives (or osiers, mulberries, vines, apples, pears, oranges, figs, almonds, or hops) as the equal of six acres of cereal in meeting the cultivation requirements of the credit selection laws, but a farm reporter who strongly favored such crops was chagrined that he could not find a single selector

[55] *The Garden and the Field* (Adelaide), June, 1878, pp. 5–6; October, 1878, and October, 1879, pp. 65–66. On the Hill River Estate after the stripper had taken the grain, the stubble was mowed and stacked for fodder, but probably it was used mainly to feed the 123 work horses needed. See *The Northern Argus* (Clare), Feb. 6, 1874.

[56] *The Garden and the Field* (Adelaide), February, 1877, and June, 1878.

[57] *The Northern Argus* (Clare), Nov. 27, 1874.

who had taken advantage of that provision.[58] Wattle for tanning bark also had its supporters.[59] Such tree crops could not, of course, be put in rotations, but they were advocated as a means toward building a more balanced economy – to diversify the sources of income for the farmer and the colony alike. The failure of many wheat growers to bother with orchards and gardens, dairy stock, swine, and poultry brought caustic comment from those who sought to promote a better agriculture. In their view every farm ought to have its grove of olives, its own vineyard; mulberries for silkworms would build a most "useful and profitable industry" which "would furnish suitable employment for the children and females of our farmers' families."[60]

The persistence of this kind of propaganda was equalled only by the dogged refusal of the wheat farmer to pay any attention to it. In 1875 a commission was established to study the question of setting up some kind of scientific agricultural research and training facilities. The testimony given to the committee is an interesting reflection of farmer attitudes.[61] Very little enthusiasm and considerable outright opposition was voiced. It was clear that none thought of farming in any other terms than wheat farming. One suggested that a suitable forage rotation crop was a great need, but attention was almost entirely focused upon the problems of wheat itself, upon hot winds and rust and the excessive costs of farm labor. "A shipload of bone and sinew would be more appreciated than any number of professors and lectures," said one frank witness; there was no need for an agricultural department, claimed another:

> The wheat-grower, with labor at £2 per week, and land at £1.10.1 per acre, has nothing before him but go on with his double or triple plough from one farm to another while new land is to be obtained. No

[58] *The Farmers' Weekly Messenger* (Adelaide), Feb. 19, 1875. *The Garden and the Field* was an especially strong proponent of olives. It should be noted that orcharding, viticulture, and truck gardening were well established in the Adelaide Hills and Barossa Valley.
[59] *Port Augusta Dispatch,* Feb. 6, 1880.
[60] *The Farmers' Weekly Messenger* (Adelaide), July 17, 1874. See also *The Garden and the Field* (Adelaide), June, 1881, p. 8, in which Yorke Peninsula farmers are urged to grow olives, mulberries, and vines.
[61] *S. A. Parl. Paper No.* 77 (1875).

professor who ever sat in a chair can persuade him out of that simple truth.

And still another agreed that an agricultural college was altogether useless:

So long as virgin soil is to be obtained at £1 per acre, so long will the average South Australian farmer prefer to spend the money in the purchase of new land, rather than in the improvement of what has been impoverished.

However unpleasant such attitudes might be to those concerned with the quality and future of farming, they were a much more realistic recognition of the facts than most of the recommendations which had been so liberally showered upon the farmers.

It is quite clear that the system of land legislation was an important influence upon the whole character of farming. Goyder, with his typical foresight, had warned of this very danger when the credit system was first established:

it may be a question how far much of the legislation in land almost offers a premium to the exhaustion of the soil by giving new or virgin soil in exchange for worked-out land. It is not difficult to suppose that too liberal land regulations may not so much induce fresh immigration as a shifting population from a locality partially exhausted to another with similar soil in a state of nature, for it cannot be denied that under a system of liberal credit, with small cash payments, opportunity is given to the selector to abandon his holding when it is cropped out, not only without loss, but as a matter of fact, with great profit to himself.[62]

It was a prophecy soon fulfilled. Hardly had settlement in the North begun than it became apparent that it was being accomplished almost wholly by farmers from the older districts. As early as 1873 the speculative possibilities of the new legislation were becoming well recognized: "many of the settlers have with frank audacity avowed that they never intended to complete their contract with the Government."[63] Under the credit laws the initial payment became only a modest fee for the right to hold a block of land for several years, the interest payments became a very modest rental, a succession of crops could be harvested until the

[62] *S. A. Parl. Paper No. 23* (1870–71), p. 8.
[63] *Yorke's Peninsula Advertiser and Miners' News* (Moonta), June 3, 1873.

final payment came due and then the selection could be turned back to the government and another obtained. For the most part the successive alterations in credit legislation only served to reduce these fees, lengthen the schedule of their payment, and magnify the speculative possibility.[64] An obvious curb upon this system would have been to prohibit re-selection, to allow each person the right to purchase land on credit only once. If he forfeited, his only recourse for another farm would be cash purchase.[65] But such a limitation was not imposed, and the results were rationalized: to be sure, "this flocking to the North" was depopulating the South, "but as there has been no immigration lately, it is the only means that the character of the country for agricultural purposes can be tested."[66] There was an "anxiety" to settle the country, and it was argued that the depressive effects upon the older areas would be only temporary. Once the limits of the new agricultural domain were established there would be a gradual filling up, and a re-occupation and rehabilitation of the old farms. It was generally agreed that this was a lamentable but necessary phase.[67]

If the government offered, in effect, to sell virgin soil fertility for a small sum and allowed the customer to return for more when his supply was exhausted it would hardly be fair to place the entire blame for the results upon the buyer. If the great majority of the spokesmen for the colony pointed with pride to a constantly enlarging agricultural prospect, it was, under the existing circumstances, only by means of this speculative instability that frontier expansion could be maintained.[68] If the spectre of American com-

[64] Under the original Strangways Act a 20 per cent deposit was required and final payment after four years; under the 1872 amendment, only 10 per cent was required initially, 10 per cent after three years, and the remainder at the end of six years; in 1877 the payment schedule was extended over nine years. These latter liberalizations undoubtedly gave a great boost to the practices under discussion.

[65] See Goyder's statement of the consequences of failure to insist upon this restriction, *S. A. Parl. Paper No. 60* (1890), p. 35.

[66] *The Northern Argus* (Clare), Jan. 3, 1873.

[67] For example, *The Farmers' Weekly Messenger* (Adelaide), May 29, 1874, citing a parallel experience in the United States.

[68] It should be noted that this instability of settlement was by no means wholly because of abandonment and reselection, but also because of sale and reselection by those who had completed a credit purchase. For example, in *Mannanarie* Hundred, of the fifty-eight credit selectors who completed their contract during the years 1877–79, sixteen had sold their farms by late 1879;

petition was constantly voiced and the need for greater efficiency emphasized, it was largely because of the much criticized large acreages, new machinery, and "skimming" techniques that South Australian production costs were kept low and competitive. If the farm "advisers" always complained that the farmers insisted that "it won't pay" to add "butter, cheese, bacon, ham, eggs, and poultry to the products of their farms,"[69] there was precious little proof that it would pay on any general commercial scale. As the evidence is examined it becomes increasingly clear that there was simply no meeting of the minds between those who were doing the farming and those who were advising how it ought to be done. And this difference was very far from being a gulf between the ignorant and the learned – it was, in fact, a gulf between two distinct concepts of agriculture.

A NEW KIND OF AGRICULTURE

When the critics of South Australian frontier farming insisted upon the superior merits of a "small farm well tilled" in contrast to what they saw around them, they were evoking the image of an old ideal: the small, freehold farm of the sturdy, independent yeoman; worked by the family which it in turn supported from its own produce of field, garden, orchard, woodlot, and livestock; yielding a modest surplus from a variety of crops carefully planted and tended. It was a concept based upon the rich heritage of a deeply-rooted European peasantry, emancipated and up-graded by the social and economic changes of the seventeenth and eighteenth centuries, idealized by the utopian social philosophers of the most recent century, and ardently embraced by the theorists who half a century before had conceived the very idea of a South Australia.

But the pioneer on the wheat frontier in South Australia, as in all the "new" lands of the time, was working within an entirely different context. He had no emotional ties to his land, he could not have – there was no heritage to bind him to this new and strange kind of country. His land had not been passed down to

in *Pekina,* five out of six had sold; in *Tarcowie,* eighteen out of twenty-six; in *Yongala,* four out of fourteen. See *S. A. Parl. Paper No. 71* (1879) for these and additional data.

[69] *The Garden and the Field* (Adelaide), September, 1881, p. 49.

him through the generations, it had been purchased – it was not a legacy but an investment. Land was potential wealth and wheat was the proven means of reaping the potential. His wheat was not for his family and the village grist mill, it was wheat for the millions of the new industrial world. He farmed not as a member of an intimate, stable, localized society, but as a member of a world-wide, dynamic, competitive society. Success was measured by his cost per bushel. Anything that promised to raise yields and lower costs was of interest, anything that promised to divert his energies from wheat, that required more time and labor, was of no interest. The invention of the stripper had opened the way toward this new agriculture, but a generation of experience had proved that in these precarious sub-humid lands under intensive competitive conditions it had to be grown on each farm by the hundreds instead of mere tens of acres. Labor, not land, was the scarce factor, and a whole array of new, enlarged, and efficient machinery now allowed a whole new scale of agriculture. Those who viewed the stripper, the harvester, and the stump-jump plough as implements of ruin were simply anachronistic. And the railroad, the great instrument of regional specialization, was basic to it all. The day was arriving when the products of the orchard and garden and dairy could be shipped to the wheat farms instead of being grown there. And the day had arrived when the farmer at a relatively trifling cost in time or money could go to the city and partake of all the amenities of the new urban civilization; it was the first step toward healing the age-old cleavage between rural and urban life. For these farmers, wheat was the springboard for a sudden leap into a new way of life.

In short, the one group was still thinking largely in pre-industrial terms, the other was working directly within the context of the new age. For the one land was "home," for the other it was "capital." While the one tended to preach the familiar practices of old lands, the other was evolving radical practices for the new. To be fair, it must be admitted that the dichotomy was not complete and the frontier farmer should not escape from criticism. There was, undoubtedly, an excessive degree of crudeness and slovenliness on many farms. Some greater permanence of settlement and pride of ownership was certainly a theme worth promoting. Some higher standard of housing and better care of livestock was clearly desirable. The absence of gardens and orchards and milch cows was justifiable only if their products actually were being purchased, not if their neglect meant an impoverished diet. And in farming techniques it must be admitted that the publicists, while often advocating untried or unsuitable practices, were at least very alert to new developments elsewhere in the world, and, on the other hand, local farmers often stubbornly resisted innovations even after they had been experimentally proved as locally sound.

On balance, however, the evidence would certainly seem to confirm the South Australian frontier wheat farmer – and his companion, the country machinist – as uncommonly industrious, adaptable, and inquisitive pioneers who rapidly developed a new and basically successful farming system to meet the peculiar challenges of new environmental and economic situations. The new seasonal rhythms of activity, new tillage techniques, new implements for clearing, cultivating, and harvesting were all folk-inventions. Working directly with the realities of local climates and soils, these pioneers, through trial and error, had either solved or at least made important progress toward solving most of the basic problems insofar as they could be met with the materials at hand.

The great persistent deficiency of this agriculture was its chronically low average yield of wheat. But the removal or at least amelioration of that defect was to come primarily from the realms of biology and chemistry, as yet beyond the grasp of the pioneer. And the way was opened for such contributions from the laboratory just at the close of this period. Despite a discouraging disinterest and even opposition, the Agricultural and Technical Education Commission of 1875 filed a recommendation for the establishment of model farms and an agricultural college. In 1879 the proposal was approved, two years later J. D. Custance was appointed as the first Principal, and in March, 1882, the experimental farm and college was begun at Roseworthy (amidst loud cries from Gladstone and Jamestown which regarded themselves as the center of the agricultural domain and therefore the logical location).[70] The heavy drought was then in its second year and

[70] *Ibid.*, pp. 91–92, and April, 1883, p. 162; *S. A. Parl. Paper No. 33* (1883–84).

the alarmingly low yields over the entire wheat country underscored the urgency of this incipient partnership of farmer and scientist. The latter gradually assumed the dominant role in innovations. New disease- and drought-resistant wheats, new exotic rotation pasture plants, and chemical fertilizers would in time bring this agriculture to a new level of productivity, but they did so not by a rejection of the old farming system, but by modification and improvement within its basic context.[71]

This brief period of frontier expansion, then, almost exactly circumscribes a distinctive phase of "industrial-age folk-agriculture" in South Australia. A whole new agricultural region had been defined, its domestication initiated, and a system of farming established. Some elements of that system had been brought forward intact from the older regions, most had been altered, some were completely new – but the whole complex had been worked out by the settlers themselves. The scientist entered the local scene to grapple directly and systematically with farming problems just when the frontier had reached its outermost limits in the North. It was a propitious time: the fresh land was now gone and the farmer was faced with the necessity of settling in and improving that which he had.

[71] The first important result of this new farmer-scientist partnership was the development of new wheat varieties. The whole topic of wheat varieties is of basic importance in the study of such colonizations, but it has been omitted simply because the primary sources were curiously silent about the specific wheats being grown during these years. Dunsdorfs also notes this lack of information (*op. cit.*, p. 189), but he does give a good summary of developments up to this period. Quite naturally, English wheats predominated in the early years, with White Lammas probably the leading variety until about 1850. By 1860 South Australian Purple Straw, probably a field variant selected from English Red Straw, became prominent. Because it matured much earlier it has been credited with being an important factor in making possible the advance into drier regions. The 1880's mark a new phase of experimentation. Dr. Schomburgk, of the Botanic Garden, imported DuToit wheat from South Africa in 1881 (for a local notice of its trial in the North see *The Agriculturist and Review* [Jamestown], Dec. 7, 1881). From a plot of this wheat a farmer near Port Pirie selected some rust-free variants and developed Ward's Prolific which soon became the most successful wheat in the colony. Two other important varieties, Steinwedal and Early Gluyas, were also discovered and developed from local variants by South Australian farmers. All of these preceded the famous scientifically-created hybrids of Farrer and others and this again illustrates how folk experimentation anticipated that of science. See Dunsdorfs, *op. cit.*, pp. 147–48, 189–92. See also Callaghan and Millington, *op. cit.*, pp. 261–63 on South Australian variety selections, and Chapter 17 on scientific wheat breeding.

VII.

Setting the Patterns of Circulation

> The time has arrived when our iron roads should be extended to connect many of our agricultural and mineral districts with the Metropolis and Shipping Ports of the Province.
>
> — Report of the Select Committee . . . on Railway Extension, *S.A.Parl. Paper No. 161* (1866-67)

> At the present rate of building jetties a map of our gulf coast lines would show in a few years time a more than distant resemblance to a . . . comb.
>
> —*The Jamestown Review,* Aug. 7, 1879

PORTS AND RAILWAYS

Wheat fields within sight of the sea are a distinctive feature of South Australia. They were nearly unique within the patterns of development of the important new grainlands of the world during the latter nineteenth century. The greatest of those areas lay deep in the continental interiors of North America and Eurasia, and lesser regions nearer the coast, such as California, the Willamette, and the Columbia Basin of America and the Pampa of Argentina, still faced serious overland transport problems. Among South Australia's export competitors only the relatively minor Canterbury Plains of New Zealand fronted the ocean and even there the relationship between farms and the sea was less advantageous. No other region had the penetrating embayments and peninsularity of South Australia, and thus no other region developed anything like the astonishing density of small direct grain shipping points.

Yet despite the fact that the wheat belt developed into a narrow strip no more than sixty-five miles (air-line distance) wide from the coast to its inland margins, railways, here as elsewhere, were an essential tool of colonization. Long bullock teams did cart the harvest, with grinding slowness, as far as sixty miles to a port, but though colorful in retrospect these were inordinately laborious in reality and were regarded at the time as but a necessary pioneer expedient. Only the confident expectation of railways induced settlers to range so far inland. Though locally satisfactory, by any world standard even the best years in South Australia gave a low average yield per acre, and the government, ever conscious of competition from other export regions, was convinced from the first that the cheapest possible means of getting the harvest to the ports must be obtained.

Thus, aside from the survey, sale, and settlement of the land itself, no activity was more fundamental to the development of this new farming region than the construction of railways. And just as in the case of its land disposal policies, the government exerted full control and sought to shape developments according to a preconceived pattern, and, as with land legislation, the original design was soon modified in response to local demands and conditions in the frontier. Further, the pace of railway construction closely reflected the accelerating surge of settlement expansion: without a mile of track completed in 1869, by the end of 1882 this new agricultural realm had nearly five hundred miles of line in operation as the result of a near frenzy of construction in the years immediately preceding.

The sheer magnitude of this railway program was an impressive achievement, but its importance must be measured in more than mileage. For, inevitably, the evolution of this network necessitated basic decisions on the objectives, patterns, and density of lines and on the character of facilities which left an indelible imprint not only upon the transportation system but upon many another feature of the region. The most notable decisions were the following:

1. The gradual shift in emphasis from a centralized system focused upon Adelaide and its port to a dispersed system oriented to northern outports.

2. The selection of particular outports as terminals and the determination of hinterlands by the patterns of railway construction.
3. The authorization of two different gauges and the selection of the junction points between the two networks.
4. The establishment of a general policy of placing all farming districts within at least fifteen miles of a rail line.

Another decision, less basic to the agricultural region but in part related, was the determination to build a few long feeders far into the sparsely settled pastoral interior.

Underscoring the importance of these decisions was the fact that in this instance, unlike its course in the history of land legislation, the government, though altering its program from time to time, never relaxed its firm control over the pace and pattern of railway extension. In the absence of private entrepreneurs who might build when and where they chose and compete for the traffic of various districts, the South Australian network was therefore developed by conscious design and as it passed through each district it set a relatively stable framework for the development of related features.[1]

INITIAL RAILWAY SURVEYS AND CONSTRUCTIONS, 1860–70

The confidence of South Australian colonists that railways would soon follow the march of the plough was solidly based upon the achievements of the dozen years preceding this northward expansion.[2] The first road was that between Adelaide and its port. In

[1] By the time of this colonization period, government control of railways was a generally-established policy. The only private lines were the local tramway of the mining company at Moonta-Wallaroo-Kadina, and a short passenger railway between Adelaide and the beach at Glenelg. Consideration was given to a proposal by a syndicate of British capitalists to build a transcontinental from Adelaide to Darwin in return for a huge land grant, following American precedents, but their demands were considered exorbitant. With the slight exception of the short Laura branch which will be noted later, construction and operation by private concerns was not really a live alternative in this wheat country. That the type of control is worth emphasizing, however, will be obvious to anyone who is acquainted with the stark contrast with the history of railways and regional developments in the United States.

[2] A very useful study of the early phases of construction and policy is that of A. W. Cheesman, "Railways in South Australia: 1839–1875," Honors Thesis, History, University of Adelaide, 1958.

the following year, 1857, the North Line was completed to Gawler and three years later extended to the copper center of Kapunda. Although the mining traffic was a principal inducement, this line cut diagonally through the main agricultural region in the hills and valleys north of the metropolis and it soon garnered a brisk traffic in wheat and other farm produce. And as early as 1860 the future transport needs of the country farther north were given some attention. The Burra copper developments were rich enough to be assumed as the next likely terminus of extension, but a survey was also made from that point to Melrose at the foot of Mt. Remarkable. To be sure, the intention was to secure the reservation of land and not immediate construction, but it was an important indication that the railway was already being regarded as a pioneering instrument of regional development.[3]

Significantly, the Engineer-in-Chief who reported on the Mt. Remarkable survey stated that when that district required a railway it should be served from nearby Spencer Gulf and not by extension of a line all the way north from Adelaide. With this, the major issue of the geographical nature of the incipient rail system of the province may be said to have been opened: whether to focus a network of lines upon the capital city and main port or to construct a series of shorter feeders to scattered local outports. As long as agricultural development remained anchored in the hill country logically served by Port Adelaide, no decision was necessary, but even before the settlers began their rapid northward advance the question was faced, and although not directly answered in any final way a program of construction was initiated which was to influence subsequent developments.

The issue arose over how best to provide rail service to the rich farming section in the hills of the Upper Wakefield and Clare districts. This area was almost equally distant from the Kapunda rail line and the head of St. Vincent Gulf. On the gulf, Port Wakefield had long been established, first as a copper and coal port serving the Burra and later as a wool export point. Despite its primitive facilities and very serious navigational disadvantages (all goods had to be lightered out to ocean vessels) it was an obvious possibility, and a series of examinations was begun in 1865.

[3] *S. A. Parl. Paper No. 38* (1860).

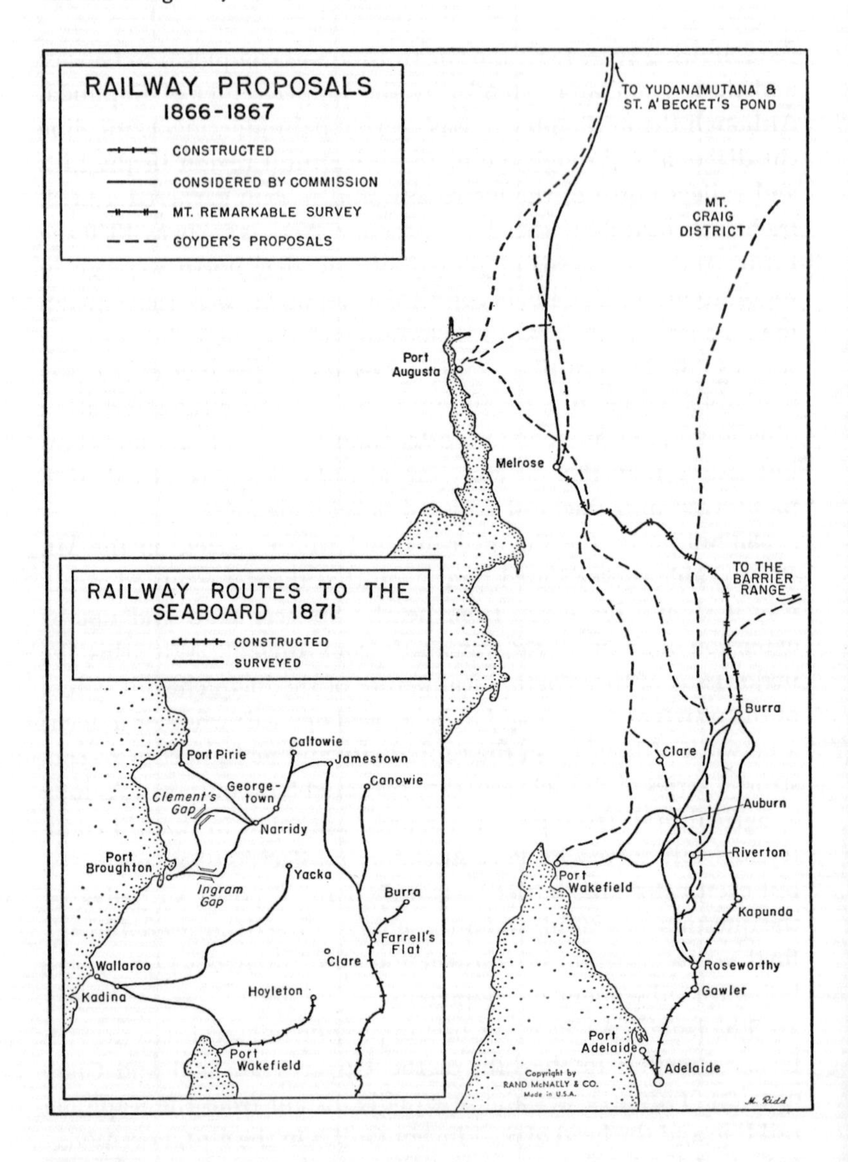
RAILWAY PROPOSALS
1866-1867
CONSTRUCTED
CONSIDERED BY COMMISSION
MT. REMARKABLE SURVEY
GOYDER'S PROPOSALS
TO YUDANAMUTANA &
ST. A'BECKET'S POND
MT.
CRAIG
DISTRICT
Port
Augusta
Melrose
TO THE
BARRIER
RANGE
Burra
Clare
Auburn
Riverton
Port
Wakefield
Kapunda
Roseworthy
Gawler
Port
Adelaide
Adelaide
RAILWAY ROUTES TO THE
SEABOARD 1871
CONSTRUCTED
SURVEYED
Port Pirie
Caltowie
Jamestown
Canowie
Georgetown
Clement's
Gap
Narridy
Port
Broughton
Yacka
Ingram
Gap
Burra
Farrell's
Flat
Clare
Wallaroo
Kadina
Hoyleton
Port
Wakefield
Copyright by
RAND McNALLY & CO.
Made in U.S.A.
M. Ridd

Map 15

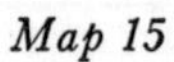

The report of that year described its defects, was uncertain as to whether deepening or a jetty would be the best solution, but noted that 8,000 bales of wool had been shipped that season and that the potential shipment of grain could be "very large."[4] In the next year a survey for a horse-traction tramway inland to the vicinity of Auburn was made. The engineer concluded that the cost of building along the Wakefield River into the hills would be too great and recommended a line terminating on the plains just to the west. Such a route would have a very gentle slope to the coast, could be readily reached by roads leading over the hills, and would open up the agricultural lands along the western base of the ranges.[5] The committee charged with examining further the port itself agreed with this recommendation, noted the important advantage of easy extension of the line much farther north when settlement expansion warranted, and concluded that "the evidence is decidedly in favor of the desirability of the construction of a tramroad to the seaboard, rather than any plan of connection with the Northern Railway."[6] The significance of this report was not only in its emphatic commitment to a policy of developing local feeders to minor ports, but in its diversion of emphasis from the provision of service to the older settled district to the importance of planning for railroad construction into fresh agricultural regions.

The whole issue of railway extension was by now sufficiently alive to warrant comprehensive study, and a special committee was established to explore the question. Attached to their report was a map showing lines tentatively considered by the committee and also those suggested by Goyder, who as Surveyor General and a man who knew more about the nature of the country than anyone else, was invited to prepare an over-all program of future development (Map 15).[7] The importance of the Burra and the studies already made for a Port Wakefield line were sufficient to insure common agreement on the general pattern of construction which ought to be undertaken immediately beyond the present Kapunda line, although specific route locations in each case were

[4] *S. A. Parl. Paper No. 129* (1865–66).
[5] *S. A. Parl. Paper No. 39* (1866–67).
[6] *S. A. Parl. Paper No. 62* (1866–67).
[7] *S. A. Parl. Paper No. 161* (1866–67).

yet open to consideration. It is the proposals for extension well beyond the existing agricultural region that provide the most interesting insight into the perspectives of the time both as to the prevailing geographical outlook and the objectives of railway construction. The committee based its initial view of northward extension upon the Burra–Mt. Remarkable survey. The town of Melrose, isolated in the pastoral domain, was an obvious anchor upon which to hang proposals for lines into the Far North. Beyond, a route was plotted through the Willochra toward the Yudanamutana copper district. Goyder's program was similar but considerably more ambitious. In addition to a choice of possible routes to Melrose and a generally parallel line to Yudanamutana, he added a line far into the pastoral zone to St. à Becket's Pond near the southern margin of Lake Eyre, a line north from near Burra to the Mt. Craig mining and pastoral area, and a route curving northeastward to the Barrier Ranges "to annex the whole of the valley of the Darling and Bogan to this Colony."

Out of this range of possibilities, the committee recommended the following: a line branching from near Roseworthy to Burra via Saddleworth; a northern extension from ten miles southwest of the Burra to near Mt. Remarkable (via the middle route on the map); and a Far Northern line from Port Augusta to near St. à Becket's Pond, 200–250 miles distant, to open up mineral and pastoral districts.[8]

The Port Wakefield route, already surveyed, was generally assumed to be part of the evolving program, although, in deference to one committee member who condemned that port as a miserable mudhole and tried to hammer every witness into agreeing that Wallaroo was the logical terminus, a preliminary survey of a line from Clare to Wallaroo was also recommended. Nevertheless, it is clear that nearly all were assuming that the main system should be focused upon Adelaide. The country beyond Clare was believed to have but limited agricultural potential; traffic from such inland districts would consist primarily of wool and copper and, periodically, of sheep sent south from drought-stricken runs, with station and mining camp supplies inbound. Port Augusta

[8] See *S. A. Parl. Paper No. 52* (1870–71) for a detailed map of possible routes north of Port Augusta.

would serve as a minor outlet but the over-all plan revealed both a strong centralization bias and a commonly-assumed duty to build very extensive lines deep into sparsely settled non-agricultural regions.

In 1867 a special committee studied the question of a Clare to Wallaroo railway. There was ample evidence that Wallaroo with its deep-water harbor was far superior to Port Wakefield, but by now a tramway to the latter had already been authorized and despite a favorable recommendation, the Wallaroo route was too much a duplication to gain legislative approval.[9] In 1870 the only lines actually authorized from this series of studies, from Roseworthy to the Burra and from Port Wakefield to Hoyleton, were completed. Although still not directly served (a matter of deep local disappointment), the Auburn-Clare district had a much improved situation, with stations at Farrell's Flat, Saddleworth, Riverton, and Hoyleton relatively easily accessible.

THE TRIUMPH OF THE OUTPORTS, 1871–74

By the time this nearly one hundred miles of new line was completed in 1870, the credit legislation of the previous year had initiated a whole new pattern of demands for service. The principal zone of the new colonization was in the Broughton district, forty miles and more beyond the nearest railway. The new Agricultural Areas were hardly opened before a petition was forwarded to Parliment pleading for extension of the still uncompleted Port Wakefield tramway on north to the River Broughton.[10]

Settlement proceeded so rapidly that by 1871 a new railway study was initiated. Submitted by the Deputy Surveyor General and entitled "Railway Routes from Northern Areas to Seaboard" this report showed how strikingly the needs of the country had changed, not only in urgency but in direction (Map 15, inset).[11] Of three possible extensions northward from the Adelaide-Burra line, all equally feasible insofar as terrain was concerned, the one from Burra to Hallett was listed as preferable because it was "least

[9] *S. A. Parl. Paper No. 141* (1867).
[10] *S. A. Parl. Paper No. 74* (1869–70).
[11] *S. A. Parl. Paper No. 40* (1872).

likely to be brought into competition with short lines leading westward to the seacoast." As the Burra area was the least important sector of the northern agricultural frontier this meant in effect a rejection of older programs of metropolitan centralization. The principal area of concern was the Jamestown–Middle Broughton area which had already proved to be a rich farming region. Direct service from Spencer Gulf was now assumed, the only questions centered on ports and exact routes. A Port Pirie–Georgetown–Jamestown line received the strongest recommendation, although Port Broughton was suggested as possibly a better outlet. The great superiority of the deep-water harbor and existing facilities at Wallaroo continued to attract attention, but the longer distance to the main region to be served and the broad belt of poor scrubland intervening forced a reluctant rejection.

The railroad question was now thoroughly alive in the North. Petitions began to pour in pleading both the urgent need of service and the clear superiority of some particular route. The fate of ports, inland towns, and whole districts was in the balance, rivalries were intense, and politicians quickly responded by introducing a host of bills calling for the immediate construction of various lines. The issues were obviously complex enough to warrant thorough inquiry, and in 1873 a new committee of the Legislative Council on railway construction was formed[12] and other surveys of the several ports were initiated.

The least controversial recommendation of this new committee was the extension of the Port Wakefield tramway about thirteen miles to Blyth Plains. The terrain was nearly level, the plains were becoming settled, Wakefield was clearly the nearest port, and the added traffic would enhance the profits of the existing line.

Farther north the issue was far less simple. At least a short railroad inland from Spencer Gulf was assumed as desirable by all, but from which port and by which route was a matter of heated argument. Periodic inundations and cramped wharfage space at Port Pirie led to suggestions that a terminus be established at Mt. Ferguson just across the inner bay to the north. However, after lengthy inquiry Pirie won the recommendation, largely because

[12] *S. A. Parl. Paper No. 141* (1873).

of prior development (Map 16A).[13] Next came the problem of which of two surveyed routes inland would prove most advantageous: one looping southward via Georgetown or one cutting directly around the southern end of the Flinders to Gladstone. The former would cross good agricultural lands nearly all the way, the latter would closely skirt the ranges but would be shorter and would better serve the upper Rocky River district of Laura and Wirrabara to the north. Petitioners from each area, and especially from the youthful towns so vitally affected, strongly argued the merits of their favored routes.[14] The Gladstone line was chosen, principally because it was shorter and would capture the Georgetown trade anyway. A third question was how far this line ought to be extended. This was a more significant issue for it once again raised the problem of centralization versus coastal feeders. Jamestown, already a flourishing town in a developing farming area, was the focus of the controversy: should it be tapped by extending the Port Pirie line eastward, or by a branch from the Burra line northward? Petitioners in favor of the latter pointed out that it coincided with the existing flow of traffic, wheat being carted from forty to sixty-five miles to the Farrell's Flat station, and that "such a line would have the advantage over any other proposed in placing your memorialists in direct communication with, and attracting all the northern trade to, the metropolis."[15] Attractive as this might appear to influential Adelaide interests, insofar as getting wheat to the seaboard was the principal objective, Port Pirie was far closer, and most persons in the Jamestown area favored an east-west line.[16] But in view of the conflict the railroad committee dodged the issue and recommended construction only as far as Gladstone for the present.

The situation at Port Broughton was somewhat analogous to that involving Port Pirie. Again, although stores and meagre shipping facilities were already established, there was some question as to whether it might not be better to lay out a township at

[13] See *S. A. Parl. Papers Nos. 107, 133, 137* (1873).
[14] *S. A. Parl. Papers Nos. 57, 60, 66* (1873), *No. 206* (1874); also *No. 92* (1873) for a detailed map of these rival routes.
[15] *S. A. Parl. Paper No. 99* (1873).
[16] Many of the petitioners of *Paper No. 99* were residents of *Anne* and *Ayers,* an area between Jamestown and Burra which would not be served by a Port Pirie line.

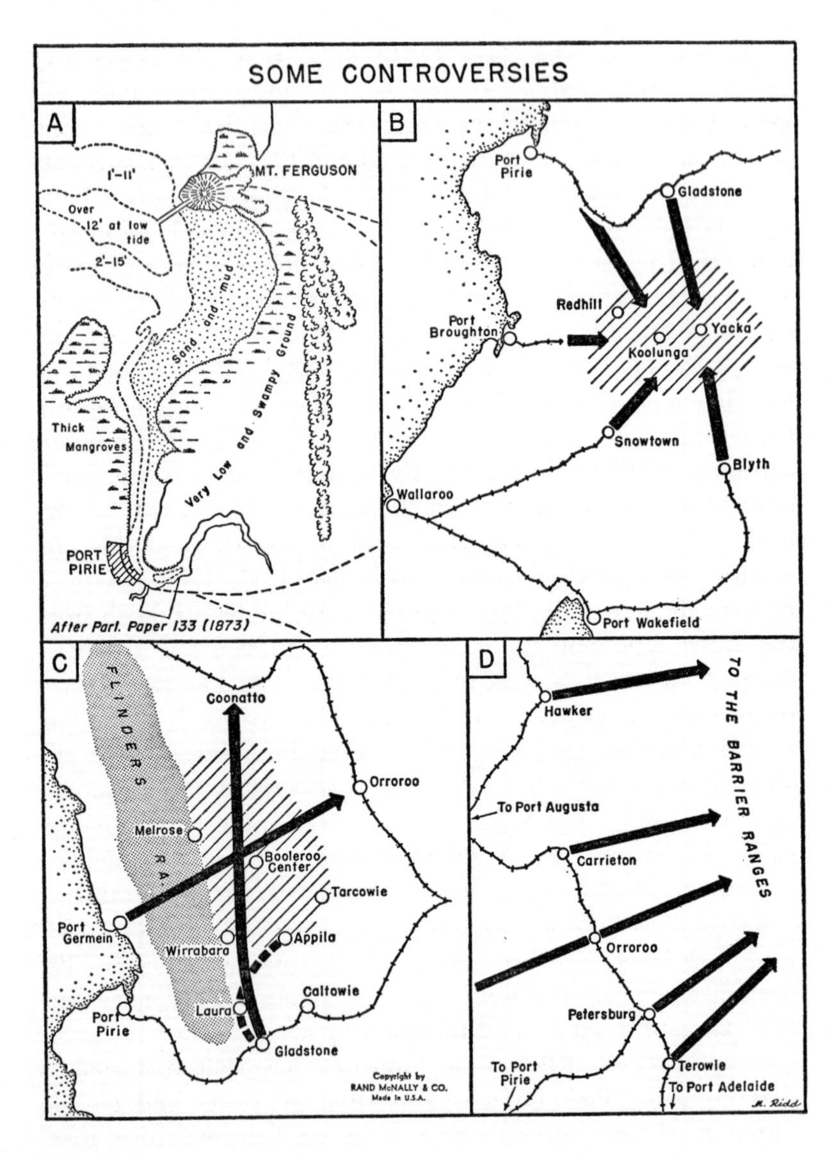
SOME CONTROVERSIES
A
1'–11'
MT. FERGUSON
Over 12' at low tide
2'–15'
Sand and mud
Very Low and Swampy Ground
Thick Mangroves
PORT PIRIE
After Parl. Paper 133 (1873)
B
Port Pirie
Gladstone
Redhill
Port Broughton
Yacka
Koolunga
Snowtown
Blyth
Wallaroo
Port Wakefield
C
FLINDERS RA.
Coonatto
Orroroo
Melrose
Booleroo Center
Tarcowie
Port Germein
Wirrabara
Appila
Caltowie
Laura
Port Pirie
Gladstone
Copyright by RAND McNALLY & CO. Made in U.S.A.
D
Hawker
TO THE BARRIER RANGES
To Port Augusta
Carrieton
Orroroo
Petersburg
Terowie
To Port Pirie
To Port Adelaide
M. Ridd

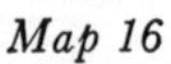
Map 16

a new site. And again two possible tramway routes inland were debated. One would lead northeast toward Clement's Gap, the other directly east toward Ingram Gap (Map 15, inset).[17] Although Clement's offered a lower crossing of the Barunga Range and could be extended into the Redhill and Narridy districts, the prior decision in favor of a Port Pirie line eastward made this route too much a duplication. Therefore, a short horse-tramway directly eastward to bridge the long, dry haul across the unfarmed mallee was recommended.

Finally, and somewhat curiously, a tramway from Wallaroo to Port Wakefield was endorsed. Although service to Green's Plains was a local inducement, the function of this line was not clearly explained. That the "large" mining market needed a rich agricultural hinterland was an unreal but persistent belief, but it appears likely that this line was offered chiefly to stop the persistent outcry by Wallaroo interests and to give them some feeling of equality with the rising ports to the north. The agricultural regions showed little interest in such a road.

These four lines were all authorized by Parliament and were the only ones approved for the North. Construction was begun on the first three in 1875 and completed in the following year. The Wallaroo–Port Wakefield line was not begun. Obviously the policy of shallow feeders to local Northern outports had, for the time being, won the day.

THE NEW PROGRAM, 1875

Even before any of these new lines were completed a new commission was formed and directed to make a thorough study of "the probable direction of traffic, and the requirements of the country for railway accommodation." There were several reasons why still another examination of the railway question was initiated. For one thing a new government had been formed and proposed to undertake a greatly enlarged program of public works. For another, the new land act of 1874 had removed Goyder's Line as the limit of agricultural advance, and the acceleration of expansion would obviously soon bring a new rash of demands for

[17] *S. A. Parl. Papers No. 107 and No. 136* (1873).

rail service. Finally, there was considerable dissatisfaction in the government and in the capital with the recent authorizations. The whole problem had been considered in piecemeal fashion and there was some feeling that decisions had been influenced too heavily by the pressures of very local demands.

Thus, unlike the studies of the past few years, this new commission sought to formulate basic policies related to engineering, equipment, and operations, together with a comprehensive design for a provincial rail system and a schedule of construction sequence.[18]

Among the most important conclusions was that related to the density of the network:

> In deciding the question of how far apart railways might be constructed to afford the necessary accommodation to the public, in the more settled Districts of the Province, the Commission considered that so long as the distance to the nearest railway did not exceed fifteen miles, the object in view would be fairly attained.[19]

Such a policy, if rigorously followed, would give an added portent to each route decision because each line constructed would stabilize the railway question for a broad belt of territory. Short branch lines would tend to be excluded, a fearful thing for the ardent promoters of the many small townships to contemplate, for if once by-passed by a line within fifteen miles there would be little hope of ever obtaining a connection.

With this general objective in mind the needs of every district were examined, alternative roads considered, and an extensive network of new lines recommended. With the realization that the entire program could not possibly be undertaken at once, and that the urgency of service varied from area to area, a classifi-

[18] *S. A. Parl. Paper No. 22* (1875). This study was made during the period December, 1874, to August, 1875.

[19] *Ibid.*, p. ix. It is of interest that Isaiah Bowman, in his discussion of railways as instruments of pioneer expansion, reports that a survey by the Kansas City Southern railroad in the pre-motor era found that fifteen miles was the "effective economic distance" of its service, while most of its basic freight was drawn from a belt only ten miles wide. See Isaiah Bowman, *The Pioneer Fringe,* American Geographical Society Special Publication No. 13 (New York, 1931), p. 70. See also Dunsdorfs, *op. cit.*, p. 214, note 3, for the testimony of a Victorian farmer that fifteen miles was a maximum daily haul.

cation of construction priority was suggested. The program was as follows (Map 17):[20]

First Priority

1. Extension of the Port Pirie–Gladstone line east to Jamestown.
2. A branch from Gladstone north to Wirrabara, to tap the Rocky River district.
3. A link from Hamley Bridge to Balaklava to connect Adelaide with the Port Wakefield–Blyth line.
4. Extension of the latter from Blyth to connect with the Port Pirie line near Gladstone. (Together these lines would provide a direct connection between Adelaide and the Broughton region.)
5. Extension of the Burra line north to Gottlieb's Wells (near Terowie).
6. A long line deep into the northern interior from Port Augusta, via Pichi Richi Pass and the Willochra Plains, to the Yudanamutana copper district.
7. A route from Port Hughes–Moonta across upper Yorke Peninsula to Ardrossan.

Second Priority

8. A connection between the Adelaide-Gladstone system and the Far Northern line by extension of the Wirrabara branch to Willochra.
9. Further extension of the Burra–North East line from Gottlieb's Wells toward Waukaringa.

Third Priority

10. An additional segment of the North East line from near Waukaringa to Mannahill Well.
11. Extension of the Port Pirie–Jamestown line to Yatina.
12. A wholly new line from Kadina on Yorke Peninsula across the Barunga Range to Blyth Plains.
13. A short link between Moonta and Kadina.

Fourth Priority

Two final segments of the now great North East line:

14. Mannahill Well east to the New South Wales boundary.
15. Mannahill Well north-northeast toward Cooper's Creek and the Queensland border.

And, finally, a short feeder from the Willochra Plains east via Coonatto to Oladdie Plain (16).

[20] Both the map and the discussion are restricted to lines north of Adelaide-Kapunda. The map, like that in the report, does not show the Port Broughton tramway.

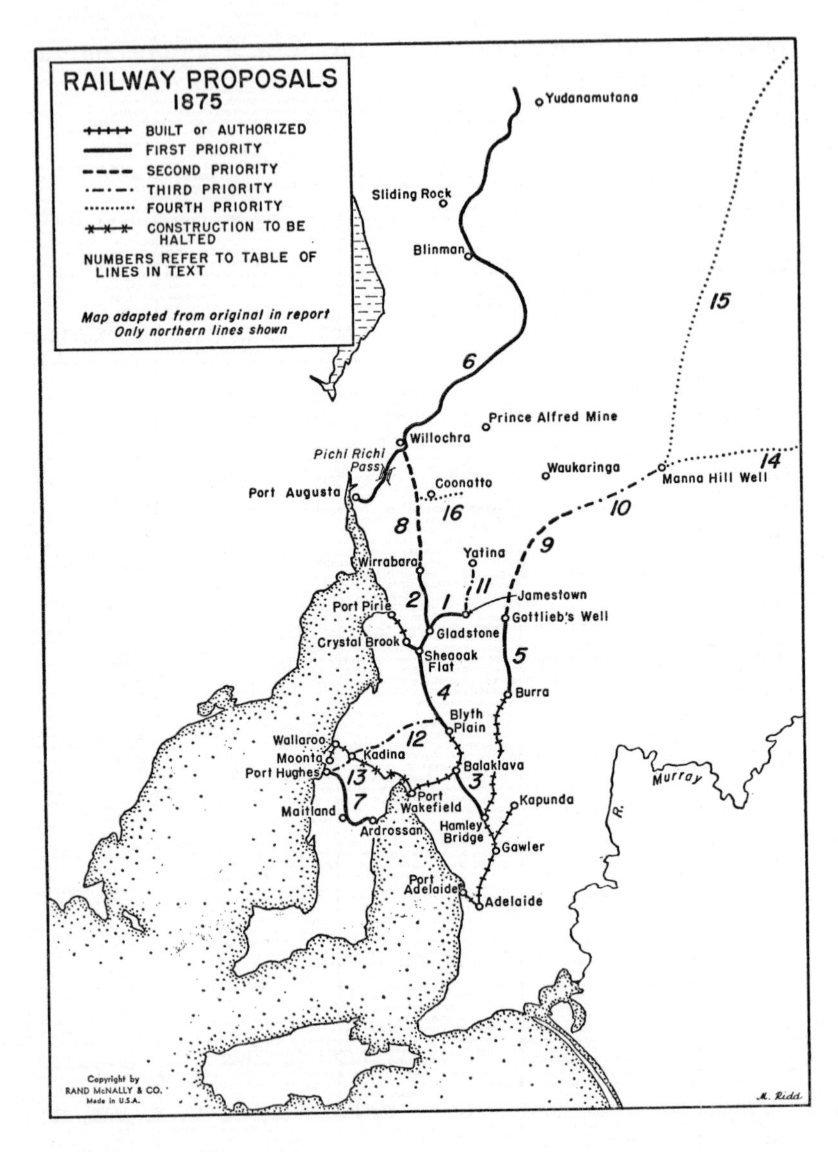
RAILWAY PROPOSALS
1875
BUILT or AUTHORIZED
FIRST PRIORITY
SECOND PRIORITY
THIRD PRIORITY
FOURTH PRIORITY
CONSTRUCTION TO BE HALTED
NUMBERS REFER TO TABLE OF LINES IN TEXT
Map adapted from original in report
Only northern lines shown
Yudanamutana
Sliding Rock
Blinman
15
6
Prince Alfred Mine
Willochra
Pichi Richi Pass
Waukaringa
14
Manna Hill Well
Port Augusta
Coonatto
16
10
8
9
Yatina
Wirrabara
11
Jamestown
Port Pirie
2
1
Gottlieb's Well
Gladstone
Crystal Brook
Sheaoak Flat
5
4
Burra
Blyth Plain
Wallaroo
12
Moonta
Kadina
Port Hughes
13
Balaklava
3
Murray
R.
Port Wakefield
Kapunda
Maitland
7
Ardrossan
Hamley Bridge
Gawler
Port Adelaide
Adelaide
Copyright by
RAND McNALLY & CO.
Made in U.S.A.
M. Ridd

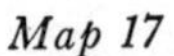

Map 17

In addition, the Commission specifically recommended no extension of the Port Broughton tramway, and, interestingly, that the Kadina–Port Wakefield line already approved be halted at Green's Plains and no connection be made on to Wakefield.

This proposed network abounds with interesting and important features. It is almost possible to infer from the map alone what was in fact the case: that the Chairman of this Railroad Commission was G. W. Goyder, for the whole design carries the imprint of his ideas first outlined in 1866–67. Two major features stand out. First is the reimposition of a metropolitan focus. Upon completion of construction through the first two stages, Adelaide would have direct linkage with every northern line except the distinctly minor Port Broughton feeder and those on Yorke Peninsula, and it was anticipated that a regular Port Adelaide–Ardrossan boat service across St. Vincent Gulf would provide a good connection from the latter area to the metropolis. The key lines in this strategy were those of Hamley Bridge to Balaklava and Blyth to Crystal Brook, neither of which would be necessary (if the Kadina-Blyth extension were given equal priority) if the sole objective was to place wheat farmers within fifteen miles of a railway and give them access to the nearest port. Still more revealing of Goyder's purpose was the diversion of the Port Pirie line beyond Jamestown abruptly northward to Yatina, leaving all lands to the east to be served by Port Adelaide via the Burra. When a witness argued in favor of tying the Hallett-Terowie (Gottlieb's Wells) district directly westward to Spencer Gulf, Goyder questioned him sharply whether he thought the mere saving in cost of delivery of wheat to the seaboard was sufficient "to justify the Government in making Port Pirie the principal port, instead of taking it to Kooringa [Burra] and on to Adelaide?"[21] The witness insisted that it would certainly save the farmers a great deal of money, but obviously Goyder was not guided so strongly by such a consideration. Thus while his western north-south line linked up nearly all the short branches with Adelaide, he sharply curtailed the eastward penetration of outport feeders. Each of the minor ports of Wakefield, Wallaroo, Pirie, and Augusta would

[21] See *ibid.*, pp. 127–33, for the testimony relating to this problem of routes.

have a relatively limited agricultural hinterland, and in fact that of the first would be much reduced from what it now enjoyed.

The other outstanding feature persistent in Goyder's designs was the emphasis upon long extensions deep into the interior, not only to serve the pastoral and mining regions, but also as instruments of grand strategy to capture a major share of the interior trade of neighboring colonies.[22] Both the priorities accorded to such lines and their links with the metropolis showed that Goyder's perspective on the railway problem was similar to his views on the colonization question: an outlook shaped by his judgment of the long-term interests of the colony as a whole rather than by the immediate local demands of agriculturists.

CONTROVERSIES AND CONSTRUCTIONS, 1875–80

This report of 1875, though elaborate and specific, was of course merely a report and not a law, but it did serve as a general guide for railway policies for many years. Certainly its recommendations were not rigidly adhered to insofar as specific routes were concerned, but it persisted as a basic framework for the consideration of new alternatives. The metropolitan-outport issue was far from settled but it was now placed in a more general perspective. Actually no rigid program could be initiated, for the tide of settlers was only beginning to surge into the lands beyond the Broughton and no one knew how far they might go or what the ultimate pattern of settlement might be. Thus the next few years would inevitably raise many new demands, and, as surely, new controversies.

In fact the most immediate complaint came from an old district. It was rather ironic that the very region whose demands for rail service had prompted some of the first surveys in the North, the Clare-Auburn area, should have been so completely by-passed. The 1875 Commission specifically ruled out the line these communities so anxiously sought on the basis of their proximity to stations on lines already built: to Hoyleton on the Port Wakefield tramway, and to Farrell's Flat on the Adelaide-Burra line. This ruling was the first fruit of the density policy and

[22] The proposals to tap the River Murray at Northwest Bend (Morgan), though outside the area under discussion, were of course important designs relating both to the policy of centralization and that of intercolonial competition.

it left a bitter taste with those affected. "Such a statement," wrote the Clare editor, referring to the idea of placing every locale within fifteen miles of a railway, "may sound well, but when practically tested may prove utterly worthless," for when the roads over the hills were nearly impassable during the wet season any distance was too far.[23] And so, wearily, new "monster meetings" were called, new petitions signed, and the agitation for a line renewed – but with a now somewhat blighted hope.[24]

The settlement nucleus at the base of Yorke Peninsula, Wallaroo-Kadina-Moonta, was more fortunate, although disputes over routes caused a brief setback and delay. Contrary to the Commission's recommendation, the Kadina–Port Wakefield link was not canceled, although its construction proceeded at a desultory pace. Retention of this line made the Hamley Bridge–Balaklava connection, so vital to the over-all network envisioned, of even greater significance, for it now would provide a direct tie between Adelaide and Yorke Peninsula as well as with the northern feeders.[25] As usual there was argument over specific routes. Although the government defended its original proposal as being most central to the colony as a whole, looking forward to an eventual link northward with the Port Pirie line, this long-range objective was almost completely overshadowed by the immediate concern for service between Adelaide and the Peninsula. Focus upon this objective brought an obvious challenge that a route from Salisbury to Port Wakefield (Map 5) would be far superior, and as both the residents on the Peninsula and Parliament itself were badly divided on the question the first bill of 1876 was defeated.[26] Reintroduced in the following year, the old issues were revived and compounded by suggestions of routes also from Gawler or Wasleys, via Mallala to Wakefield, chiefly to meet the objections that a Salisbury line would be too near the coast, However, this time the original proposal was approved, although probably more because of its relative shortness (twenty-two miles)

[23] *The Northern Argus* (Clare), Oct. 5, 1875.
[24] For example, *ibid.*, Aug. 17, 1875.
[25] Evidently retention of the Kadina–Port Wakefield line canceled the Commission's support of the Moonta-Ardrossan route which had been given a top priority.
[26] *S. A. Parl. Debates,* Aug. 29, Sept. 5, Sept. 12, 1876.

and cheapness than of its general functional merits, and also because Peninsula opinion was more or less resigned to accept this more devious route than none at all.[27] During all these considerations it was assumed that the government would purchase the private mining tramways connecting the three Peninsula centers and in March, 1878, this was done for a sum of £90,000.[28] As the original lines were broad-gauge horse-powered facilities, new parallel narrow-gauge tracks suitable for locomotives were constructed. The Kadina-Wakefield connection was completed in October, 1878, and the Hamley Bridge link in January, 1880, giving at last the long desired through service (with one break of gauge) between the "two most populous centers" of the province.

Farther north the issues were much more complex. The most bitter controversy of the next few years raged over the several schemes to tap the rich Redhill-Koolunga-Yacka district (Map 16B). A memorial from 182 petitioners in that area pleaded for a connection with Port Broughton, "the natural port of these districts."[29] Immediately 412 signatures were gathered in Port Pirie "and surrounding districts" citing all the advantages of that city, which was obviously "the natural port of the district."[30] Soon the Port Pirie newspaper ran an alarming editorial warning of Wallaroo's plot to get the Barunga Gap line extended to Yacka. This was a far more serious threat and public meetings were called to intensify the agitation for a Crystal Brook to Koolunga branch.[31] A further complication arose when Gladstone renewed its demands for a direct route via Yacka to Blyth, with explicit anticipation of the Hamley Bridge–Balaklava link to Adelaide.[32] For Port Pirie such a route would be a more devious branch, would still leave Redhill and Koolunga unsecured, and would allow metropolitan merchants direct access into her own hinterland.

Surveys were made of each of these proposed routes. In 1878 bills were submitted for a Gladstone to Georgetown branch and

[27] *Ibid.*, Sept. 17, Oct. 23, Oct. 30, 1877.
[28] *S. A. Parl. Paper No. 34* (1878), p. 5.
[29] *S. A. Parl. Paper No. 165* (1877).
[30] *S. A. Parl. Paper No. 175* (1877).
[31] *The Port Pirie Gazette and Areas News,* July 27, 1877, and nearly every issue two months thereafter.
[32] *Ibid.*, Sept. 21, 1877, *S. A. Parl. Paper No. 141* (1877).

for an extension from Blyth to Magpie Creek a few miles north. Both were defeated.[33] In the following year to meet the argument that the previous bills had offered "the two ends without the body," a complete Blyth to Gladstone railroad was submitted. But despite impressive figures of the potential traffic from the rich area to be served ("perhaps the finest wheat-growing country in the whole of South Australia") and its important role as a link in an eventual trunk line from Adelaide to Quorn, the proposal foundered on a host of objections. The Barunga Gap line was nearing completion to Snowtown and the advantages of Wallaroo were once more detailed;[34] objections were made to the specific route location as being too near the hills to the east; and, as always with proposals for construction in districts already settled, it was argued that it was not a "development" line but one of "accommodation" and money would be better spent in opening up new country where railways would foster settlement and increase the value of unsold lands and enhance the Crown assets.[35] The Port Pirie paper hailed the defeat of this bill as a great triumph and then turned its full resources of logic and scorn against Wallaroo's scheme for extension east from Snowtown.[36] But the end result of this competitive fury was a complete stalemate: no line was built into the district at the time, and the local farmers and trades-

[33] *S. A. Parl. Debates,* Nov. 14, 1878, and Nov. 19, 1878. The proponents of the Georgetown branch were accused, evidently with some justification, of trying to placate that town after having voted previously in favor of the Port Pirie–Gladstone route. That the government could not build railroads just "to make things pleasant" for some township but a few miles away from existing lines was a telling argument against the proposal, and one more implicit expression of the "density policy."

[34] The Kadina-Snowton branch had, as one Member pointed out, a "comic" and "tragic" history, well illustrating the dangers possible when politicians plan railways. The original bill proposed a line of twenty-six miles and the debate raged over the various merits of Wallaroo, Broughton, and Wakefield; this was finally approved in September, 1876. In the following year the government, somewhat sheepishly, offered a bill for an extension of six miles to Snowtown as they now realized that the original terminus was at Barunga Gap at the crest of the range and was of very little use to the agricultural region it was designed to serve. Members who had opposed the first bill made the most of the mistake in debate, but even they admitted that the only way now to make the investment pay off was to approve the extension See *S. A. Parl. Debates,* Sept. 5, Sept. 12, Sept. 27, 1876, and Nov. 6, 1877.

[35] *Ibid.,* June 17, cols. 215–18, and June 26, cols. 256–59, 1870.

[36] *The Port Pirie Gazette and Areas News,* July 18, 1879; cf. *The Areas Ex press and Farmers' Journal* (Gladstone), Oct. 15, 1879.

men must have shared a common disgust with all their self-appointed friends in surrounding ports and townships whose belligerent competitive eagerness to serve them had canceled, for the moment, any hope of service.

The proposal to extend the Port Pirie line from Gladstone via Caltowie to Jamestown, in keeping with the recommendations of 1875, received an unusual, though understandable, unanimity of support. The first section to Gladstone had proved marvelously successful, draining as it did the most productive of all the new farming districts, and Port Pirie's now-assured position as a feasible wheat port removed doubts about the advisability of extending the line at least a short distance farther inland.[37] Similarly, construction of the broad-gauge Adelaide-Burra line on north to Hallett was essentially non-controversial and was approved at the same session.[38] But with the completion of these two projects in May, 1878, and service to the region beyond contemplated, the old issue of Adelaide versus Port Pirie was revived. In June, 1878, a meeting was called at Port Pirie to spread the alarm that the government was planning to push the Burra line on to Yongala, giving Adelaide access to the great North East, "the natural outlet for which was Port Pirie." This "centralization" policy was denounced as economically absurb for the distance was so great that "not a bushel of wheat would go to Port Adelaide" and such a railroad "would not pay for the grease of the wheels."[39] Actually, the government's plan was not so iniquitous and did have a built-in protection for Port Pirie's interests. Both construction eastward from Jamestown and northward from Hallett was proposed. The critical issue was where to break the gauge between the metropolitan broad-gauge system and the northern narrow-gauge lines. Terowie (near Gottlieb's Wells) was selected for this key point on the basis of several considerations:

1. Traffic from the North East would be principally wool which would be shipped on the broad-gauge directly to the established wool market at Adelaide rather than to Port Pirie where it would have to be transhipped by

[37] *S. A. Parl. Debates,* July 4 and July 20, 1876.
[38] *Ibid.,* July 20 and Aug. 8, 1876.
[39] *The Port Pirie Gazette and Areas News,* June 21, 1878.

coastal vessels. (Also wool was now beginning to be exported in large steamships via Suez which could only load directly at a deep-water port.)

2. Wheat from the agricultural frontier in *Terowie, Gumbowie, Yongala* and vicinity would have direct access via the narrow-gauge to Port Pirie, the nearest coastal point.
3. The specific site at Terowie had an excellent supply of fresh water necessary for a major engine terminal.[40]

But another line was also proposed which would connect these points with the long discussed and now approved Port Augusta–Government Gums line into the Far North. The route selected was via Orroroo, Eurelia, Coonatto, and Quorn, skirting the whole northern agricultural fringe, and this raised the next controversy: where would the Port Pirie line intersect this northern narrow-gauge arc between Terowie and Quorn? The government had decided to make this junction in *Yongala* Hundred some six miles northeast of Yongala township. That township naturally vigorously objected and found some supporters in Parliament who considered that it ought to be "the entrepôt of the district." Much the loudest cry was raised by Jamestown, which looked upon itself as the logical "head-centre" of railroad facilities in the area and insisted that a Hallett-Jamestown line was the only fair choice. Unfortunately for these aspirations an engineering survey proved that this would be a very difficult and expensive route. Furthermore. Jamestown's campaign was so vehement that it alienated many who might have been sympathetic and stiffened their resolve not to be influenced by "every little township" which "felt aggrieved because the line was not dragged down to suit the residents there." The junction point was thus stabilized in Section 216 of *Yongala* Hundred where the town of Petersburg[41] was later established.

The proposed line from that point to Quorn in the Willochra was subjected to two criticisms: that it did not cut through the best agricultural land and that it was a remarkably indirect trunk line from Adelaide to Port Augusta. Opponents advanced arguments in favor of a Blyth-Gladstone-Coonatto route as much more

[40] *S. A. Parl. Debates,* July 11 and July 18, 1878.
[41] Now "Peterborough."

direct, but the government refused to acknowledge that question as relevant and defended the scheme entirely on its service to the farming frontier. In that way it made a sharp departure from the proposals of 1875, and it did so because of the whole new prospect for agricultural expansion which had unfolded since that year. If this route would be an accommodation to the existing frontier margin it was even more importantly a line to open up the North East. That country "would be developed in a manner that would be perfectly startling" argued the Commissioner of Public Works. All the signs of the times were in support: Granville, Herbert, Lytton, and Derby counties had been declared, the surveyors were hastily marking off the hundreds, and selectors were ranging far out into the saltbush searching for farms. Finally, it was repeatedly emphasized that this railway completed "a great trunk system which brought into harmony the three great ports of the colony": Adelaide, Pirie, and Augusta. Port Pirie's apprehensions were quieted by anticipation of an extension eastward via Manna Hill (where the experimental farm was just getting underway) to the Barrier Range: "every inch of such a line would develop wheat-growing country" and her hinterland would be enormously enlarged. Riding with the high tide of expansionist optimism the bill was approved in October, 1878.[42]

With this series of approvals the railway question was temporarily stabilized. Throughout these debates warnings had been sounded against the "railway mania" that seemed to have gripped the country, and in fact this recent frenzy of agitation had committed the colony to a prodigious construction program in the North. In the opening years of settlement, 1869–70, ninety-seven miles of line (the Burra and Wakefield routes) had been completed. Then followed a lull, ended by the building of fifty-five miles in 1875–76. But the combined total in 1878 of those actually under construction or approved was 477 miles! Of these, that portion of the Far Northern line from Hawker to Farina, 133 miles, was to reach far out into the pastoral country, but the remaining 344 miles were all within the new wheatlands opened during the last decade.

[42] *Ibid.*, July 11, July 18, Sept. 12, and Oct. 3, 1878; see cols. 357, 358, 942, 946 for specific quotations.

CONTROVERSIES AND CONSTRUCTIONS, 1881–84

The onset of the drought in 1880 inevitably altered the context of railway considerations, but it by no means brought an end to an interest in further construction. It did suggest that the need for "developmental" agricultural lines – those designed to open new districts to settlement – was ended for the time being at least. Even before completed, the northern arc from Burra through Terowie, Orroroo, Carrieton to Quorn could be understood as skirting the outer margins of agricultural colonization; there would be no need for further extensions in that sector. Yet interest remained high in two other kinds of areas. On the one hand, there remained districts well within the main block of farming country which were inadequately served; on the other, there was a continued interest in extending lines far into the pastoral and mining outback. Indeed, the drought actually intensified the question of the latter because of the urgency of having some means of exporting sheep off of the stricken pastures; without it, tens of thousands simply died of thirst and starvation.

Within the older area of settlement the Redhill-Koolunga-Yacka remained a vacuum which seemingly had to be filled, and in October a new Blyth-Yacka-Gladstone bill was introduced (Map 16B). This time it carried the endorsement of a Select Committee which had studied all the rival schemes, but it again became entangled in the same web of conflicting designs.[43] Residents in the Clare district, utterly frustrated at being once more left out of the government's program, were especially strong in opposition.[44] And the question was further compounded by a fresh conflict which had arisen over the area north of Gladstone which would be greatly influenced by the pattern of construction south. Once more such complexities forestalled any action and the bill was defeated.[45]

Construction of the Terowie-Quorn line created a situation north of Gladstone somewhat similar to that south. Lying east of the Flinders Range and at fifteen to twenty-five miles inside the remaining perimeter of narrow-gauge railways was the rich

[43] *S. A. Parl. Paper No. 109* (1881). The other routes examined were: Blyth–Crystal Brook, Riverton-Clare-Yacka-Gladstone, and Snowtown-Yacka.
[44] *S. A. Parl. Papers Nos. 141, 168* (1881).
[45] *S. A. Parl. Debates,* July 14, Oct. 18, and Oct. 20, 1881.

Booleroo district with growing townships such as Melrose, Wirrabara, Appila-Yarrowie, and Tarcowie about its margins. Need for a railroad in this area was accentuated by considerable tracts of hilly country and numerous deep creekbeds which lay athwart many of the market roads. Furthermore, after difficult cartage to the nearest railway station, such as Gladstone or Caltowie on the south or Hammond on the north, the wheat was still a considerable distance from a port. The 1875 Commission had anticipated this need and had given first priority to a branch north from Gladstone to Wirrabara (Map 17) which would be extended in the next construction phase, to some point along a Willochra–Port Augusta route. By the end of the decade the settlement pattern within and around the district had become sufficiently developed to foster two specific railroad proposals: a north-south line from Gladstone to Coonatto (Hammond area) and an east-west route from Port Germein to Orroroo (Map 16C). Each scheme had strong support, and as they were completely contradictory the issue became one of the most intensely contested of this entire railroad construction period. The problem was faced in 1881.

Despite very active agitation already well underway in favor of the Port Germein line,[46] the government announced its intention to support the Gladstone-Coonatto route.[47] The positive features cited in favor of that line were that it would place every farmer within ten miles of a railway; it would be an important feeder to existing lines both north and south, with Port Pirie and Port Augusta sharing the traffic; it had easy gradients and would be relatively inexpensive to construct; and, finally, it would eventually be a link in a direct trunk line from Adelaide to the Far North. In addition, there were many disadvantages peculiar to the east-west route: the first twenty miles through the Flinders Range would be both unproductive of traffic and costly to build and operate. Orroroo already had rail access to three ports, and Port Germein would require very extensive and expensive improvements before it could become a really good port.[48] On the other hand, proponents of the Port Germein line emphasized that

[46] *S. A. Parl. Papers Nos. 62, 67, 89* (1881).
[47] *S. A. Parl. Debates,* Aug. 3, 1881.
[48] *Ibid.,* esp. col. 476.

it would provide a much shorter haul for all the localities to be served and that this would be especially important for the area east of Orroroo which was already being rapidly settled and would soon need a railroad extended. Furthermore the entire feasibility of a line through the Flinders was stressed, as were the immense potential advantages of Port Germein over Port Pirie as a shipping place. To forestall a quick and perhaps unfavorable decision the Port Germein advocates were able to get a select committee formed to inquire into the two proposals.

This Committee intensively examined a very large number of witnesses. Insofar as the main agricultural district was concerned, opinion was principally in favor of the direct line to Port Germein. But the situations at the terminals of that route were a very different matter. The advantage of Port Germein over Port Pirie, even with a major extension of its jetty and improvement in shipping facilities, was simply not clear-cut and the testimonies of pilots, ship captains, engineers, and wheat merchants were strongly divided. At the other end of the line, advocates had made a serious mistake in emphasizing the importance of serving the lands beyond Orroroo, for the great drought was now on and, although not a single farmer who testified admitted that he had any intension of abandoning his selection, few could cite any successful harvests. Goyder agreed that this route would well serve the intermediate Booleroo country but he was certain that agriculture at Orroroo and beyond could never succeed. Thus, while finally recommending this east-west route, the Committee was forced to append that it ought not be commenced "until further experience has proved the permanence of that settlement."[49]

The fate of this east-west railway and of Port Germein as an aspiring wheat port was therefore to be sealed by the persistent drought of the 1880's. But the railway question for the region was still not resolved, for the Committee recommended the immediate construction of a line from Gladstone to Laura and Appila. This was obviously an attempt to placate those southerly districts most favorable to a connection with Port Pirie and at the same time to divert and truncate the proposed north-south route in order to protect the core of the area concerned for a future railway from

[49] *S. A. Parl. Paper No. 127* (1881).

Germein to Orroroo. In 1882 a bill to authorize this branch was offered. Although most agreed that it would carry a considerable traffic there was one very serious flaw in the proposal: it ran almost parallel with the Jamestown line and the terminal was but ten miles from Caltowie (Map 16C). It was therefore flatly contradictory to the established policy of keeping parallel railroads approximately thirty miles apart, although it would be of some advantage to the more isolated Booleroo sector.[50] Curiously, the legislature proceeded to lop off the upper twelve miles of the route and proposed to build only to Laura. Against the obvious criticism that the remaining stub of seven miles was even less defensible on the same grounds, it was argued that it could be extended more directly north in the near future. Probably more important was the fact that Laura was a thriving township and its residents had had the unusual initiative to make a serious effort to construct their own branch to connect with the line at Gladstone. The government had forestalled that effort with a promise to build the line.[51] Although authorized at this time and begun the following July the contractor was so dilatory that these seven miles were not opened until June of 1884.

The remaining proposals of this time concerned constructions far into the interior. One of these, an extension of the Port Augusta–Farina line about a hundred miles on north to Hergott Springs (now Marree) was not really relevant to the agricultural region for the present terminus was already well beyond the limit of farming.[52] The concurrent proposal for a line from Terowie via Manna Hill toward the Barrier Ranges on the New South Wales border, however, directly related to the agricultural network. Originally conceived as a development line which would serve an eastward-expanding agricultural as well as the pastoral country, the great drought altered the context but did not end the agitation. It was debated and modified over the next three years

[50] See *Parl. Papers Nos. 122, 124* (1882) for petitions against and for this line. Much of the opposition came not from Booleroo but from Caltowie which would be robbed of much of its trade area.
[51] *S. A. Parl. Debates,* Aug. 17, Aug. 29, Sept. 19, Sept. 26, and Oct. 10, 1882.
[52] This was part of a policy of advancing "bit by bit" in order to increase settlement, traffic, and the value of the land. Extensions could be made either toward Port Darwin or northeast toward Queensland, and it was anticipated that both would probably be done "at no distant day." *Ibid.,* Aug. 3, 1881.

and sporadically unleashed flurries of controversy among rival ports and aspiring junction towns. Initially the Terowie editor was not enthusiastic and argued that it was premature, as agriculture was not expanding in that direction very successfully as yet. It may be suspected, however, that he feared that the loss of the heavy freighting traffic already focused upon this terminus of the broad-gauge would not be offset by the advantages of a mere railroad junction.[53] However, when a year later it appeared that the government had shifted its proposal from Terowie to Petersburg, he quickly changed his tune, hailed the railroad as highly desirable to "open up and develop a vast track of country, eminently suitable for grazing and in many places for agriculture," and mounted an attack against his rival: "to found Petersburgh was a mistake" and to make a railroad from there would be even worse; Terowie was the only logical terminal – "nature has decreed."[54] At the same time Port Augusta interests read the government's original Terowie plan as part of "the ruinous process of centralization" and called for a branch from the Great Northern line to bring the North East into cheap and rapid communication with its "natural outlet."[55] Representatives of other centers, Burra, Port Pirie, Port Germein, and Orroroo, quickly joined the fray. In 1883 the government ran surveys on several routes, each related to a particular junction and port: from Terowie (broad-gauge to Port Adelaide), from Petersburg (Port Pirie), from Orroroo (Port Germein), from Carrieton and from Hawker (both Port Augusta) (Map 16D).[56]

In the winter of 1884 this North Eastern railway scheme was given fresh impetus with news of a big silver discovery in the Barrier Range. A mining camp immediately formed and the railway question took on new meaning:

> The prospects of Silverton as a mining centre are . . . immense, and the magnitude of the trade which must arise if these prospects are realized may be judged from the part which Nevada silver mines have played in the development and settlement of the western half of the United States, and in the construction of the American transcontinental railway.[57]

[53] *The North-Eastern Times and Terowie News,* July 22, 1881.
[54] *Ibid.,* June 16 and Oct. 6, 1882.
[55] *Port Augusta Dispatch,* June 27, 1882.
[56] *Ibid.,* June 9, 1883, *S. A. Parl. Papers No. 63* (1883–84), and *No. 142* (1884).
[57] *Port Augusta Dispatch,* June 23, 1884.

As the new mines were located some fifty miles south of the previously planned terminus new surveys were ordered. However, this had no major effect upon the competitive position of the several routes and the same patterns of rivalry remained, though intensified by the suddenly magnified prize in contention. Port Augusta's reactions were typical. When a new survey from Terowie was ordered, the editor pointed up the advantages of Carrieton and insisted that there was "no valid reason why trade should be taken nearly 80 miles out of the way to aggrandize Port Adelaide." A week later a Petersburg survey was attacked with the claim that "it was pretty generally acknowledged that Port Pirie is a gigantic mistake" for it could never be made into a decent harbor.[58] In Parliament, despite vigorous argument in favor of the others, the debate was largely narrowed to a consideration of Terowie and Petersburg.[59] The Terowie route ultimately foundered on the question of gauge. Few members were willing to consider building a more costly broad-gauge line all the way to the New South Wales border, therefore traffic to Adelaide must encounter an interruption no matter which junction was chosen. Petersburg won the day because there a single junction offered access to three ports (Augusta, Pirie, and Adelaide), the wool traffic would have but a very short deviation to Adelaide, and if the mines did develop there would be a heavy inbound movement of flour, grain, chaff, and other farm products which could best be drawn from the country bordering the Port Pirie line. On the fourteenth of November the Barrier Range extension was authorized.

This was the last of the great railway controversies of the era. The drought, depressed economy, and abrupt halt of frontier expansion brought a complete cessation of railroad extension in the agricultural North. It would be many years before another mile of track would be laid down in the area.

THE RAILWAY SYSTEM

A simple map showing only the routes of the network in 1884 would be deceptive for there was really not one but two systems serving the agricultural North: the 153 miles of 5′3″ gauge from

[58] *Ibid.*, July 4, 1884.
[59] *S. A. Parl. Debates*, July 29, Oct. 30, Nov. 4, and Nov. 5, 1884.

Terowie to Adelaide, and the 396 miles of 3′6″ gauge south of Hawker and west of Petersburg (Map 18). That difference in gauge began with the first of the purely agricultural lines, the Port Wakefield tramway, constructed in the opening year of Northern expansion. It became a practical operational problem ten years later when the completion of the Hamley Bridge–Balaklava line introduced "for the first time in the history of the colony that most objectionable feature in railway construction, a break of gauge."[60] In the following year the Terowie-Petersburg line made the second junction between the two systems. From that moment on South Australia was saddled with a problem which was to harass every government, sap the annual revenues, and plague the shipper with a persistence and magnitude rivaled by no other feature of economic development.[61]

The problem did not arise suddenly and unforeseen. Before a mile of narrow-gauge had been built the question had been debated many times. The Railway Committee of 1866–67 explored the idea of converting the existing broad-gauge to 4′ 8½″ and building all subsequent lines on that scale, and the merits of other widths were also examined.[62] But cost was the deterrent to conversion and it was the obvious argument in favor of narrow-gauge. Yet it would be a mistake to explain the development of two gauges as the legacy of a blindly parsimonious administration. Many persons very early foresaw an eventual linking of all lines into a state-wide network and yet advocated the furtherance of both gauges. The really decisive factor was the prevailing geographical view of logical traffic patterns. The narrow-gauge system in the North was justified primarily on the assumption of a single, simple axiom: *wheat would always move to the nearest port.*[63]

The choice of Hamley Bridge and Terowie as the points of

[60] *S. A. Parl. Paper No. 29* (1880), p. 5.
[61] It was of course a problem shared by other colonies and compounded as the continent-wide network was evolved. Queensland and Western Australia lines are predominantly 3′ 6″, those of New South Wales 4′ 8½″, and those of Victoria 5′ 3″. Lines constructed by the federal government are 4′ 8½″ and a general change to that gauge is envisioned although deterred by the staggering costs.
[62] *S. A. Parl. Paper No. 161* (1866–67). The three common gauges were already in existence in Australia and it is interesting to note that Goyder advocated for South Australia still another, a gauge of 4′ 3″ as advantageously combining all the merits of "narrow" and "standard."
[63] *S. A. Parl. Paper No. 141* (1873).

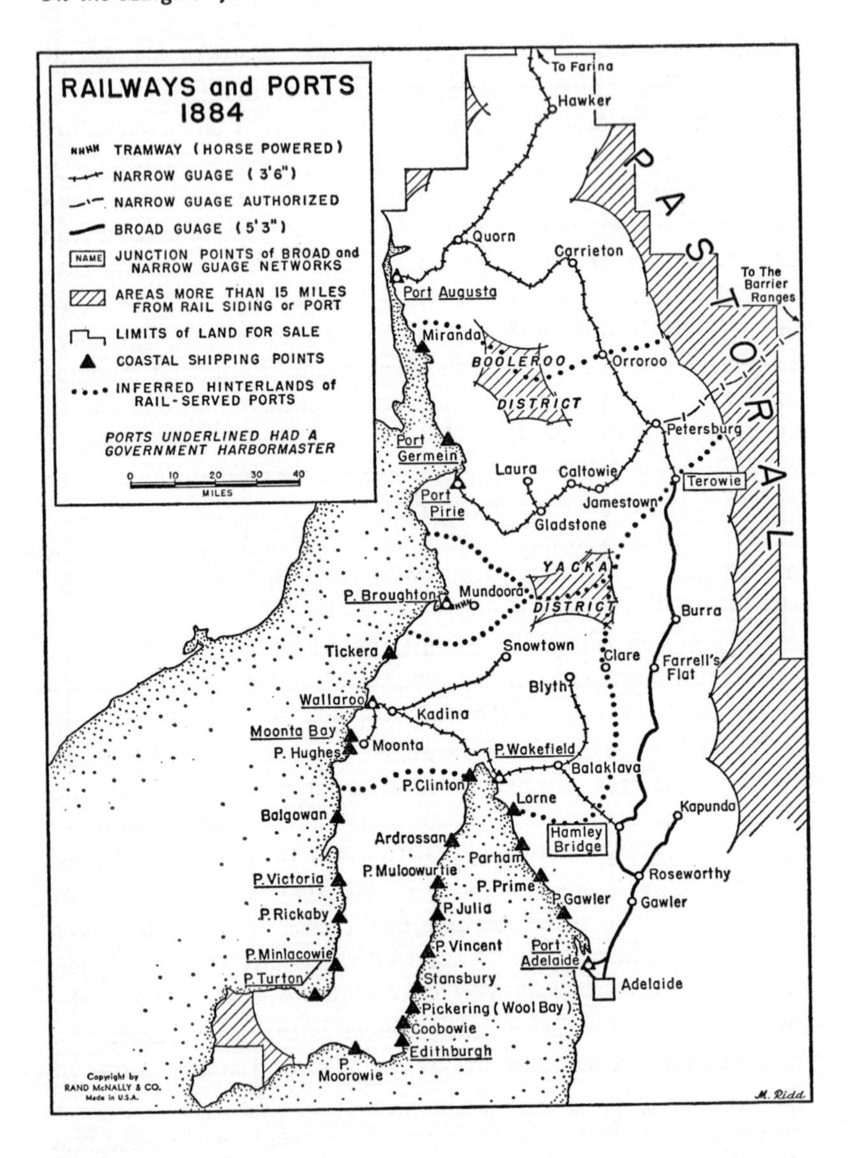
RAILWAYS and PORTS
1884
TRAMWAY (HORSE POWERED)
NARROW GUAGE (3'6")
NARROW GUAGE AUTHORIZED
BROAD GUAGE (5'3")
JUNCTION POINTS of BROAD and NARROW GUAGE NETWORKS
AREAS MORE THAN 15 MILES FROM RAIL SIDING or PORT
LIMITS of LAND FOR SALE
COASTAL SHIPPING POINTS
INFERRED HINTERLANDS of RAIL-SERVED PORTS
PORTS UNDERLINED HAD A GOVERNMENT HARBORMASTER
0 10 20 30 40
MILES
To Farina
Hawker
PASTORAL
Quorn
Carrieton
To The Barrier Ranges
Port Augusta
Miranda
BOOLEROO
DISTRICT
Orroroo
Petersburg
Port Germein
Laura
Caltowie
Terowie
Port Pirie
Jamestown
Gladstone
YACKA
DISTRICT
P. Broughton
Mundoora
Burra
Tickera
Snowtown
Clare
Farrell's Flat
Blyth
Wallaroo
Kadina
Moonta Bay
Moonta
P. Hughes
P. Wakefield
Balaklava
P. Clinton
Lorne
Kapunda
Balgowan
Ardrossan
Hamley Bridge
Parham
P. Muloowurtie
P. Victoria
P. Prime
Roseworthy
P. Gawler
Gawler
P. Rickaby
P. Julia
P. Vincent
Port Adelaide
P. Minlacowie
P. Turton
Stansbury
Adelaide
Pickering (Wool Bay)
Coobowie
Edithburgh
P. Moorowie
M. Ridd

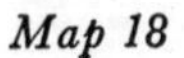

Map 18

contact between the two systems was the product of this view. Each was considered to be in a logical separation zone of hinterlands between Port Adelaide and Port Wakefield and Port Pirie, respectively. The very existence of the two systems, therefore, represents the rejection of a policy of metropolitan centralization and that crucial decision was dictated by the one great commodity of the agricultural North. The one line which did not fit the logic of this framework was the extension to the Barrier Range, and it was precisely upon this branch that by far the greatest discussion of gauges was focused. Here the colony faced a dilemma and cost did force the choice. The outbound traffic of wool, livestock, and ores should logically move to Adelaide, yet the times were depressed and the added expense of a broad-gauge over that distance was simply too great. But there was an awareness that the decision was contradictory to the general railway scheme, and proposals were strongly advanced at that time to convert all lines north of Adelaide to narrow-gauge, or to lay a third rail from Terowie to the capital to accommodate the equipment of both systems.[64]

The nagging question of cost influenced the railway system in many other ways. The construction of horse-powered tramways was a prominent example. Such facilities would seem more appropriate to an earlier, experimental phase of railways than to the 1870's when the utility of steam locomotives had been thoroughly proved and ever-heavier and more elaborate facilities were being extended rapidly over every continent. But locally certain positive advantages could be cited and cheapness was foremost. Horses were plentiful, replacements could be made "at once for £30," and every associated facility, from track to engine shed and drivers, was comparably inexpensive. Not only would there be no costly import of fuel but "the horses would eat the produce of the district, and would be, so to say, customers of the farmers."[65] Moreover, wheat traffic would be seasonal, overhead costs could be kept low, and it was even considered that farmers might be allowed to hire tramway trucks and haul their produce to port with their own teams. There were of course many obvious disadvantages

[64] *S. A. Parl. Debates,* esp. Sept. 2, cols. 815–17, and Nov. 5, 1884.
[65] *S. A. Parl. Paper No. 141* (1867), pp. 15, 36, 52–53.

also, and as with nearly every aspect of the railroad question opinion was divided.[66] Perhaps the deciding point was that inexpensive horse lines could later be easily converted for locomotives, although the cost of such refitting was probably underestimated.

The Port Wakefield tramway provides a good illustration of the mode and scale of such operations. In 1875 seven horses were used to haul passenger coaches (Fig. 11), eighteen regularly for goods trucks, with five extra during the busy season. The line, twenty-eight miles long, was operated in three divisions with changes made at Saint's and Balaklava. A team could haul six empty trucks up and six loaded down. On line the goods were supposed to move at four and a half miles per hour, and the schedule from Port Wakefield to Hoyleton covered nine hours.[67] Such facts make the local impatience with these facilities more understandable, and their advantages over the bullock cart more obscure.

Economy in construction was a basic policy for the entire system laid down by the Railroad Commission of 1875: "every penny that is saved . . . enhances the profit to producers, . . . increases the value of more remote lines, and enables the Government to construct additional lengths of line. . . ."[68] And it was a policy generally supported. Certainly the country press was ready to sacrifice quality for quantity, for hundreds of miles of line were suddenly needed. Neither speed nor high daily capacity was essential. Trains run at ten to fifteen miles per hour would allow the use of light rails, little ballast, and obviate the need of fencing. After all, the prospect of daily service in all seasons to all points along the line was a remarkable enough improvement:

[66] *S. A. Parl. Debates,* Aug. 12, cols. 67–69, Aug. 17, cols. 94–102, and Sept. 3, 1869, cols. 219–24. One Member accused the horse advocates of deliberately seeking to make the Port Wakefield tramway an inferior line to protect Port Adelaide. See also W. Hanson, "The Comparative Merits of Different Gauges for Locomotive Railways," in *Adelaide Philosophical Society, Annual Report and Transactions for the Year ending 30th September, 1867* (Adelaide, 1867), for an argument that locomotives are actually cheaper than horses on the basis of ton-mile costs.

[67] *S. A. Parl. Paper No. 22* (1875). The schedule was as follows: leave Port Wakefield 7 A.M., arrive Hoyleton 4:30 P.M.; leave Hoyleton 10:30 A.M., arrive Port Wakefield 3:43 P.M.

[68] *Ibid.,* p. viii.

Surely, for providing means of intercommunication throughout the country, it is not necessary that we should at once jump from a condition in which, for four months in the year, heavy traffic is almost stopped, to one in which we can rush along with 150 tons at 30 miles an hour.[69]

And it was a reasonable view. For the farmer any kind of railway promised both a saving of his time, teams, and labor and a higher price for his wheat at inland markets. The comparative costs of wagon and railway haulage were cited so variously and self-interestedly (especially when alternative routes were being contested) as to obscure the actual facts, but the following table comparing the wheat quotations before the Port Pirie–Gladstone line was built with those during the same week in the following year after its construction gives some indication of the economic impact of a railroad during this era:

	March 17, 1876	*March 15, 1877*
Crystal Brook	6% less than Pt. Pirie	4% less than Pt. Pirie
Gladstone	16% less than Pt. Pirie	4½% less than Pt. Pirie
Georgetown and Laura	16% less than Pt. Pirie	8% less than Pt. Pirie*

**In 1877 Georgetown and Laura were now seven miles from a railroad station.*

Fortunately for the farmer that impact could now be felt to some degree in every district. Measured by the 1875 policy of fifteen miles maximum access, service had been provided for all but two small areas of the main wheat region, the Yacka and the Booleroo districts (Map 18). Those hundreds in the northeast and east which also lay beyond that belt of service, such as *Eurilpa, Minburra,* and *Ketchowla,* could now be dismissed as also beyond the belt of reliable farming. To be sure, difficulties of terrain undercut the practical suitability of that arbitrary policy in numerous localities, and in others the nearest railway station was to the east, away from the sea, and might in fact be a more costly point of shipment than a more distant siding closer to a port. Nevertheless, even the longest cartage would rarely have to cover more than twenty miles, and the average haul was surely less than half that distance. Certainly no district could claim to be crippled by inadequate transport.

[69] *The Farmers' Weekly Messenger* (Adelaide), July 23, 1875. See *Port Augusta Dispatch,* March 16, 1878, for similar statements.

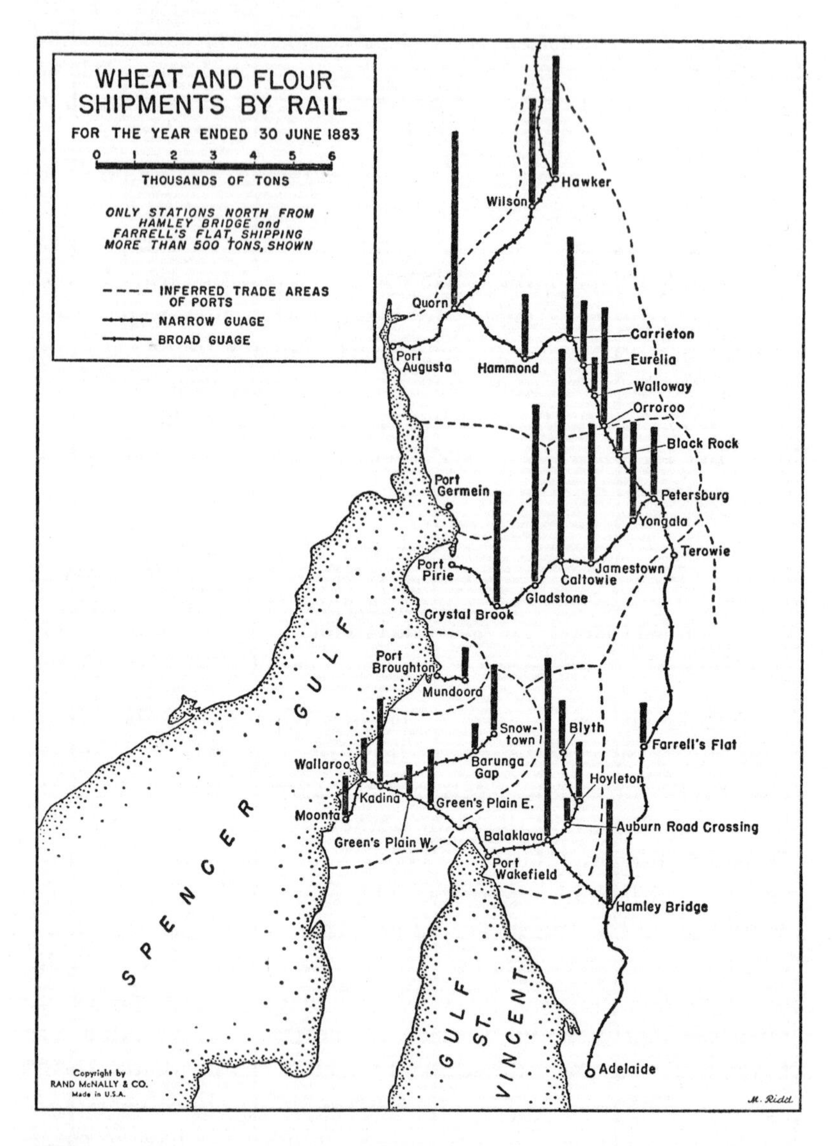
WHEAT AND FLOUR SHIPMENTS BY RAIL
FOR THE YEAR ENDED 30 JUNE 1883
0 1 2 3 4 5 6
THOUSANDS OF TONS
ONLY STATIONS NORTH FROM HAMLEY BRIDGE and FARRELL'S FLAT, SHIPPING MORE THAN 500 TONS, SHOWN
INFERRED TRADE AREAS OF PORTS
NARROW GUAGE
BROAD GUAGE
Hawker
Wilson
Quorn
Port Augusta
Hammond
Carrieton
Eurelia
Walloway
Orroroo
Black Rock
Petersburg
Yongala
Terowie
Port Germein
Port Pirie
Jamestown
Caltowie
Gladstone
Crystal Brook
Port Broughton
Mundoora
Snow-town
Blyth
Farrell's Flat
Barunga Gap
Hoyleton
Wallaroo
Kadina
Green's Plain E.
Moonta
Auburn Road Crossing
Green's Plain W.
Balaklava
Port Wakefield
Hamley Bridge
SPENCER GULF
GULF ST. VINCENT
Adelaide
M. Ridd

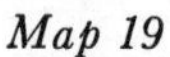

Map 19

PATTERNS OF TRAFFIC AND SERVICE

Statistics of the amounts of principal commodities loaded at each rail station allow some impression of the patterns of outbound freight movement. Those of wheat and flour for the year 1882–83 are shown on Map 19. That was the first full year of operation of the entire northern agricultural lines, excepting only the short Laura branch. It was, of course, also a year of drought, and the total shipments are far below those of a few years before, yet the proportionate patterns remain fairly representative.[70]

The combination of productivity and extent of line and station hinterlands is well revealed. The heaviest concentration of wheat traffic was along the Port Pirie–Petersburg railway, which not only cut directly through the best agricultural land of the North but drew much of the trade of the two principal locales still inadequately served by the system, the Yacka and the Booleroo districts. Caltowie was the largest grain shipping station in the colony, an eminence its strenuous opposition to the proposed Appila branch, which would cut into the area just to the north, was obviously designed to protect. Quorn was the major focus of trade in the Willochra, and the fairly large shipments at Wilson, Hawker, Carrieton and Orroroo, despite the devastating drought, suggest that such points drew from extensive trade areas. On the other hand, the absence of any significant export from stations on the broad-gauge north of Farrell's Flat reveals the smaller acreages and almost complete crop failure in the Burra sector of the frontier. Balaklava stands out as the most productive locale in the mallee plains country west of the hills, while Mundoora shows what failure to extend the Port Broughton tramway east beyond the Barunga Range meant – it was the only line that consistently lost money.

Shipments of wool and sheep naturally show a very different pattern. Most revealing is the heavy focus of wool traffic upon Terowie. The 8,445 bales loaded at that station as compared with fifty-seven at nearby Petersburg showed the power of the broad-

[70] The 1882–83 shipments are derived from *S. A. Parl. Paper No. 29* (1883–84), pp. 56–58. These have been compared with the statistics showing wheat (but not flour) shipments in the prosperous year 1879–80 in *S. A. Parl. Paper No. 177* (1880).

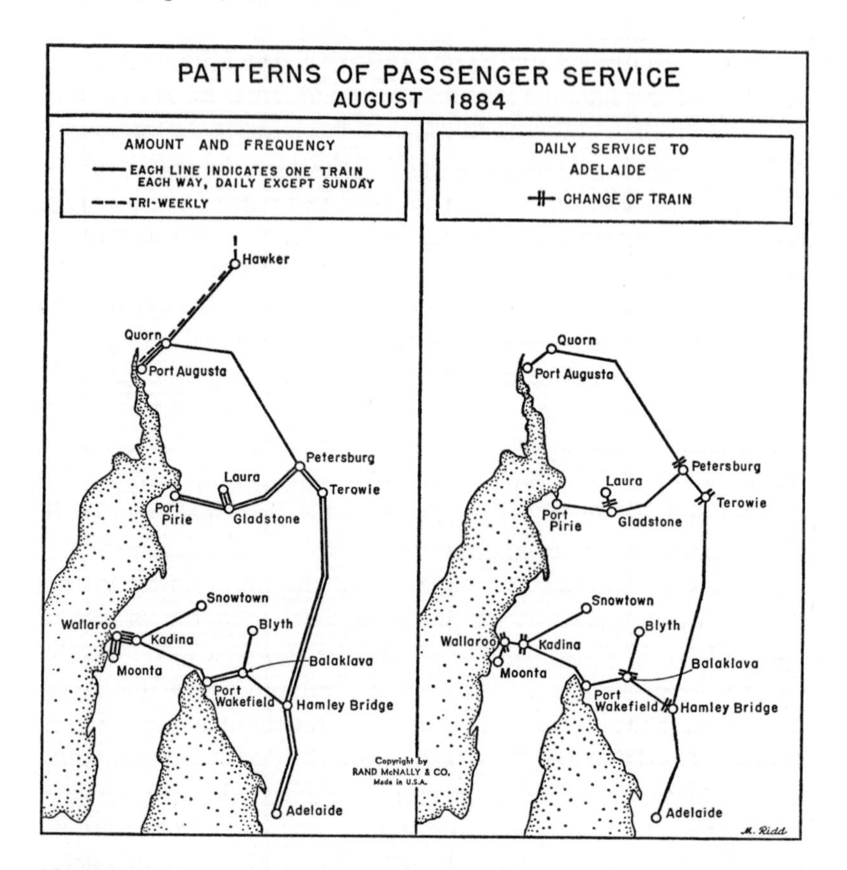

Map 20

gauge to Port Adelaide over the much shorter narrow-gauge to Port Pirie. Equally striking are the 106,066 sheep loaded at Terowie and 74,379 at Farrell's Flat, which two stations together accounted for nearly two-thirds of the total shipments for the entire Northern system. Farrell's Flat was the main shipping station for all the large runs just beyond Clare for which, if mere distance to the seaboard had governed, could have in some cases more advantageously loaded at Blyth or Snowtown. Such facts underscored the arguments in favor of the broad-gauge extension northward, cutting behind the east-west wheat feeders. Relatively large wool and sheep loadings at Quorn, Hawker, and Carrieton showed that these had become new contact points between the agricultural and pastoral domains in the Far North.

Although in the debates over the construction of these various railways, potential passenger traffic was almost always a secondary consideration, many in the North must have thought that rapid and almost effortless conveyance to townships and the metropolis as by far the most exhilarating prospect. The patterns of service offered are illustrated in Map 20.[71] Although the trunk lines connecting the capital with Wallaroo, Port Pirie, and Port Augusta had in each case evolved by fragments undesigned for through service and provided very indirect connections, the outstanding fact was that every point on the system from Quorn south had daily (except Sunday) service to Adelaide. The trip from Port Augusta took 13½ hours, including two changes of carriages (Fig. 12); from Port Pirie 11½ hours and one change; from Wallaroo 7½ and two changes. Wheat might move to the nearest port, but from the moment these various feeders were linked into a network, people moved to and from Adelaide, and this in itself was to have a subtle, belated, but perhaps in the long run an almost decisive influence upon the eventual triumph of centralization.

PORTS AND EXPORTS

At least twenty-eight wheat ports beyond Port Adelaide were used to some extent during this era (Map 18). Yet no one of these enjoyed that ideal combination of a safe, deep-water harbor and an easily accessible, productive hinterland. Thus, again, the government exerted a powerful influence through its programs of public works; its decisions as to which harbors to improve and which feeder railways to build largely determined the patterns of outport development. The competition for governmental favors was therefore keen and the following description of the successive steps to greatness was not grossly exaggerated:

> One not uncommon dodge is to get the Government to erect a wharf or jetty . . . at the head of a shallow creek. They are next told that the outlay is utterly useless without the channel be cleared and deepened so that vessels may come up to load. This being done the discovery is made

[71] Based upon timetables in *Sands & McDougall's Monthly Diary,* August, 1884. This later date was chosen in order to include the Laura branch.

that this famous jetty or wharf being at last approachable from sea is still inaccessible by land, and a railway is the only thing that will put things to rights.[72]

Certainly the railway was the prime arbiter of the relative importance of ports. The copper from the Wallaroo-Moonta mines was the only major export traffic logically oriented to a particular port, elsewhere the railroad pattern very largely determined the direction and scale of movements. Assuming the inferred hinterlands shown on Map 18, in 1882–83 rail shipments of wheat, flour, and wool to the outports were approximately as follows:[73]

	Wheat and flour (long tons)	*Wool (bales)*
Port Augusta	20,555	16,082
Port Pirie	22,002	3,031
Port Broughton	672	19
Wallaroo	8,639	297
Port Wakefield	9,718	1,289

The status of Port Broughton, so keen a rival of Port Pirie at the onset of northern development, vividly illustrates the harsh penalty of the failure of railway aspirations. Port Wakefield was the best example of a port gaining a considerable importance only to lose a portion of it to a rival. Failure to extend its rail line beyond Blyth and the extension of the Wallaroo feeder to Snowtown caused a reduction of its trade.[74] Also serious was the construction of the Kadina–Port Wakefield link which evidently caused some of the traffic formerly exported at shallow Wakefield

[72] *Jamestown Review,* Aug. 7, 1879.
[73] Total from the data in *S. A. Parl. Paper No. 29* (1883–84), pp. 56–58. Actually the wheat and flour totals are not exact, as some wheat loaded at rail sidings must have been shipped to nearby townships for milling and then reshipped as flour to the port. Unfortunately, no comprehensive records were found of the volumes of various commodities or of total tonnages shipped from each port. Various incomplete figures appear in special Parliamentary Papers and in local newspapers. The *Statistical Register* only lists the total declared value of exports of leading customs districts. In 1884 these were as follows (in £000): Augusta 703, Pirie 757, Wallaroo 341, Broughton 76, Wakefield 63, Victoria 55, Minlacowie 22; *Statistical Register of South Australia, 1884* (Adelaide, 1885), p. 76. However, these figures are made even less satisfactory by the fact that some customs districts include more than one actual port. Although as thorough a search as time permitted was made, it still seems likely, considering its significance and the propensity of the government to keep detailed records, that the data sought are somewhere extant.
[74] *S. A. Parl. Paper No. 27* (1881), p. 85.

Fig. 12 Passenger and goods train on Saltia Creek Bridge between Port Augusta and Quorn, *c.* 1880. (S. A. Archives)

Fig. 13 Wheat ships at Port Augusta, *c.* 1883. (S. A. Archives)

Fig. 14 Wheat at the docks, Port Pirie, *c.* 1880. (S. A. Archives)

to move on to the deep-water harbor at Wallaroo.[75] Port Pirie not only won direct access to a rich hinterland, but flourished on the limitations imposed upon its rivals. The shallowness of the feeder lines of its southern competitors and decision not to build the Port Germein–Orroroo railway on the north protected its trade. Port Germein was the outstanding case of a port gaining only half of the essential combination of public works: it got the longest jetty in the colony (5,459 feet), but the shortest railway—one locomotive operating upon the jetty itself.[76] Had it been successful in getting a line across the Flinders its level of development would certainly have been considerably greater. Instead it remained just another small outport in which the very adjacency to its hated rival kept it from being declared a separate customs district and thus doomed it to "being a fief of Port Pirie."[77]

Among these railway-served ports, Wallaroo and Port Augusta had the best natural harbors (Fig. 13), Port Wakefield the worst. At the latter, large vessels had to lie out as far as nine miles and be loaded by lighters. Port Pirie was also far from ideal. By 1880 half of its wheat exports were loaded by lighters but because of its importance the government was deepening the channel to allow direct loading of larger vessels (Fig. 14).[78]

Competition for the wheat trade among the score of minor ports on Yorke Peninsula and the coast north of Port Adelaide was influenced by many local factors, such as the relative costs of wharfage and lighterage, the number of wheat buyers and prices

[75] No measure of this diversion was possible, but it is apparent that in this case the hinterland of Wallaroo partially overlapped that of Wakefield, and therefore the volumes of exports calculated by rail station loadings are somewhat misleading.

[76] *S. A. Parl. Paper No. 29* (1882), p. 13.

[77] This meant that its trade was credited in the published statistics to Port Pirie. The government refused to separate the two because they shared the same outer bay, ships often loaded at both ports, and it was more efficient to administer them together. See *S. A. Parl. Papers Nos. 78* and *91* (1882). This sharing of the outer anchorage had its amusing features: newspaper reports from Port Germein often listed an impressive array of vessels at anchor as a measure of its progress, which caused the Port Pirie paper to point out angrily that they were lying off Germein either awaiting entry to or to be loaded by lighters from Port Pirie, which was largely correct. The only figure found of the relative trade of the two was for the year ended October 1, 1882: Pirie, 1,103,491 bu. (foreign export only); Germein 262,728 bu. (foreign and coastwise); *S. A. Parl. Paper No. 194* (1882).

[78] *S. A. Parl. Paper No. 27* (1881), p. 135.

offered, and the frequency and types of vessels attracted. Thus, for example, Port Vincent had a relatively good harbor and jetty while nearby Port Julia had neither, and the teams and wagons had to be taken out into the sea to small vessels. Yet some farmers who had a choice chose the latter because the owner of the Port Vincent jetty was the sole wheat buyer and consistently offered a lower price.[79] These ports which had the facilities and volume of trade to attract many ships had an obvious advantage. At smaller ports the only buyers might be those who came with the ships, or even if agents were in residence a good price might hold only while a vessel was loading then drop until another came by seeking cargo. Minor shallow ports could be served only by ketches, which were far from satisfactory:

> Ketches . . . provoke a good deal of temper on the part of the unfortunate people who have to depend upon them for supplies they may require and for the shipment of produce. No one ever seems to know even when they will sail for a given destination, and certainly no one can venture upon any conclusion as to when they will arrive where they are always long and anxiously expected.[80]

In the absence of actual statistics, no comprehensive measure of comparative importance among such small ports is possible, but some relevant evidence is at hand. It appears that the building of the railroad from Roseworthy to Hawley Bridge and Balaklava rather completely severed the hinterlands of the succession of muddy landings — Ports Gawler, Prime, Parham, and Lorne — along the eastern shore of Gulf St. Vincent. Deeper water along much of the opposite shore and on the Spencer Gulf side of Yorke Peninsula prompted the construction of numerous jetties. Port Vincent, Stansbury, and Edithburgh were apparently the principal loading points on the eastern side of the peninsula; Port Victoria was definitely the most important on the western side, with Minlacowie and Turton also of considerable local significance.[81]

In the early years of colonization most of the wheat was shipped from the smaller ports to Adelaide, although Port Wakefield was

[79] *S. A. Parl. Paper No. 27* (1881), pp. 120–25.
[80] *The Farmers' Weekly Messenger* (Adelaide), Nov. 30, 1877.
[81] This estimate is based upon an array of miscellaneous facts and references in the newspapers and reports. The locations of government harbormasters is a further indication of importance; in 1884 these were in residence at all the railway-served ports and at Germein, Moonta Bay, Victoria, Turton-Minlacowie (combined), and Edithburgh.

sending cargoes direct to overseas markets as early as 1866–67.[82] The elimination of this trans-shipment lowered costs, and loading for immediate export reduced the hazards of price fluctuations, resulting in higher prices for grain and giving those ports which could establish this direct service an important advantage. As the network of facilities was developed – wharves, jetties, telegraph lines, pilots, customs agents, and wheat buyers – an increasing proportion of the total produce was sent out directly to foreign markets. Those for which there is specific evidence of such export during these years were: Wakefield, Broughton, Pirie, Germein, Augusta, and Victoria.

The pattern of that export trade had changed significantly during these years of expansion. New South Wales and Queensland took nearly 60 per cent of the flour, and other long-standing markets such as Mauritius, Cape Colony, and Natal took most of the remainder.[83] None of these, however, could absorb the huge increase in unmilled wheat, and this era marks the major shift to Great Britain as the one big outlet. In 1884 the mother country purchased 86 per cent of the total, and another 3 per cent to France, though minute, further emphasized the almost complete re-orientation from Australian and other neighboring colonies to distant Europe. The great three- and four-masted, square-rigged wooden sailing fleet, which loaded in the gulfs from January to June and then headed out onto the high seas for a tedious voyage of four months to England (with a choice of nearly equidistant routes via Cape Horn or the Cape of Good Hope), was vivid evidence that South Australia was now inextricably bound into the rapidly developing global network of the wheat trade. The movement of grain bags from field to farmstead to rail siding to port to vessel to market half a world away was now the vital pulse of her circulation.[84]

[82] *S. A. Parl. Paper No. 191* (1867).

[83] Exports statistics are for 1884, derived from *The Statistical Register of South Australia, 1885* (Adelaide, 1886).

[84] I have briefly presented the concurrent problems of developing export transportation facilities in a major competitive wheat region and some further perspective on the world wheat fleet and patterns of competition in "Wheat Sacks Out to Sea, The Early Export Trade from the Walla Walla Country," *Pacific Northwest Quarterly*, XLV (January, 1954), 13–18. For the contemporary development of California wheat exporting see Rodman W. Paul, "The Wheat Trade Between California and the United Kingdom," *The Mississippi Valley Historical Review*, XLV (December, 1958), 391–412.

VIII.

Townships and Tradesmen

> In travelling over South Australia one cannot fail to be struck with the abundance of small townships which everywhere prevail . . .
>
> — Melbourne reporter
> *The Farmers' Weekly Messenger*
> (Adelaide), Nov. 13, 1874

TOWNSHIPS AND SETTLEMENT EXPANSION

The country township is the forgotten feature of the frontier. In the literature describing the drama of nineteenth-century expansion into new lands the stage is almost monopolized by the farmer; his hopes and problems, failures and achievements provide the grand theme. The very terms "pioneer," "settler," and "colonist" have become rather curiously narrowed to refer most usually to the farmer and rural settlement. Yet the country township was an important form of land settlement and the tradesman was no less a pioneer than the farmer. Townships did not just "appear" as a sort of belated, commonplace, and logical development; they were an indigenous and complex part of the whole frontier process.

This is especially apparent in South Australia where the tradition of land planning included townships as well as farms. There all policies relating to the survey and sale of land, all attempts at guiding the direction and governing the pace and magnitude of frontier expansion directly related to township colonization also. And these communities, no less than the farms, reflected the differing resource qualities of the countryside – the capricious variations of good seasons and poor — and, to an even greater extent, mirrored all the speculative instabilities so generally characteristic of the time and region.

A brief review of the historical geographic patterns of township foundation reveals how intimately the development was bound to the sequence of frontier expansion. In the years from 1869 through 1884 the government surveyed exactly one hundred townships in the new wheat country of the North and Yorke Peninsula (Map 21). In addition, several private townships were also established. Prior to 1869 a dozen or so surveys had already been made in the area, and several of these centers, though founded for other reasons, were to be of importance to the farming developments which were soon superimposed upon the surrounding country. Port Wakefield, the old copper port laid out in 1850 and enlarged in 1866, was the first government town in the North, and mining developments were responsible for most of the others in the pre-agricultural period: Burra, Kadina, Wallaroo, Moonta, Port Hughes, Port Clinton (all surveyed in the years 1857–63).[1] In the Far North, Port Augusta, the wool and copper port, was surveyed in 1856 (and Port Augusta West ten years later) and a few very small township sites had been staked out along the trails leading northward into the mining and pastoral outback, such as Willochra and Kanyaka, but no actual communities had developed in these latter. There was also a third cluster shown on the early maps just north of Clare. When the hundreds of *Hart, Milne, Andrews, Hanson,* and *Anne* were surveyed for sale, each included a township: Anama, Hilltown, Euromina, Davies, and Canowie, respectively. But the entire area was purchased by pastoralists and these "townships" were nothing more than patterns of surveyors' stakes in the midst of huge freehold estates.

The anomaly of such "paper towns" arose from a general policy of surveying a township within each hundred, a program which heretofore had not been rigidly adhered to but which was to receive much greater emphasis as the North was opened. When the new idea of Agricultural Areas for credit selection was pro-

[1] The dates of township surveys and all subsequent material on the acreage of such surveys have been obtained from the records held in the Office of the Surveyor General, Adelaide.

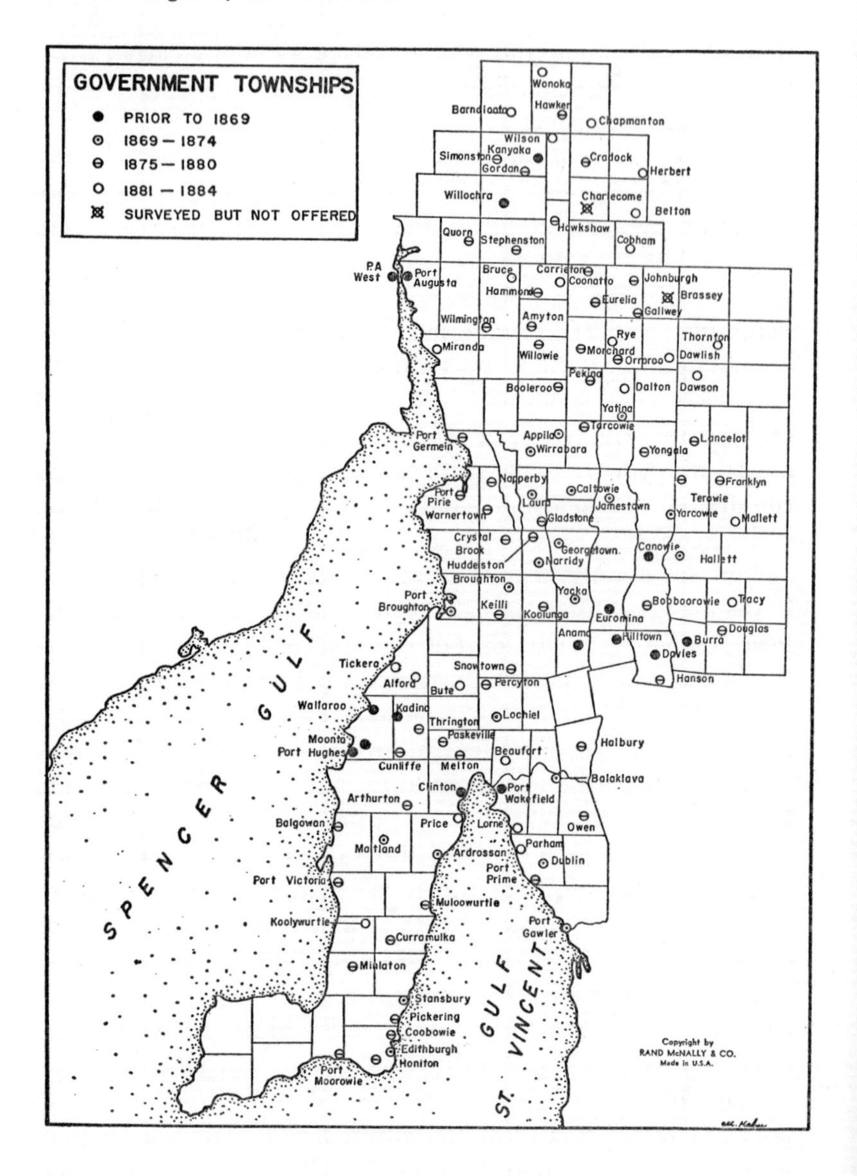
GOVERNMENT TOWNSHIPS
PRIOR TO 1869
1869 — 1874
1875 — 1880
1881 — 1884
SURVEYED BUT NOT OFFERED
Wonoka
Hawker
Chapmanton
Wilson
Kanyaka
Simonston
Gordon
Cradock
Herbert
Willochra
Charlecome
Belton
Hawkshaw
Quorn
Stephenston
Cobham
P.A West
Port Augusta
Bruce
Carrieton
Coonatto
Johnburgh
Brassey
Hammond
Eurelia
Gallwey
Wilmington
Amyton
Rye
Thornton
Miranda
Willowie
Morchard
Orroroo
Dawlish
Pekina
Booleroo
Dalton
Dawson
Yatina
Port Germein
Appila
Tarcowie
Wirrabara
Yongala
Lancelot
Napperby
Caltowie
Franklyn
Port Pirie
Laura
Jamestown
Terowie
Warnertown
Gladstone
Yarcowie
Mallett
Crystal Brook
Georgetown.
Canowie
Hallett
Huddleston
Narridy
Broughton
Port Broughton
Yacka
Keilli
Koolunga
Booborowie
Tracy
Euromina
Douglas
Anama
Hilltown
Burra
Davies
Tickera
Snowtown
Hanson
Alford
Bute
Percyton
Wallaroo
Kadina
Lochiel
Thrington
Moonta
Paskeville
Halbury
Port Hughes
Beaufort
Cunliffe
Melton
Balaklava
Clinton
Port Wakefield
Arthurton
Price
Lorne
Owen
Balgowan
Maitland
Ardrossan
Parham
Dublin
Port Prime
Port Victoria
Muloowurtie
Koolywurtie
Port Gawler
Curramulka
Minlaton
Stansbury
Pickering
Coobowie
Edithburgh
Honiton
Port Moorowie
SPENCER GULF
GULF ST. VINCENT
Copyright by
RAND McNALLY & CO.
Made in U.S.A.

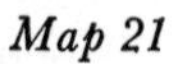

Map 21

posed a township within each was advocated and was very largely carried out (Maps 7 and 21).[2] Those townships resulting from this policy were Edithburgh (Troubridge Agricultural Area), Broughton (later Redhill) (Broughton A.A.), Narridy (Narridy A.A.), Georgetown (Gulnare A.A.), Laura (Booyoolie A.A.), Caltowie (Caltowie A.A.), Jamestown (Belalie A.A.), Yarcowie (Yarcowie A.A.), and Dublin (Dublin A.A.). Kalkabury, Penton Vale, and Mannanarie Agricultural Areas had no townships within but could each be served by a newly-established adjacent one: Maitland, Stansbury, and Jamestown, respectively. Each of these townships was laid out on an ample scale and obviously had a head-start in the soon intense rivalry to capture the trade of surrounding districts. Four other new port towns were surveyed, Port Gawler, Port Pirie, Port Broughton, and Ardrossan, each having been initiated by the wheat shippers themselves (Ardrossan was near the old landing at Parara). Aside from these, only Balaklava, Lochiel, Yacka, and Hallett, widely spaced over what were still non-credit agricultural districts at the time, were set out prior to 1874.

The application of the credit provision to all rural lands quickened the spread of farms and townships alike. Whereas seventeen townships were established in the first five years of the new wheat frontier, thirty-six were put up for sale in the next five. Most of these were in hundreds which had been proclaimed earlier but had suddenly become more attractive under the new laws. Thus the density of distribution within the original skeletal framework of "Agricultural Areas townships" was greatly increased. Along the northern margin Wilmington, Morchard, Eurelia, and Orroroo were the earliest centers; Douglas and Lancelot marked the northeastern fringe; and, in 1878, Quorn, as an assured railway town, was the first center established to serve the new surge of colonists into the Willochra.

In the final six years of this era, from 1879 through 1884, forty-seven new sites were marked out. Thirteen of these were surveyed within the older region which was in general already well studded with townships. In several instances these relatively tardy ap-

[2] *S. A. Parl. Debates,* Oct. 20, 1868, col. 647.

pearances occurred because farm colonizations in the local district had been retarded by poorer land and dense scrub. Muloowurtie, Balgowan, Lorne, Alford, and Tickera were examples of this factor. Others were founded directly in conjunction with new railroad lines, such as Owen, Percyton (Barunga Gap), and Snowtown. The remaining thirty-four were all in the broad, new, and final pioneer fringe in the North and North East. Port Germein and Miranda were established to serve the narrow strip west of the Flinders Range along the head of Spencer Gulf. Tracy, Mallett, and Franklyn marked the limits of colonization in the North East frontier. A string of new sites appeared along the Terowie-Quorn railroad: Dalton (later Black Rock), Rye (later Walloway), Coonatto (later Moockra), Hammond, and Bruce. The Great Northern line also prompted a series of new settlements: Gordon, Wilson, Hawker, and Wonoka. But a dozen townships were laid out well beyond the assuring touch of the railroad, each a tangible measure of the confident march of settlers far into the saltbush plains. Nearly all of these were surveyed in 1879–80, but, in keeping with the common practice of delaying sales of township lots until some time after farm sections had been offered, many were not actually put on the market until 1881–83. Thus the onset of the great drought during their gestation period between survey and sale had a withering effect. A few, like Cradock, Belton, and Johnburgh, got a meagre, stunted start; others, such as Dawlish, Gallwey, Cobham, and Chapmanton were stillborn — offered for sale but never came to life as towns; and Brassey, staked out on the parched ground of *Yalpara,* was never born at all — no lots were ever put on the market.[3]

Thus the "township frontier" displayed all the space and time characteristics of the general wheat frontier: initially a slow and selective development in districts of greatest promise, soon a more rapid filling in as the goodness of the land was proved, then a quickened movement outward as both confidence and speculation gained strength, accompanied by continued minor developments in previously by-passed localities of special difficulty, until finally

[3] Charlcome in *Uroonda* was also not offered for sale at this time; it was put on the market in 1891, evidently with no success for the lands were resumed (i.e., township survey was canceled) in 1943.

the drought imposed a limit and left a belt of "marginal lands" defined as much by marginal townships as by marginal farms.

GOVERNMENT CONTROL OF LOCATION AND DESIGN

This survey has been charted only in terms of government townships simply because they represented nearly the whole of such development in these areas. The policy of surveying a township within every hundred was very closely followed. Where it was not, it was in almost every case either because one already existed nearby just over the boundary of an adjacent hundred, or because the land was unlikely to become densely settled, as in the poor country at the tip of Yorke Peninsula and along the extreme North East frontier which even agricultural expansionists acknowledged as pastoral land. On the other hand, twenty-two hundreds had two or more government townships, a feature which prompted some blunt criticism: "the absurdity of placing two in one Hundred is ridiculously apparent."[4] On examination the absurdity is not quite so obvious. In nearly every instance the reasons for departing from the standard practice are quite clear: to include both an interior town and a port (e.g., Honiton and Edithburgh in *Melville*); or to include two ports in the same hundred, each useful to a local hinterland (e.g., Stansbury and Pickering in *Dalrymple*); or a second town was established on a railroad line which had bypassed the first (e.g., Dalton, after Yatina was bypassed in *Black Rock Plain*); or the two were located near the borders at opposite extremities (e.g., Franklyn and Mallett in *Wonna*). The common policy of one township within each hundred had important geographic implications, for it tended to implant a relatively uniform pattern of density of township sites. Because the hundreds were rectangular or nearly rectangular units of approximately one hundred square miles, townships tended to be fairly evenly distributed at intervals of approximately ten miles. This distribution was made even more uniform when the few privately-developed townships are added, filling in a gap here and there in the over-all pattern. The general result of such a theoretical design would be to place all the agricultural lands within five miles of a township.

[4] *The Agriculturist and Review* (Jamestown), Aug. 27, 1881.

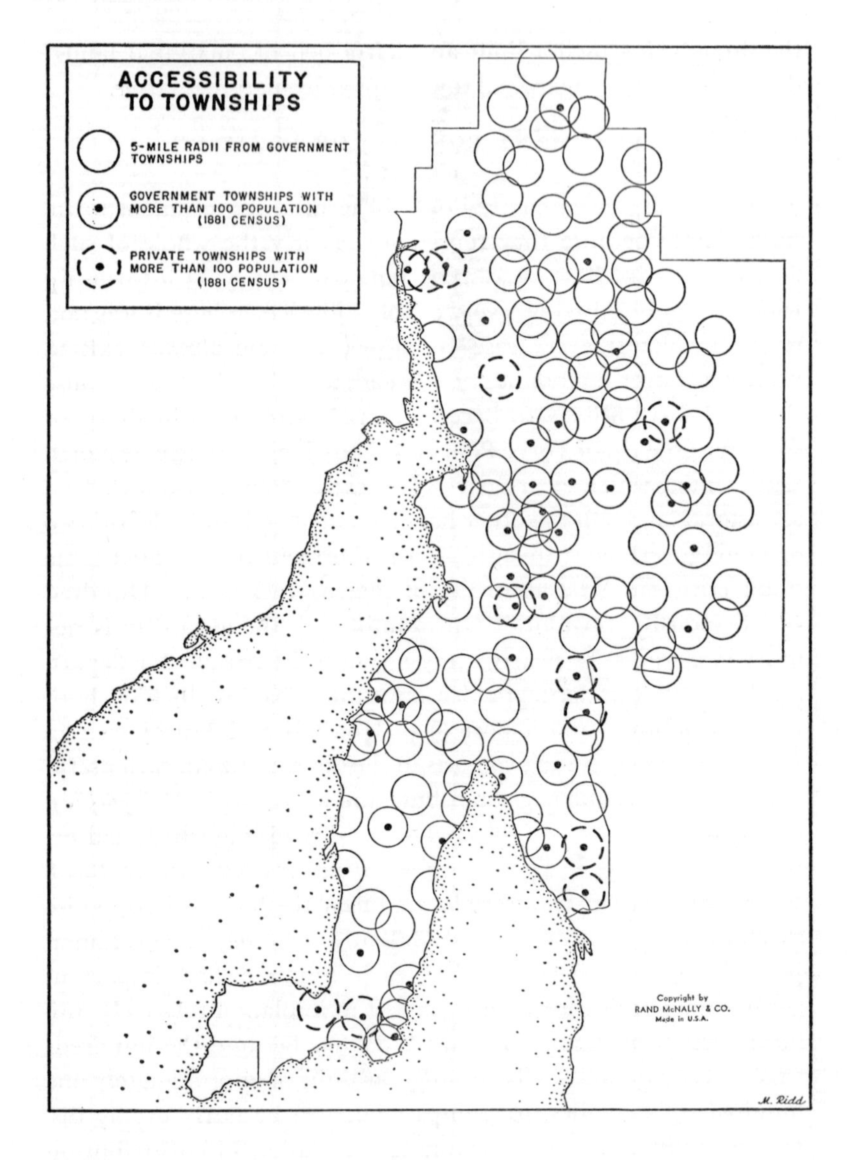
ACCESSIBILITY TO TOWNSHIPS
5-MILE RADII FROM GOVERNMENT TOWNSHIPS
GOVERNMENT TOWNSHIPS WITH MORE THAN 100 POPULATION (1881 CENSUS)
PRIVATE TOWNSHIPS WITH MORE THAN 100 POPULATION (1881 CENSUS)
Copyright by RAND McNALLY & CO. Made in U.S.A.
M. Ridd

Map 22

Whether such was a conscious objective of the government's program is not clear, but the actual result was not far short of that general schematic pattern (Map 22). Whether such an interval was a reasonable one to imprint upon such an agricultural region is another matter. With farms ranging in size from about three hundred acres to a thousand, a five-mile radius did not enclose much of a tributary rural population for each township, certainly not sufficient, in most localities, to support a full range of basic services. Those communities which aspired to grow into full-fledged functioning townships – as all which got the least start did dream of doing – had, in most instances therefore, to capture the trade of a considerably larger area, and hence had to win out in the competition with adjacent centers. The government, therefore, did not really found townships, but only potential townships. It set a general geographical framework for competition among incipient communities, and it continued to play a major role in that rivalry by such means as timing the date of sale of lands within each site, and by its decisions on railway routes, telegraph lines, and port improvements. But the government had still another very significant part to play in the geography of townships before any such competitions actually got underway, for it not only shaped the general patterns of distribution, it also controlled the micro-geography of township designs.

The internal plan of a township or city is a mirror of its heritage. Those that grow gradually without advance planning have fixed in their evolving street and block patterns some reflection of the social and economic conditions of their growth. These that are designed before they are actually colonized reveal something of the whole context of that colonization in the design itself. This is vividly illustrated in South Australia. Adelaide was a physical expression of the ideals of its founders: a carefully planned city for a carefully planned colony, laid out on a scale commensurate with the measure of wealth and development envisioned, and laid out on a new design to foster a new kind of society. That design was, of course, like the society it was to serve, not original in its several elements but only in its over-all plan. Whatever the sources of Colonel Light's ideas for the particular geometrical patterns of streets, blocks, and squares, the split focus of the central district,

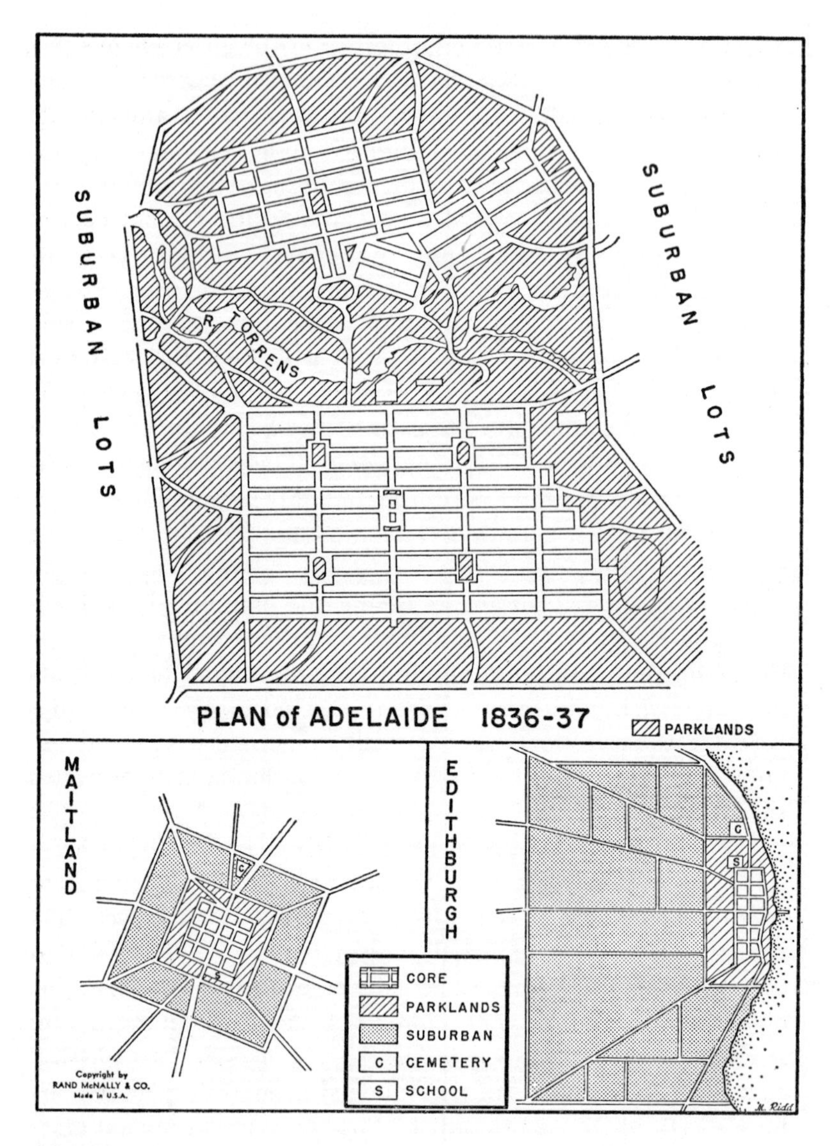
SUBURBAN LOTS
SUBURBAN LOTS
R. TORRENS
PLAN of ADELAIDE 1836-37
PARKLANDS
MAITLAND
EDITHBURGH
C
S
CORE
PARKLANDS
SUBURBAN
CEMETERY
SCHOOL

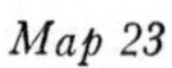
Copyright by
RAND McNALLY & CO.
Made in U.S.A.

Map 23

the reservation of the intervening riverine strips, and the separation of city and suburbs by a parkland belt which would be used for recreation and public buildings, these features were combined into a fresh idea in city planning (Map 23).[5] Adelaide was not only an expression of the ideals of its society, it was an artistic creation and a functional invention which invariably elicited praise from visitors and expressions of loyal pride from its steadily-growing body of citizens. Once the government set itself the task of designing other communities it was almost inevitable that this "ideal city" should become the model, and thus the mark of Adelaide became imprinted upon every government town in the wheat frontier.

The basic elements of the model were a central core of rectangular blocks designed for shops (and shopkeepers' residences in the early stages of development); an encircling belt of parklands reserved for public use; beyond, a perimeter of suburban residential blocks; and a radial pattern of straight roads leading from the central district. This combination of features provided the framework, and in application resulted in a widespread unimaginative repetition of a generally stereotyped design. Nevertheless there was opportunity for considerable internal variation and an interesting range of differences did appear. So unusual and important was this governmental influence upon township design that it warrants some detailed examination.

EXAMPLES OF TOWNSHIP DESIGN

A rather rare example of almost perfect geometric symmetry was the plan of Maitland (Map 23). The set of concentric squares of business blocks, parklands, and suburban lots, each with a perimeter road, was the simplest combination of the model features, and the ten radiating roads gave nearly perfectly-balanced access to the surrounding countryside. The reservation of school lands in or adjacent to the core area and of a cemetery block at the periphery

[5] There has been considerable speculation as to the source of Light's ideas. Philadelphia, Turin, and Catania, the last a Sicilian city which Light had visited and praised, have been suggested as influential examples, as well as various theoretical designs current in England at the time. Certainly it was not a direct copy of any existing city. See Price, *Founders and Pioneers of South Australia*, p. 131.

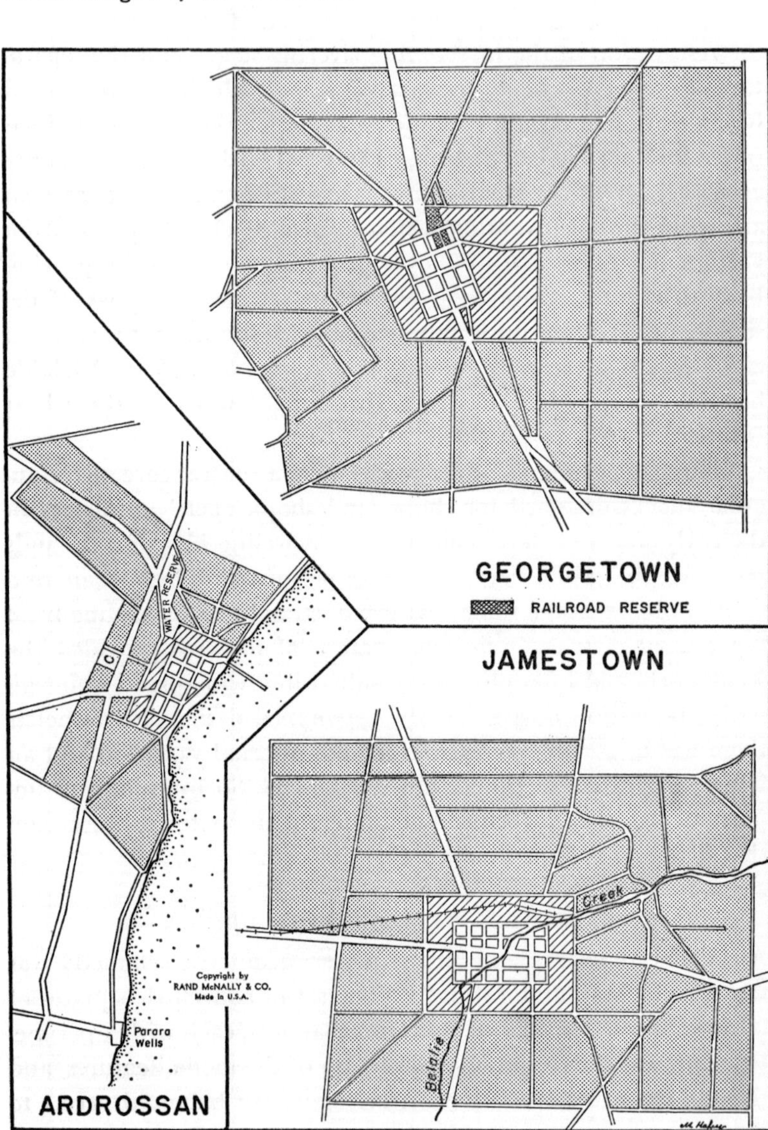
GEORGETOWN
RAILROAD RESERVE
JAMESTOWN
ARDROSSAN
WATER RESERVE
C
Parara Wells
Copyright by RAND McNALLY & CO. Made in U.S.A.
Creek
Belalie

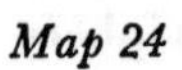

Map 24

were common minor features. Edithburgh was an example of the application of the same basic design to a port (Map 23). The coastline severed the eastern half and its curve was partially imposed upon the business frontage and coastal road. The radial pattern of access roads crossed the township, but the natural eccentricity of the site was accentuated by an enlargement of the suburban area inland, which, in turn, required local access streets. Another different feature was the gradation outward in the size of suburban lots. Those nearest the center were house and garden lots, those farther out were of small farm size.

Georgetown (Map 23) had a similar variation in lot sizes which, in effect, added a fourth, though incomplete, member to the set of concentric zones: core, parklands, small-lot residential area, large-lot suburban area. Georgetown also had the distinction of being the largest township surveyed in the North, with a total acreage of 5,523, and is a good example of similarly large plans laid out for several neighboring towns. A detail of the Georgetown scheme which added further to the imitation of Adelaide was the designation of the streets bounding the central area along the parklands as North, East, South, and West Terraces, and the same feature was applied to many other townships.

Few township plans were designed to fit intimately with local terrain features, although some minor departures from the standardized model do appear. Jamestown (Map 24) was laid out astraddle Belalie Creek which disrupted the straight-line street pattern in the northeast corner of the suburban area. The northern suburban zone also had fewer north-south than east-west streets, a feature of interest chiefly because it is such a marked peculiarity of the Adelaide central district. Ardrossan (Map 24) is an example of a beach-town backed by moderately sloping ground. Thus the design was given a more elongated pattern paralleling the shore, with a narrow suburban extension up the gully facing onto the main road to the hinterland. The most striking feature, however, is simply the persistence of the general model despite the terrain handicaps. Douglas (Map 25) illustrates the asymmetry resulting from the application of a small-scale plan to a creek-side. Some such distortion was fairly common and often was not related to terrain at all, but as in the case of Curramulka

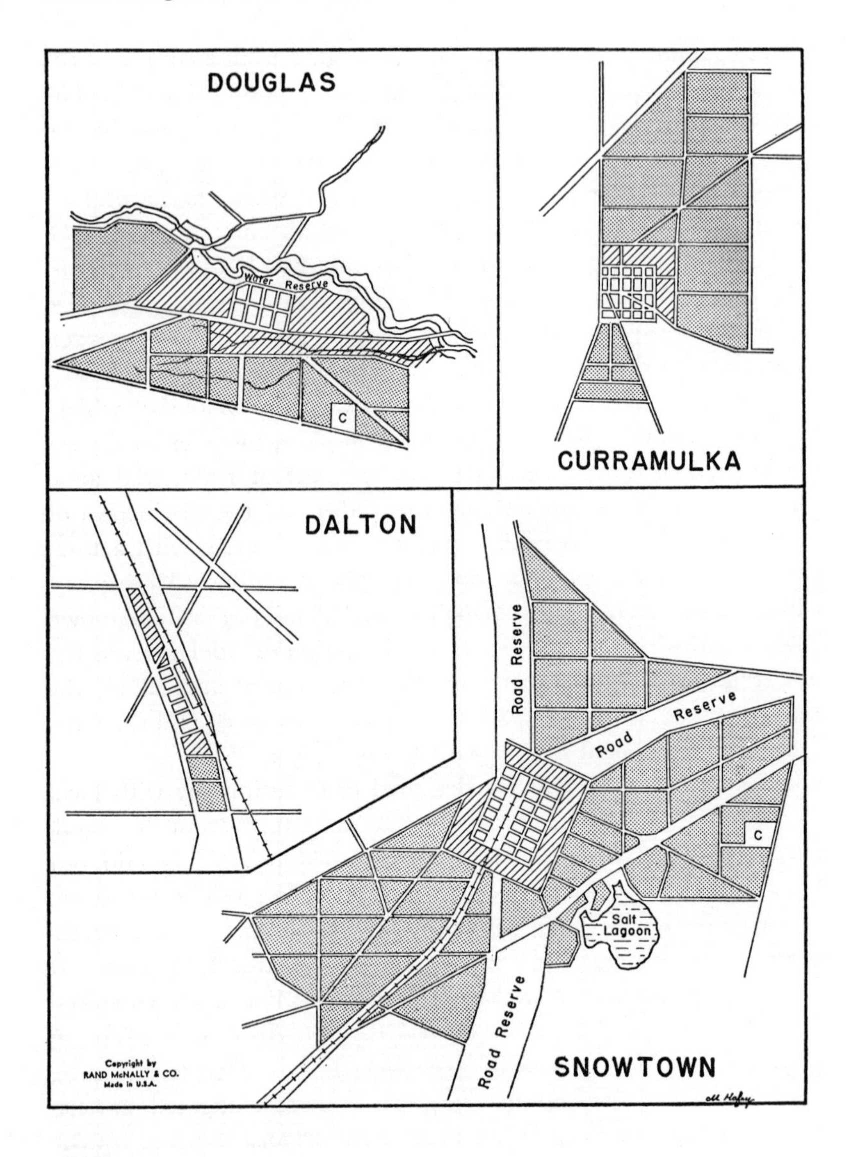
DOUGLAS
Water Reserve
C
CURRAMULKA
DALTON
Road Reserve
Road Reserve
C
Salt Lagoon
Road Reserve
SNOWTOWN

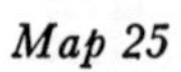

Map 25

Fig. 15 Jamestown, *c.* 1876. (S. A. Archives)

Fig. 16 Georgetown, July, 1876, six years after its founding. Although the largest over-all township survey, the main street was but half the width of that of Jamestown, illustrating another of the capricious variations in township designs. Both Jamestown and Georgetown were located in open grassy country without so much as a clump of mallee to hide the rawness of their early years. (S. A. Archives)

(Map 25), arose from the sequence of survey procedures which first set the country road pattern, then delimited the farm blocks, and finally surveyed townships within the bounds of one or more of the latter.[6]

The railroad was given a more powerful influence upon design. Some towns were of course laid out prior to railroad construction and without anticipation of possible routes. One of the redeeming features of the model plan was that it allowed entry with a minimum disruption. Jamestown is a good example of how a portion of the parklands could be used for a station near the center of town (as it was in Adelaide). That the railway station should be near the center was indicative of the central importance of such service to these country towns at the time. And this importance is more vividly illustrated in the plan of Snowtown, which was specifically designed as a railway terminus (Map 25). There the line was taken through half the suburban area, imposing six street crossings, and directly into the central core which was laid out around the terminal. Far from being viewed as a necessary but lamentably dirty, noisy, dangerous, disruptive intruder, the railroad thus became the organizing focus — which, in turn, was, of course, but a specific example of the town plan as a mirror of the social outlook and economic conditions of its time. The power of the railway was perhaps best illustrated by the fact that it was the only factor able to disrupt completely the over-all concentric pattern. Dalton (later Black Rock) (Map 25) was surveyed in conjunction with the railway survey as a minor shipping point, and its business blocks, parklands, and residential area were placed in a linear pattern parallel with the rail line. Yet, though it could drastically distort the stereotype, even the railway could not completely destroy it, and the three zones were retained, with a tiny park separating the business and residential areas.

Aside from such adaptations to terrain and the railway, little basic variation was evident. In the early years a few slight departures from the common scheme were made within the central blocks: Port Wakefield was focused upon a small oval park; Port

[6] See Chapter VI, pp. 96–99, for the example of *Pekina* Hundred and township.

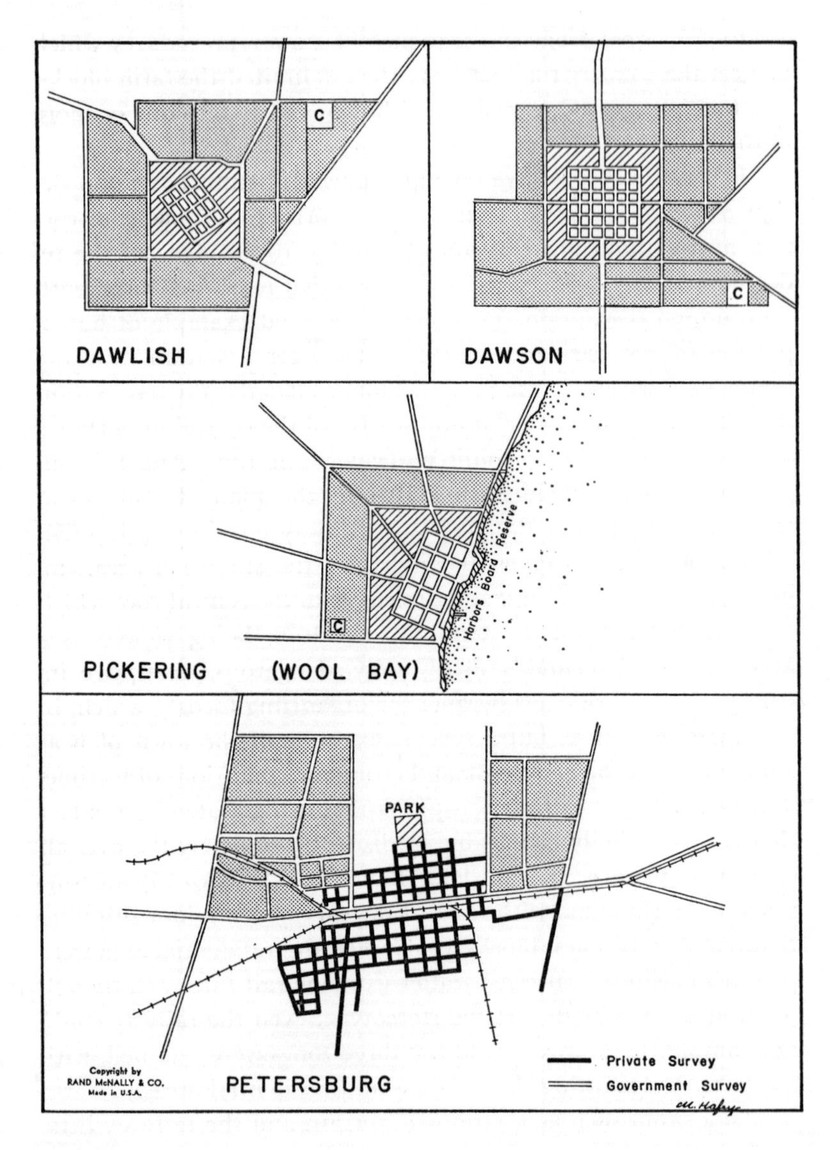
C
DAWLISH
C
DAWSON
Harbors Board Reserve
C
PICKERING (WOOL BAY)
PARK
Private Survey
Government Survey
PETERSBURG

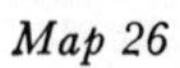

Map 26

Pirie had the distinction of a curved main street paralleling the wharf line along the creek; Crystal Brook's central Adelaide Square was a unique copy of Victoria Square in the metropolis. But as the need for new surveys increased, the plans took on a more rigid uniformity. Some minor differences in the patterns of residential blocks or the angling of the whole central district within the parklands were seemingly all that busy designers could be bothered with. Dawson and Dawlish (Map 26) were typical of a score of others in the North, that of Pickering (later Wool Bay) (Map 26) was common to several minor ports. And so townships were stamped out by the dozen from the standardized plans turned off the drawing boards of the Surveyor General's Office in Adelaide.

CRITIQUE OF SITES AND DESIGNS

But designing a town and living in one are radically different matters. How well did these "model towns" serve their purpose? An answer could only come from intimate historical study and perhaps personnal experience, yet some evidence is at hand and some tentative judgments may be offered. The only extensive discussion of this township policy in the local country press of the time was found in the *Jamestown Review.*[7] The editor of that paper was an unusually shrill critic of any governmental action which did not suit his tastes or failed to advance the interests of his community; nevertheless his comments on the method and results of this town planning raised matters worthy of notice. His editorial had been prompted by one in the *South Australian Advertiser* which had called for greater care in the selection of town sites and recommended that it ought to be made the specialized duty of "some capable official high in the service of the Lands Department."[8] The Jamestown editor thoroughly agreed, and looking about at the examples in his own region he decided that the present instructions issued to the officials in charge must be as follows:

[7] Sept. 26, 1878.
[8] *South Australian Advertiser* (Adelaide), Sept. 21, 1878. Just who was in charge of such matters and what criteria were used is a problem requiring detailed research into the records of that Department.

> Avoid all sites that are naturally high and dry and possess natural facilities for easy drainage. If there be a gentle slope, sheltered by friendly upland, avoid that also; eschew any elements of the picturesque, and select rather the flattest, most uninteresting site possible; if a flat with a creek running through it and subject to overflow, by all means get on the lower bank of the creek and peg away. If a running creek be not available get in the way of a storm channel. A mangrove swamp with sinuous cozy channel is a combination of favorable conditions too good to be often hoped for, and if subject in addition to direct tidal overflow, consider it perfection.

It was crude sarcasm but it was backed by disconcerting facts. "Sinuous cozy channels" subject to "tidal overflow" was an all too real and notorious situation at Port Pirie,[9] and for the rest Jamestown itself could serve as an example, as he went on to point out. Belalie Creek cut right through the center, periodically overflowed one side and gave poor drainage to the other, and yet "within a mile or so . . . there are in more than one direction beautifully verdant slopes, upon any of which Jamestown would have been infinitely more picturesque, more enjoyable, and more healthy." The degree of improvement which might have been realized from these alternative sites may be questionable, but that the surveyors were strongly attracted by the "flattest, most uninteresting sites possible" is certainly clear. And the reason seems equally obvious: the rigid predetermined geometrical model. These designs which appeared so beautifully balanced on the drafting board could obviously best retain that beauty and balance if transferred to an equally plane surface on the ground. About the only other thing in favor of such flat locations was their advantage as a balanced focus of radial access roads. But good drainage was certainly a more pressing need and many a township was chronically plagued by a lack of foresight on the part of its surveyors. Even where sloping ground was available, the main street was likely to be placed on the level ground parallel with the base of the slope and was thereby transformed into a sluggish drain fed by a whole set of new tributaries coursing down the straight streets from the adjacent slope. The winter results of such a design were enough to move even so strong a local patriot as the Glad-

[9] See *S. A. Parl. Paper No. 39* (1875), an appeal from the residents there for a levee to halt the "repeated [tidal] inundations."

stone editor to describe his own township as "a dreary, monotonous treeless mudhole."[10]

Not only the selection of site but numerous details within these plans were roundly criticized. In Jamestown the main thoroughfare cut through the business center at an angle "setting every one of the principal frontages askew." The editor called this "a wanton exhibition of cussedness," but it was not a very common nor would it appear to be a necessarily bad feature. A more usual and much more important detail was the radial road pattern angled through the suburban blocks creating "a lot of multi-angular and preposterously-shaped allotments." This certainly reduced the value of some of these pieces of land and must have resulted in a considerable amount of unused space.[11]

Even the name of his town galled him: why not "the very musical title of Belalie for the certainly horridly prosaic one of Jamestown?" The judgment was of course a matter of personal taste, but the question had been raised before. In 1872, when townships and hundreds were being rapidly blocked out over the North, a resolution was introduced in Parliament "that it is undesirable to continue the system of giving to townships and hundreds the names or surnames of ladies and gentlemen." When so many euphonious native names were available such a practice was declared to be a "gross absurdity." On the other hand, another member warned that if such a change was to be made an interpreter had better be employed for "some of those [native] names had very pretty sounds, but very dirty meanings."[12] Perhaps that danger was ominous enough, for the resolution was defeated and the names of ladies and gentlemen continued to be sprinkled liberally over the countryside. In general, these personal names were confined to townships; most of the hundreds were given native names. And whatever their meanings, these aboriginal words were not necessarily ideal; some were over-long and cumbersome, local pronunciations could bewilder the uninitiated (e.g., Booyoolie,

[10] *The Areas' Express and Farmers' Journal* (Gladstone), Aug. 20, 1879. See also *Port Augusta Dispatch,* Dec. 17, 1880, on the problem of flash floods in Gladstone.

[11] The Jamestown editor's criticism of this same practice in the countryside: that it left an excessive number of field corners that could have only been cultivated with a "narrow spade," was probably a more important point.

[12] *S. A. Parl. Debates,* Oct. 9, 1872, cols. 2209–11.

pronounced "Bowly"), and many of the most attractively euphonious invited confusion, as the later modifications to distinguish Yarrowie, Yarcowie, and Tarcowie proved.[13] Disputes over names were recurrent and heated but hardly vital to the process of colonization, although, like township designs, local toponymy may give some interesting expressions of the context of that colonization.

The *Advertiser* leveled one further criticism: "the area laid out for townships is as a rule ridiculously large." A review of plans and their acreages certainly supports the contention. A half dozen surveys covered more than 4,000 acres, a score were greater than 2,000 acres, and only a very few included less than a square mile of ground. Certainly on the basis of any reasonable prospect for the development of communities in a wheat-growing region of large farms, such dimensions would seem open to some ridicule. In addition to over-all scale there was the matter of relative scale among these many towns. Although the program led to a fairly even distribution of town sites, the growth prospects for some would certainly be greater than for others. To be sure, it would have been impossible for anyone to foresee such patterns of development with any real accuracy, but the best port sites, major road junctions, and positions central within especially productive land could reasonably be expected to enjoy greater development than many other types of locations. Certainly there is evidence of some attempt to make such judgments. Port Pirie, Port Broughton, Port Germein, and Edithburgh were surveyed on a much larger scale than other ports; Quorn was given dimensions proportionately suitable for a major railroad and trade center; Georgetown was in the midst of the rich Gulnare Plains. But there were curious inconsistencies. Thus within less than twenty miles of Georgetown, which sprawled over nearly nine square miles, were Broughton (Redhill), Crystal Brook, Caltowie, Jamestown, and Yacka, each over 2,500 acres in extent. Surveys on this scale, if completely settled with a family on each lot, would accommodate a community of several thousand people. It was perhaps conceivable at the time that one township in each district might indeed attain that size, but certainly there was no possible basis for the idea that

[13] The name of the hundred was added to the township name of the first two: Appila-Yarrowie, Whyte-Yarcowie.

any district could support a cluster of half a dozen such townships. Yatina, Orroroo, Eurelia, and Carrieton, encompassing from 1,400 to over 2,000 acres each and spaced out at intervals of fifteen miles or less, provide a further illustration. Willochra, nearby Simonston in the Willochra Plain, and Lancelot out on the saltbush plains in the North East were other surveys of enormous size which would appear to have been utterly disproportionate to any conceivable level of development, even during the height of expansionist optomism.[14]

An even greater lack of rational proportion was apparent internally in these plans. The zonation of each design into separate functional areas was an admirable idea, but the business core and suburban areas were functionally interrelated, and a model plan should presumably establish some reasonable ratio between the number of business and residential lots. In practice the most astonishing variations appear – the actual proportion was apparently a matter of mere whim – for example, the gross differences in suburban areas of the following townships with nearly equal central districts:

Township	*Central District*	*Suburban Area*
Maitland	101 acres	580 acres
Carrieton	102 acres	2,864 acres
Redhill	116 acres	4,408 acres

The most extreme example was Halbury, with a business center within the parklands of four blocks totaling 24 acres as the focus of a sprawling suburban zone of 2,573 acres. Even in the plans of the many small townships which were turned out with almost identical general designs this ratio fluctuated capriciously, as illustrated by Dawson and Dawlish (Map 26) with nearly comparable suburban allotments (944 and 882 acres) but with Dawson given twice the central area of Dawlish (148 as compared to 71 acres).

The only reasonable explanation for both the enormous size of many townships and such internal disproportions would seem

[14] Town and suburban acreages of each of these three totaled more than 2,000 acres. Simonston's 2,384 acres of suburban land were never put on the market, but Willochra's 1,925 acres were offered in 1884 after the great drought had destroyed all hopes for any dense agricultural settlement.

to be that offered by the *Advertiser*: the government was anxious to make as much money as possible from the auction of township lots. Such a policy was a serious blot upon any general merits of this unusually comprehensive program of town planning. Despite a considerable amount of speculative purchase in a few townships, most of these suburban lots remained unsold for years, locking up in total a very considerable portion of the region's farm land. Gradually some of these blocks were purchased by nearby farmers and combined into fields of adequate size; in numerous cases the government, years later, canceled all or part of the original plan and resurveyed the land into farm sections.[15]

This hunger for revenue — and, to be sure, the money was badly needed to support railway construction, port improvements, and other programs — was also apparent in the obvious discouragement given to private town developments. When Warnertown was laid out as a private venture east of Port Pirie, the government surveyed a competitive site a quarter of a mile away.[16] Terowie was originally promoted by an individual landowner; when the railway was extended the government surveyed the township of Shebbear around the terminus, directly adjacent to the private township;[17] ultimately the two were combined. Petersburg was an unusual case. The surveyors, guided by terrain, set the railway junction in Section 216 of *Yongola,* a farm allotment already in private hands which was of course promptly subdivided into township lots. However, two adjoining sections were still unsold and the government surveyed these into suburban lots. The result (Map 26) was a hybrid township, with a business and residential core subdivided as a private speculation into a fine grid of small blocks, its eastern and western margins laid out on the usual gross dimensions of government suburban surveys, with the streets patterns along the boundaries between the two only partially interconnected. A reversal of this situation also happened: private land

[15] Townships which never developed and were finally resumed for resurvey and sale (or lease) were: Anama, Amyton, Barndioota, Brassey, Charlcome, Cobham, Euromina, Gallwey, and Mallett. Many others were reduced in size and partially resurveyed.

[16] *Port Augusta Dispatch,* Dec. 17, 1880. At that time the private township had a shop, pub, blacksmith, and public school; the government town, only a church.

[17] *The North-Eastern Times and Terowie News,* Oct. 21, 1881.

adjacent to a government township being subdivided into residential allotments, as for example Wanborough and Port Wakefield North, on the eastern and northern margins of the government survey at Port Wakefield. Generally, however, the scale of the government surveys allowed no opportunity for such speculation.

Not all private ventures faced this kind of direct competition, but the government program of townships was applied so thoroughly as to leave relatively little room for individual promotion. Melrose, Saltia, and Stirling North were established before this government program was underway; the most successful of the post-1869 private townships was Yorketown; the only privately developed port township of any significance was Port Vincent; Mallala, Hoyleton, Blyth, Collinsfield, and Warooka were about the only others that got any real start at all.

This role of the government in controlling the site, design, and over-all patterns of country townships was one of the most distinctive features of the South Australian wheat frontier. In retrospect the whole program seems to reflect much the same history as the more general experience in colonization: the actual implementation and result falling short of the admirable ideals of the declared philosophy. Through control of site selection and scale of survey the government presumed to guide the density and scale of township development in order to promote the social values of concentrated settlement. In practice it proceeded without any really rationalized program carefully adapted to the physical and economic conditions of the region. Through control of township design the government presumed to set a framework to insure a high quality of living conditions within these towns, but that framework itself partially defeated its very objective. Aside from being too strongly influenced by the concern for revenue, the chief deficiency of the program was perhaps its rigid, unimaginative adherence to a stereotyped model which in origin had not been conceived for that purpose at all. The clear fact was that while Colonel Light had invented a new metropolitan design, no one invented a new country township design, and to impress the image of Adelaide upon a hundred sites across the countryside was to clothe hamlets grotesquely in metropolitan dress. The gazetteers which described "scattered" townships and the newspapers which lamented "the deserted wilderness appearance which characterizes so many of our townships" (Figs. 15 and 16)[18] were implicitly describing the consequences of the unsuitable scale of lots blocks, streets, parklands, and over-all surveys. Aside from a disheveled appearance and more social dispersal than compactness, the practical results were large areas of wasteland, and excessive costs of street maintenance, drainage systems, and water supply services.[19] To reserve land for recreational and other public use was admirable; automatically to girdle the central district with a parkland of fifty to five hundred acres was rarely advantageous. Those communities that never developed beyond village size were all too often surrounded by a weed-infested wasteland, those few that did grow to considerable size found themselves "locked up" by their parklands "as completely as many of the European towns were once upon a time hemmed in by fortifications."[20] Even in many of the larger towns both shops and residences were crammed into the central district out of sheer convenience, while the spacious suburban lots beyond the parklands lay unsold. And in fact the whole concept of "suburban lands" was largely inappropriate to the region. The lots varied from an acre to not more than forty acres, the latter usually only at the periphery of the very large surveys. But what was the land to be used for? A home garden and orchard, a small paddock for a pair of horses and a cow, perhaps, but what else? Lots of several acres were a suitable size only for market gardens, commercial orcharding, vineyards, dairying, or similar intensive activity, and thus were suitable for the periphery of a metropolis but hardly for that of a country township in the

[18] *The Australian Handbook* (1883), p. 402; *The Agriculturist and Review* (Jamestown), Aug. 27, 1881.
[19] *South Australian Advertiser* (Adelaide), Sept. 21, 1878.
[20] Charles C. Reade, "Planning and Development of Towns and Cities in South Australia," *S. A. Parl. Paper No. 63* (1919), pp. 18, 20–21. This report by the government Town Planner is a general survey of the whole question though it gives no explanation of the specific designs of the agricultural districts. It does mark a fresh beginning in town planning in the state and contains both a critique of the historic standardized model and an alternative design, perhaps the first specifically planned to meet the needs of country towns—but, of course, too late to be of any consequence for this agricultural region.

midst of a mono-economy, large-scale wheat region. After all, "suburban" presupposes an "urban" center.

In short, the whole township scheme, its basic elements, standardized patterns, gradations of lot size, and over-all scale was a metropolitan complex transplanted into a country setting and therefore could not possibly achieve the desired results. Just what results it did obtain is neither altogether clear nor within the bounds of this study, but it seems certain that any assessment of the qualities of country life in this portion of South Australia must take into account the physical anatomy of its townships. Whatever its defects this comprehensive experiment in town planning remains a unique and important facet of this nineteenth-century agricultural colonization. The contrast with the competitive, speculative maelstrom of the concurrent American frontier is stark, and that contrast was firmly rooted in the social heritage of the two countries. Despite the injection of revenue considerations, the over-all South Australian procedure was perfectly in accord with the philosophy of her founders. And despite all the now apparent inadequacies of her theories and practices, at least the idea persisted that such matters were of fundamental social importance and therefore of basic political concern. It was a kind of heritage that many another province and nation, groping in more recent years to find some means of bringing order out of urban chaos, might well envy.

COMPETITION AND PROCESSES OF DEVELOPMENT

Despite this unusually strong role of the government in setting out the framework through its control of public works the actual level of development depended upon a host of other factors. And despite the importance of local variations in site advantage and land quality, a great deal depended upon the citizens themselves. The importance of local initiative was heightened by the over-all context of township beginnings: a large number of essentially similar sites, laid out thickly and almost simultaneously over the region. To be sure, the controlled spacing of townships usually insured at least a minor potential hinterland to each, unlike

America, for example, where rival privately-initiated townships might spring up within a mile or two of one another and hotly compete for trade. Still, growth beyond hamlet size necessitated a considerable trade area, and competition among adjacent towns certainly developed.

Nearly every town that got started at all did so with the same set of pioneer tradesmen. "We have our Post-office, general store, bootmaker's and saddler's shops, boarding house, and the indispensable hostelrie," reported one resident during the initial stages of his town, and when he added that "business is brisk, and Wonoka bids fair to become one of the great commercial centres of South Australia," he had accurately described both the tangible features and the aspirations common to most of these budding communities.[21] Of these shops and services the hotel ("pub") was very important in drawing trade from the surrounding country. Thus the private speculator who laid out Collinsfield attempted to give it an initial boost by erecting "a splendid hotel."[22] Once this elemental complex had been obtained, the next and critical step was to establish a school, a church, and a blacksmith shop for farm repairs. The addition of these provided sufficient basic services to form a community focus and fairly well secure a local hinterland. Many townships reached this level, which usually meant a population of fifty to a hundred or so, and stabilized.

Townships of a recognizably higher order had other distinguishing features. A description by a traveling reporter of such centers in the older district south of Clare in 1874 could have applied equally well to those of the North eight or ten years later. He found the prevailing features, in addition to the usual shops, to be:

> a good flour-mill, hard at work; a blacksmith's shop, surrounded chiefly by double-furrow ploughs, reapers, . . . and winnowers; a public house or two, a school, several well-built churches, a representative of one or two

[21] *Port Augusta Dispatch,* Nov. 13, 1878. The boarding house was hardly common and may have been related to the railroad survey activity in the area at the time. The country papers document many similar examples of the content of new towns. For instance, Hammond had two stores, two blacksmiths, a saddler, butcher, and one hotel, *ibid.,* May 2, 1882; Morchard had exactly the same in 1878. See *The Areas' Express and Farmers' Journal* (Gladstone), Nov. 16, 1878.

[22] *The Northern Argus* (Clare), May 25, 1875.

of the banks and insurance societies, a public reading-room and library ["institute"], and a number of cottages, many having nice gardens.[23]

In these centers the community focus had been strengthened by church services for leading denominations;[24] more distinguishing features were an institute,[25] which was a good symbol of status, and banking services, essential to any real commercial development. The blacksmith's shop in such a township was also likely to be more than just a minor repair and horse-shoeing station and to include some manufacture of farm implements. The flour mill was also a good measure of success in development. Such mills provided an essential local service, were important as wheat-buying agencies, and were the most basic and likely kind of rural industry to be obtained. Their importance is indicated by the eagerness of the towns to gain such facilities. Thus, for example, the Terowie newspaper strongly supported local efforts to get a mill, arguing that "we must do our best to attract new customers, and in order to do that we must be able to supply their wants with promptitude."[26] In Yongala and Orroroo public meetings were called shortly after each community was founded to explore the means of getting a mill. Both were successful, and the Yongala mill, at least, was a locally-financed venture.[27] When Hawker was rumored to be getting a flour mill, Wilson petitioned the leading

[23] *The Farmers' Weekly Messenger,* Nov. 13, 1874.

[24] As in most British colonies the Church of England was at least nominally the largest in membership, if not the largest in active attendance. South Australia, however, had an unusually strong nonconformist population. Many of the founders and early leaders were strongly opposed to any state-supported church and thus the colony had a strong attraction for restive English dissenters. See Pike, *op. cit.,* Chapters XI and XV for a detailed discussion of the early history of churches and religious problems. The larger country townships would commonly have congregations of Anglicans, Methodists, Presbyterians, and Roman Catholics, with Congregationalists and Baptists only somewhat less common, with occasionally a chapel or meeting house of some evangelical splinter sect.

[25] These institutes were expressions of English social reform movements common in the early nineteenth century which sought to improve the educational and social conditions of industrial laboring classes. Usually known as Mechanics Institutes in the homeland, their widespread incidence in South Australia was but another reflection of the social idealism of its founders. Commonly housed in a substantial building near the center of the community, they served as a library, reading room, lecture and meeting hall, and place for social functions.

[26] *The North-Eastern Times and Terowie News,* July 29, 1881.

[27] *The Jamestown Review,* May 16 and May 30, 1878, May 12, 1881.

Northern Areas milling company to establish one there, arguing that if it would pay at Hawker "it would pay even better" at Wilson.[28] By 1883 twenty-eight towns had their own mills and Port Pirie and Quorn each had two. There was a wide variation in their capacities and, undoubtedly, in the quality of their products, but each was an important visible symbol of its township's progress and stature.[29]

The other most common country industry was an agricultural implement factory. This very era was probably precisely the period when such plants were most widely distributed among country towns. Most had evolved out of blacksmith shops. As the wheat economy unfolded an unprecedented demand was created for a wide range of fairly simple implements, such as ploughs, harrows, scarifiers, wagons, drays, and strippers, which could be manufactured in at least limited quantities by fairly small shops. As this agricultural economy continued to develop in the decades following, the size and complexity of machines increased, especially binders, winnowers, harvesters, and seeders, and at the same time the railroad network destroyed the isolation essential to the success of many small shops and allowed larger and more efficient factories to market over the whole state. But at this time every farm center of any size and pretension had its agricultural-implement maker. It is quite impossible to obtain any measure of the relative scale and importance of these local plants, but some evidence is available on a few towns of especially large works. Laura was a leading implement manufacturing center. In 1878 one company there was reported to employ thirty to forty workers, had seven furnaces, a wide array of machine tools, and turned out wagons, drays, buggies, rakes, harrows, ploughs, scarifiers, and reapers. At that same time a Georgetown plant, with thirty-five employees, was reported to have produced the following during the year preceding: 150 single- and double-ploughs, 40 triple-ploughs, 40 sets of harrows, 45 scarifiers, 34 reapers.[30] Such factories were obviously more than slightly enlarged blacksmith shops and

[28] *Port Augusta Dispatch,* Aug. 1, 1883.

[29] The location of flour mills is derived from the *Statistical Register of South Australia, 1882* (Adelaide, 1883), Vol. III, p. 60.

[30] *The Areas' Express and Farmers' Journal* (Gladstone), Jan. 26 and Feb. 27, 1878.

were not only significant to the farm economy but were rare prizes for any aspiring town to obtain. In addition to Laura and George-town, Quorn was also an important center. The fact that its three implement foundries were each a branch of a larger concern was perhaps already an indication of an important trend which would eventually nearly eliminate such manufacturing from country towns.[31]

Laura, Quorn, Melrose, Port Augusta, and Burra each had a brewery; Wirrabara, adjacent to the forest reserve, had a sawmill; and these represented about the only other manufacturing activities of significance at this time.

There were still other measures of progress and stature, however, which tended to differentiate a few of these townships as centers of a higher order. One was self-government. In 1882 there were nine municipal corporations in this area, although four were mining towns (Burra, Kadina, Moonta, Wallaroo), three were ports (Augusta, Pirie, Wakefield), and only two were purely agricultural centers (Jamestown and Yorketown).[32] Such places had, or at least claimed to have, an "urban" prestige denied to all the rest which were governed as part of a larger rural area under district councils. A far more potent instrument in the competition for trade and general advancement was a newspaper. Eight had been established in the North by 1882: at Port Pirie, Port Augusta, Gladstone, Jamestown, Burra, Terowie, Wallaroo, and Moonta. A paper, dependent upon local advertising and subscriptions, was likely to be established only in those towns which had already become leaders of a considerable district, and once in being became a very powerful agency in increasing that predominance.

RAILWAYS AND TOWNSHIP DEVELOPMENT

There remained one other factor in this growth and rivalry among these many towns which was far more decisive than any other: the railway. A rail line did not of course insure major development, but lack of one was almost certain to deny it. An Auburn

[31] The Quorn plants were those of James Martin & Co., also of Gawler and Gladstone; Mellor Bros. of Adelaide and Jamestown; and Adamson Bros. of Adelaide and Laura; Morris, Hayter & Barry, *The Commercial and Trades Directory of South Australia, 1882–83* (Adelaide 1882).
[32] *Ibid.*, pp. 472–73.

correspondent put the issue succinctly: "Auburn is desirous of having rail communication for precisely the same reason as other places, viz., to avoid dwindling down into obscurity, and to protect her trade."[33] The intense and complex agitations and rivalries for various rail lines have already been extensively described, but a few specific comments directly relating to townships may be pertinent. The danger of "dwindling down into obscurity" if bypassed by rail lines was very real. When Stephenston, for example, was put on the market, buyers were sure that the Quorn-Terowie line would pass through; but it crossed the plains four miles away and Stephenston soon lost one general store to newly-surveyed Hammond, was left with but one other, a blacksmith shop, and a wineshop – and little hope for the future.[34] This vital effect of the railroad and the fact that the locations of both railroads and townships were controlled by the government inevitably brought cries for greater co-ordination of the two programs:

> we would urge that *every* township should be surveyed with a view to ultimate railway accommodation, and that a railway reserve should tap all Hundreds and a station site be reserved in all towns. It is grossly unfair that it should be allowable for the Railway Department to survey lines completely ignoring settlements *en route*. Settlements too that have been surveyed and sold by the Government and where allotments have been purchased by a verdantly confiding public. Look at Yatina with a railway station six miles distant, completely damning any prosperity that might ultimately accrue to the town. Why was Yongala ignored and Petersburg created? . . . All places cannot have "through" lines of railways but feeders from the main lines should tap all Government townships.[35]

The plan was unrealistic but the problem was evident. Perhaps the best example of this lack of co-ordination was the case of Georgetown where the diversion of the route of the Port Pirie railway to the north more than offset all the hopeful advantages of a head start, fine potential trade area, and the largest township survey. Laura was similarly left off construction programs for years but finally got its branch, largely because of the sustained agitation of an unusually energetic citizenry. The rare initiative

[33] *The Northern Argus* (Clare), Aug. 24, 1875.
[34] *Port Augusta Dispatch,* Nov. 12, 1880.
[35] *The Agriculturist and Review* (Jamestown), Aug. 27, 1881.

of forming a private company to build its own rail connection was probably the deciding factor.[36]

The critical importance of the railroad to town rivalries led to a dog-in-the-manger attitude. If a line could be obtained it was best if it could be halted there and not extended on to other nearby centers: to be a terminus was far better than to be merely a station if a large trade area was to be captured. Thus at a public meeting in Laura one speaker warned that they must seek a line to their town but strongly oppose any extension beyond "as it would affect in a very alarming degree the interests of Laura."[37] When the line from Port Pirie to Gladstone was extended on to Caltowie, the editor of the Gladstone paper spoke of "the dreaded 'going through' of the line" which now meant that his town "henceforth must exist, flourish, or decay in proportion to the business done with the surrounding districts" – a sharp reduction in status after having served as the railhead for the entire region.[38] The whole flavor of this rivalry for railways is delightfully illustrated by the following summation of the see-saw battle over the choice of terminus for the Barrier Range line:

> The feeling in Terowie has alternated during the week, from grave to gay, from lively to severe. The triumphant passage of the bill for a line *via* Petersburg last week caused wailing and gnashing of teeth here, while in Petersburg there was general rejoicing and festivity, and bands playing "Happy are we tonight boys." Wednesday a change came o'er the spirit of our dream, with the news that the Upper House had rejected the measure. Terowie jubilant, champagne flowing, flags flying, Petersburg . . . band playing "I'd mourn the hopes that leave me," telegrams of condolence from Terowie. Thursday reversed matters again. Bill *via* Petersburg reintroduced and passed . . . Telegrams came back to roost. Bonfires and beer at Petersburg. Terowie band playing "O! Chide not my heart for its sadness!" "Toiling, rejoicing, sorrowing," such is life.[39]

[36] As an example of the strong presentation made to railroad committees by Laura see *S. A. Parl. Paper No. 22* (1878), pp. 143–47.

[37] He went on to state that "he could not see why Appila-Yarrowie wanted a railway when it was within six or seven miles of the Caltowie station already," which was certainly a dangerous argument when Laura was seeking a branch of but seven miles to Gladstone. *The Areas' Express and Farmers' Journal* (Gladstone), May 24, 1879.

[38] *The Port Pirie Gazette and Areas News,* March 8, 1878.

[39] *Port Augusta Dispatch,* Nov. 17, 1884, quoting *Terowie Enterprise.*

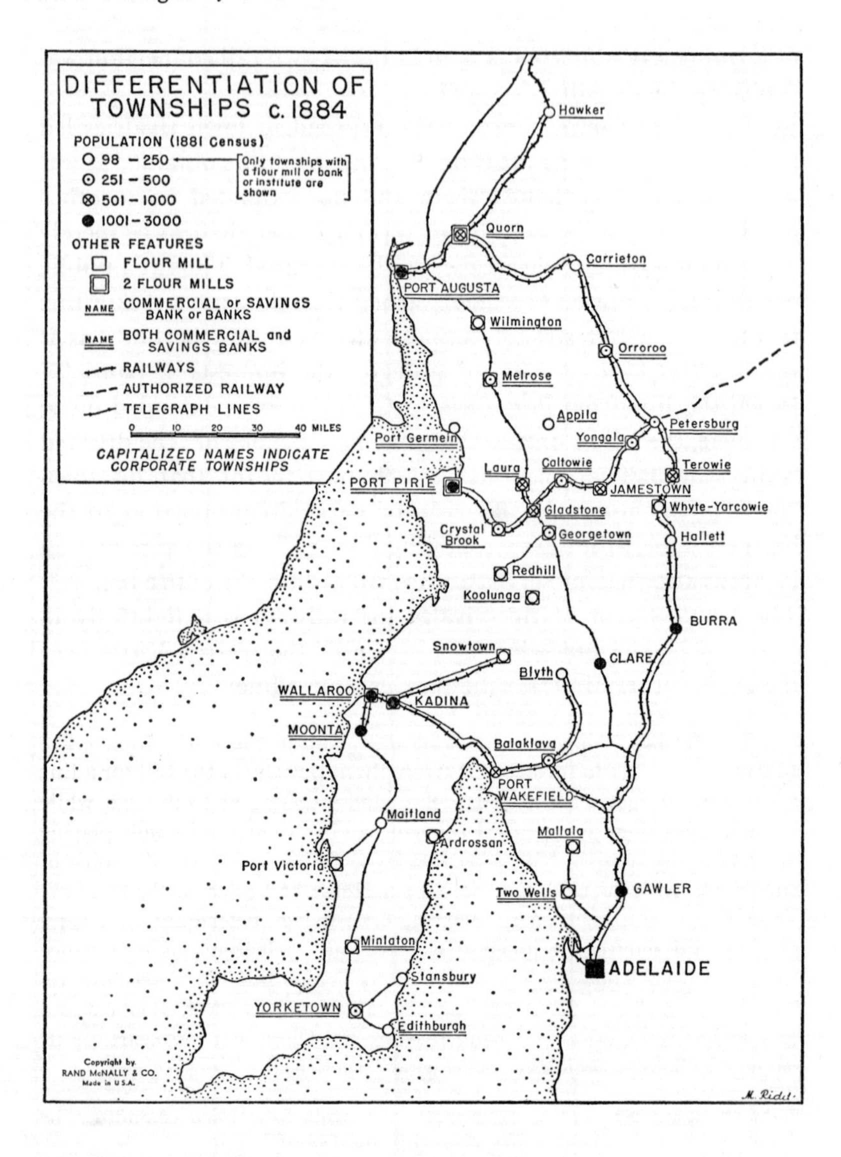
DIFFERENTIATION OF TOWNSHIPS c. 1884
POPULATION (1881 Census)
98 – 250
251 – 500
501 – 1000
1001 – 3000
Only townships with a flour mill or bank or institute are shown
OTHER FEATURES
FLOUR MILL
2 FLOUR MILLS
NAME COMMERCIAL or SAVINGS BANK or BANKS
NAME BOTH COMMERCIAL and SAVINGS BANKS
RAILWAYS
AUTHORIZED RAILWAY
TELEGRAPH LINES
0 10 20 30 40 MILES
CAPITALIZED NAMES INDICATE CORPORATE TOWNSHIPS
Hawker
Quorn
PORT AUGUSTA
Carrieton
Wilmington
Orroroo
Melrose
Appila
Petersburg
Port Germein
Yongala
Terowie
PORT PIRIE
Laura
Caltowie
JAMESTOWN
Gladstone
Whyte-Yarcowie
Crystal Brook
Georgetown
Hallett
Redhill
Koolunga
BURRA
Snowtown
CLARE
Blyth
WALLAROO
KADINA
MOONTA
Balaklava
PORT WAKEFIELD
Maitland
Ardrossan
Mallala
Port Victoria
Two Wells
GAWLER
Minlaton
ADELAIDE
Stansbury
YORKETOWN
Edithburgh
M. Ridel

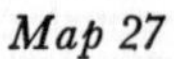

Map 27

The railway usually brought along a telegraph line as a facility necessary to its own operation, and this additional medium of communication had a special importance in this wheat country. The completion of the transcontinental telegraph to Darwin was one of South Australia's proudest achievements of the time and it was claimed that its cost of construction "was paid during the first year of its operation by the increased price obtained by its agency for the season's wheat."[40] Local lines served a similar purpose within the colony and were sought by every township which aspired to become a wheat-marketing center. Thus a group of Yorke Peninsula residents petitioned for a line "to enable the farmers, wheat buyers, and others to get the latest information of the state of the rise and fall in the Adelaide market"; doubt about the prevailing price of wheat had "caused much annoyance between buyers and sellers."[41] By the close of this period the wheat country was well served (Map 27). The telegraph paralleled most of the rail lines, the Adelaide–Port Augusta trunk line extended through Clare, Georgetown, Melrose, and Wilmington, traversing several districts without rail service; a Moonta-Edithburgh line served the length of the Peninsula, with branches to the principal ports; and other short extensions connected such non-railroad towns as Mallala and Redhill.

THE PATTERN OF TOWNSHIP GROWTH

These few years of colonization were important, therefore, not only as the era of township initiation but also of township differentiation. Because the tradesman and the farmer were fellow pioneers, because the government exercised so strong an influence and carried forward its basic program of public works concurrent with settlement, and because the drought of the early 1880's brought a sharp cessation of expansion and thereby circumscribed the general areal framework of development, the patterns of proportionate growth were already quite apparent by the end of this colonization period. This is not to suggest that such populations had already reached their peak nor that any particular rank order of size had become stabilized. There were still many local rural

[40] *The Farmers' Weekly Messenger* (Adelaide), Feb. 19, 1875.
[41] *S. A. Parl. Paper No. 208* (1877). See also *No. 137* (1880) for a similar petition for service to Port Germein.

districts which were not as yet completely colonized and there were local trade orientations which were not as yet firmly fixed, yet the processes of differentiation had already operated sufficiently to give a fairly reliable indication, measured by size and/or by facilities and services, as to what the prospects of a particular township would be.

Certainly none of these centers was very large nor functionally complex measured against even contemporary standards of development in similar type regions. In South Australia greatness and complexity of urban development remained solely a feature of the capital. Adelaide's 103,864 persons in 1881 compared with Port Augusta's 2,662 was a clear measure of metropolitan dominance. In general, the small scale and simplicity of township development was a measure of the relatively low density of rural settlement and the diffused pattern of local trade areas. Because of the narrowness of the agricultural belt, its orientation toward local ports, and the pattern of railway lines, no township in the North could become a truly regional trade center — a focal point of both distribution and collection for an extensive hinterland. Paradoxically, had metropolitan centralization become the determining principle of circulation, such a subsidiary regional trade center on some scale intermediate between that of Adelaide and the country townships might well have developed at some multiple rail junction near the threshold of the new agricultural frontier. Clare, serving as the principal portal for emigrants into the new districts for several years, had dared to entertain just such hopes — to translate its pretensions as the "Northern metropolis" into reality. Its failure to secure even a branch rail line was therefore an uncommonly hard blow and it derived no real lasting benefits at all from these years of Northern development.[42]

Yet despite this relatively meagre scale of township growth, the processes of differentiation had already sorted out the nearly one hundred communities into several levels of development or prospects. Those which had achieved at least the minimum level of growth and facilities to suggest the prospect of some permanence as local trade centers are listed, in rank order of population, in Table 1,[43] and partially depicted on Map 27.

[42] Population in 1871 was 1,004; in 1881, 1,131.
[43] Basic sources: Edward Greville, ed., *The Official Directory and Year-Book of*

TABLE 1

TOWNSHIP POPULATIONS* AND SELECTED FEATURES

Township	*Population (1881)*	*Commercial Banks*	*Savings Banks*	*Institutes*	*Flour Mills*	*Newspapers*
PORT AUGUSTA	2662	4	1	1	1	1
WALLAROO	1869	1	1	1	1	1
PORT PIRIE	1530	4	1	1	2	1
KADINA	1521	2		1	1	
MOONTA	1418	3	1	1		1
JAMESTOWN	995	2		1	1	1
Laura	828	2	1	1	1	
Gladstone	729	2	1	1	1	1
Terowie	687	2	1	1	1	1
Quorn	540	2	1		2	
PORT WAKEFIELD	506	1	1	1		
Crystal Brook	496	1		1	1	
Melrose	411	1	1	1	1	
Balaklava	354	1		1	1	
Yongala	353	1	1	1	1	
Petersburg	345	2				
YORKETOWN	340	2	1	1	1	
Caltowie	338	1	1	1	1	
Orroroo	314	2	1		1	
Georgetown	266	2	1		1	
Wilmington	250	1			1	
Redhill	245	2		1	1	
Edithburgh	234	1	1	1		
Mallala	219		1	1	1	
Snowtown	218	1			1	
Port Germein	211	1	1			
Two Wells	208	1	1	1	1	
Maitland	177	1		1		
Whyte-Yarcowie	158	1			1	
Wirrabara	156					
Appila-Yarrowie	151	1				
Hawker	142	1				
Hallett	137			1		
Stansbury	123	1				
Carrieton	120	1				
Port Victoria	113				1	
Minlaton	112	1	1	1	1	
Collinsfield	110					
Hoyleton	102					
Ardrossan	101			1	1	
Blyth	99	1				
Koolunga	98	1			1	

**Corporate townships capitalized.*

Three of the six largest communities were within but not really a part of the agricultural region. Wallaroo, Kadina, and Moonta were still very largely dependent upon the copper mines, smelter, and shipments. Wallaroo had become a wheat port, but whatever measure of increase that new function may have added it was insufficient to offset the gradual decline in mining activities which had caused a reduction in the population of all three townships.[44] Port Augusta and Port Pirie had populations commensurate with their position as the major rail-served outports, with the former functioning as a supply center for a huge pastoral domain as well. Other than these, however, relative size was almost solely a measure of immediate rural productivity and status within the context of very local rivalries for the farm trade.

The only real concentration of well-established townships was in the oldest and richest area of the Broughton district where Jamestown, Gladstone, and Laura had achieved some small margin of advantage over such nearby communities as Caltowie, Yongala, Crystal Brook, and Georgetown. All of these had acquired sufficient tangible facilities to insure development beyond that of mere crossroads communities. Terowie, at the terminus of the broad-gauge and therefore the focus of much of the North East pastoral trade, and Quorn, a rail junction and trade center for the Willochra Plains, were other townships which had significantly

Australia for 1884 (Sydney, 1884), and *The Australian Handbook and Shippers and Importers Directory for 1883* (London, 1883). Populations in both references are stated to be derived from the census of April 3, 1881; the only publications of the latter found did not list populations of noncorporate townships separately, but these two references have but very few discrepancies and may be assumed to be very nearly correct. In a very few instances a comparison of township populations with the official figures for the local hundred suggested that the former must have included much more than that of the immediate township and these places have not been included. The population of Port Augusta includes that of Port Augusta Extension and Port Augusta West, that of Port Pirie includes that listed as adjacent but outside of the corporate town. Stirling North and Saltia, just east of Port Augusta, are not included because they have no direct relation to the agricultural colonization. The "selected features" have been checked against several other miscellaneous but less complete sources but still may contain a few inaccuracies. By law, savings banks and commercial banks are separate institutions in South Australia.

[44] The three had a total population of 4,819 in 1881 as compared with 5,638 in 1876; Wallaroo's loss was 206.

outdistanced local rivals.[45] Melrose, Orroroo, and Balaklava were still others which had pulled ahead of several other communities in their local districts. Township development on Yorke Peninsula was still meagre and dispersed, yet already some differentiation was apparent in the cases of Yorketown, Edithburgh, and Maitland; and Minlaton, still but a tiny hamlet of 112 persons, already had those basic facilities — banks, an institute, a flour mill, and a telegraph — which suggested some assurance of growth, even though its peninsular location could never make it the focus of a very large district.

There were more than a score of communities of about 100 to somewhat more than 200 population which had at least one of the important facilities beyond shops and churches, but none except Minlaton and Two Wells had the full array. At this stage of township development this latter scale was apparently the base level of what may be termed firmly-established communities — those which were more than the merest crossroads convenience centers — for, with one exception, none of the dozens of townships of smaller population had a bank or an institute or a flour mill.[46] There was, of course, no certainty that some of these latter might not become more substantial centers, but developments had already proceeded far enough to place them at a disadvantage, and any marked growth would necessitate some considerable change in the context of a whole district.

Whatever the achievements or failures of individual townships, the over-all picture was impressive to the people of the time. More than 12,000 persons, a quarter of the total population influx into this new wheat frontier, now resided in these communities. Even as the drought halted all expansion and shattered all optimism, the achievements in township colonization and social services could give a measure of solid satisfaction:

> there were more townships, prosperous and flourishing townships, now than stations twelve years ago; and . . . more schoolhouses full with children now than there were boundary-riders' huts twelve years ago.[47]

[45] The Terowie-Quorn narrow-gauge line was not yet completed at the time of the 1881 Census.
[46] The exception was Narridy with a flour mill.
[47] *S. A. Parl. Debates,* July 4, 1882, col. 242.

IX.

Perspective

> To the pioneer belongs high praise because he has sought new ways in the face of hardship and has experimented with the earth and with himself. . . . He has been an explorer of homesteads and regions, a discoverer of the earth's bounty and of the places where she withholds it.
>
> — Isaiah Bowman
> *The Pioneer Fringe* (New York: American Geographical Society, 1931), p. 46

TRANSITION

The early 1880's link two of the most important eras in the history of South Australian development. They also link two of the most dissimilar, for the change was harsh and abrupt — from a dozen years of accelerating expansion to well more than a dozen of stagnation, from an era of high hopes and progress to one of shattered confidence and difficulty. This colonization era therefore stands out as a marked pulsation in the development of rural settlement. It was not the first, for that had begun a generation before, nor was it the last, for there remained whole new regions of agricultural potential elsewhere in the colony but it would, in retrospect, appear clearly as the most intense, rapid, spectacular, and certainly in many ways the most important.

All the important indicators — geography, economy, demography — clearly marked this crest of the wave and the long trough that followed. The basic areal pattern in this portion of the colony had been set. The framework of counties established by 1877 has stood unchanged; a scattered half dozen new hundreds were proclaimed in later years but only to allow the conversion of pastoral leases into freeholds – not grazing lands into cultivation. The agricultural frontier never again reinvaded into the North or North East; no new townships or new railway lines were laid out beyond the old limits. Annual colonial wheat acreages, production, and exports leveled off after 1884 to show no significant rise for a quarter of a century. Active immigration, after closely paralleling the areal expansion of the 1870's, dwindled soon after the drought of 1880–81 and was succeeded by twenty years of net emigration. The overseas inflow had not been directed primarily into the farming region, yet it expressed the buoyant progress of the colony and, the total movement of persons into the new lands was sufficient to mark the census year of 1881 as the all-time high point of official record in the proportion of rural to total population in the colony.[1]

Dry years persisted through the 1880's and the world-wide depression of the early 1890's more than counterbalanced the better seasons, which in turn were succeeded by another siege of drought. That this sequence of afflictions followed so hard upon the era of expansion caused an added strain, for the growth of the 1870's had required heavy investment in railways and other public works. Thereby, South Australia now added to her impressive record as a leader a less pleasant innovation: the first Australian income tax. All in all, it was a bitter time of change.

ACHIEVEMENTS

Despite the many disheartening features of the moment, the colony celebrated its jubilee in 1886 with some considerable satisfaction. And certainly a great many of the achievements so proudly proclaimed were a product of that recent unprecedented era of colonization. The agricultural limits had been pushed nearly 150 miles northward of those of 1869. Nearly 2,000,000 new acres had been put into cultivation and the settled area of the colony had been far more than doubled.[2]

[1] See Fenner, *op. cit.,* Chapter 13 for a perspective on cycles of economic and population change.

[2] The total increase in cultivated land in the colony from 1869 to 1884 was 1,935,000 acres of which 1,823,000, or nearly 95 per cent, were in this new wheat area.

The changes in the land acts which had opened the way for this expansion had been largely prompted by the fears of competition from neighboring Victoria. Such concern had been well justified by actual events, but there was even more ample reason for South Australia to be proud of her response to the challenge. The Victorian Wimmera was rich and attractive ground and its settlement was rapidly accomplished during these same years. Yet in 1884 as in 1869 South Australia had twice the wheat acreage of her rival.[3] That her leadership in production was considerably less was evidence of the more difficult land she had to work with; yet, in 1884, her harvest of nearly 15,000,000 bushels was equal to that of Victoria and New South Wales combined.[4] Certainly, for the time being, she clung to her well-established fame as "the agricultural colony of the continent, . . . pre-eminent in wheat."[5] Wheat was now firmly established as the great staple, wool was distinctly secondary, and copper, an old mainstay, had declined to a minor position.[6]

The world situation was also satisfactory. The threat of California which had loomed so large in 1869 had continued to be of concern. Pessimists, year after year, had seen a promise of certain ruin in the scale and reputed efficiency of that Pacific rival. Yet, somehow, these dire predictions never came to pass. In part it was because of the continued rapid expansion of markets, but it was also true that the perfection of California as a wheatland was the product of a distant vision: to the California farmer economic life in the Sacramento and San Joaquin was quite as capricious as on the South Australian frontier; droughts were frequent, yields low, labor scarce, and costs high. And, indeed, although it was

[3] "Australasian Statistics," an appendix to *The Statistical Register of South Australia, 1885* (Adelaide, 1886); Dunsdorfs, *op. cit.*, pp. 532–35 also lists annual acreages and average yields of wheat for each colony, but not productions.

[4] In the years 1880–83 the combination of severe droughts in South Australia and relatively good harvests in Victoria had given the latter a slight lead, but the former did not finally relinquish her leadership for some years.

[5] Edward Greville, *op. cit.*, p. 112.

[6] As measured by declared value, the proportions of total exports in 1884 were: wheat and flour 37 per cent, wool 28 per cent, copper 7 per cent. Lower prices for wheat in that year and the usual retention of a greater proportion of wheat than wool within the colony somewhat mask the full relative importance of wheat to the colony's economy.

not yet apparent, these years were to mark the zenith of California wheat production; in two decades her agriculture was to be transformed, diversified, and largely reoriented to serve a newly-industralized America.

More than 50,000 people had been added to the population of the new South Australian agricultural area in the decade following the 1871 census.[7] A quarter of this increase lived in the several scores of new townships so densely and evenly spaced over the area. While Adelaide celebrated its jubilee, the spokesmen of a dozen aspiring Northern communities as proudly proclaimed what they had achieved in fifteen years or less. The whole scale and rapidity of the growth of their region – much of which was popularly thought to have been accomplished over the opposition of a condescending parental Adelaide – fostered a kind of adolescent ebullience. At best, such spokesmen expressed the fact of a new region more than equal in size and somewhat different in character and orientation to that of the older core; at the worst, they gave vent to typical parochial extravagance. In the common public view Yorke Peninsula, now settled in some degree throughout its length, was regarded as a separate area. Most of the remainder of the new agricultural country was distinguished as "the Northern Areas," or just "the Areas," whose residents felt some community of interest separate from that of the metropolis.[8] Such feelings of regional consciousness received overt expression in discussions of the need for realignment of electoral districts. Few would go to the extreme of suggesting that the Northern Areas was a region so discordant with the old that it might look toward the formation of a new "independent colony" which eventually,

[7] The total population of the area in 1871 was 22,760; in 1881 it was 73,128. About half of the 1871 total was in the Moonta mining district; much of the remainder was in areas just beyond the 1869 agricultural limits, and many of these people were recent selectors. Thus the total post-1869 increase was probably a few thousand greater than the census figures indicate.

[8] The term "Areas" undoubtedly stemmed from the special Agricultural Areas of the original credit legislation. Note the use of the term in the titles of the Port Pirie and Gladstone newspapers. The popular conception of discrete regions within the colony is implicit in much of the contemporary literature. A good example of an explicit delineation is in the business gazetteer of Morris, Hayter & Barry, *op. cit.*, which groups country townships and tradesmen into the following: North (Enfield to Clare), Northern Areas (beyond Clare to Farina), Yorke Peninsula, South (of Adelaide), South-East (Mt. Gambier district), and Western (Eyre Peninsula).

as the "province of Augusta or Spencer, would take an honorable place" within an Australian confederation.[9] But all local spokesmen were agreed that a new region existed, that Clare was no longer the focal point of "the North," that the Areas had little in common with the Burra, and still less with Adelaide.[10] Despite the expectable morass of petty local controversies over such a topic, this cleavage of interests, this feeling of separateness from the older region, was clear evidence that a new regional pattern had been imprinted upon minds as well as upon the maps.

Further, a great geographical experiment had been made – an empirical testing of the qualities of the land, farm by farm, district by district. No longer need the arguments rage over where the limits of agriculture lay, for those limits, as well as the existence of the marginal lands, and the extent of the fertile, reasonably reliable country had been defined. Not that experimentation was at an end, but the general qualitative patterns of the agricultural region had been roughed out and further efforts would bring refinements rather than major alterations.

All of this had been accomplished by the farmers themselves. Through a rapid succession of moves the controlling hand of the government had been withdrawn. But it is important to realize that the relinquishment of such controls was not simply an act of obvious political expediency in the face of public demands for land; it was also a conscious decision to rely upon the farmers as the best agents for testing the land. To be sure, there was little scientific information available, but there was some and more could have been gained. Goyder's plea for a reliance upon experimental farms was at least a rational alternative even if a politically difficult one. And however difficult, a retention of some large degree of political control over the pace and pattern of colonization would have been thoroughly in keeping with the political heritage, whereas the abandonment of control was a marked departure. But there was another kind of heritage which had grown up over the years. Ever since the first breaking of ground in the

[9] *The Jamestown Review,* Aug. 22, 1878. Just how seriously this view was advanced is not clear, for it was an extreme statement typical of this particular paper. Certainly the immediate object was to hasten local redistricting.
[10] For example, *The Areas' Express and Farmers' Journal* (Booyoolie), Oct. 20, 1877; *The Port Pirie Gazette and Areas News,* Aug. 23, 1878.

colony, agriculture had been developed in the face of much doubt about its success in these new lands. Each expansion of the margins of cultivation crossed over bounds which many people had judged as marking the limits of agricultural productivity. Yet in every significant instance up to this time the pioneers had been right and the doubters wrong. Thus confidence in those who dared try — in the farmers themselves — as the most reliable means of evaluating the quality of the land became an ever more firm part of the South Australian heritage. To unleash settlers into the Northern Areas, therefore, was not really a rejection of her heritage but only a shift in emphasis from one part of it to another: a sharp curbing of the predilection for controls in favor of a heightened reliance upon folk experimentation with the land.

The result was a typical nineteenth-century episode: a quick mass-testing of the land and the revelation of its qualitative patterns at an incalculable social and economic cost. But whatever the cost of the empirical test it was definitive, for Goyder's Line is still boldly drawn across official maps of South Australia. On those which also depict regions of land use the close correspondence in the North between that famous "Line of Rainfall" and the limits of reliable farming country are clearly evident (Map 28).[11] Toward Spencer Gulf the concordance is not great, but east of the Flinders Range areas of permanent grain agriculture are found only in a narrow strip along the lee of the mountains and among the nearby hills. Beyond lie the "Marginal Lands," the very idea and delimitation of which is one of the indelible legacies of the colonization experiment of eighty years ago. Even further beyond appear the empty rectangles of Lytton and Derby counties, their very presence a measure of the buoyant optimism of that exciting era, their utter emptiness of any subdivision a witness of how abruptly and permanently that optimism was quelled.

CONTRIBUTIONS

Whereas the empirical discovery of the limits of agriculture was a major folk contribution to the development of South Australia,

[11] These patterns as shown on Map 28 are derived from "Map of South Australia Showing the Principal Land Utilization Zones, June 1959," compiled in the Drawing Office of the Department of Lands under the direction of the Surveyor General.

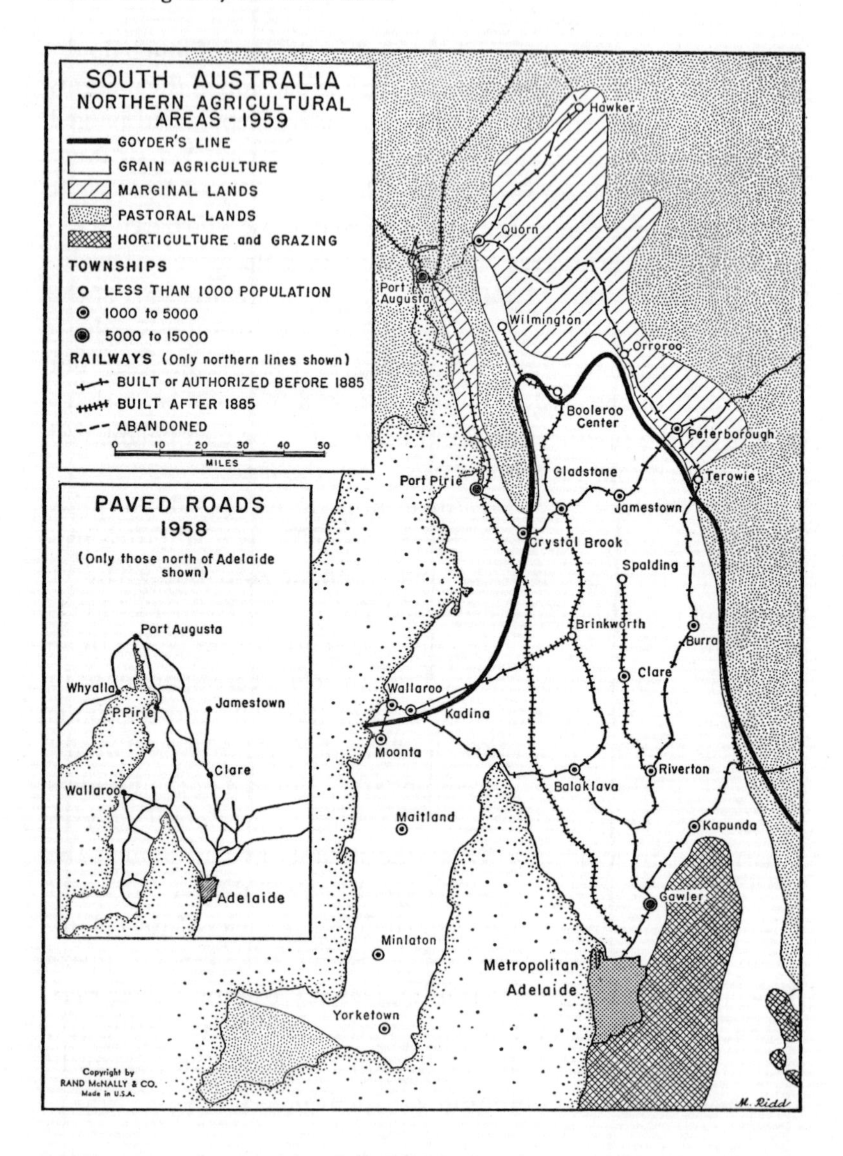
SOUTH AUSTRALIA
NORTHERN AGRICULTURAL AREAS - 1959
GOYDER'S LINE
GRAIN AGRICULTURE
MARGINAL LANDS
PASTORAL LANDS
HORTICULTURE and GRAZING
TOWNSHIPS
LESS THAN 1000 POPULATION
1000 to 5000
5000 to 15000
RAILWAYS (Only northern lines shown)
BUILT or AUTHORIZED BEFORE 1885
BUILT AFTER 1885
ABANDONED
0 10 20 30 40 50
MILES
PAVED ROADS 1958
(Only those north of Adelaide shown)
Port Augusta
Whyalla
P.Pirie
Jamestown
Clare
Wallaroo
Adelaide
Hawker
Quorn
Port Augusta
Wilmington
Orroroo
Booleroo Center
Peterborough
Terowie
Gladstone
Port Pirie
Jamestown
Crystal Brook
Spalding
Brinkworth
Burra
Clare
Wallaroo
Kadina
Moonta
Riverton
Balaklava
Maitland
Kapunda
Gawler
Minlaton
Metropolitan Adelaide
Yorketown
M. Ridd

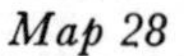

Map 28

the concurrent local evolution of a new system of agriculture was important to the development of the whole of Australia. This new system was neither begun nor completed during this particular era, but it was a time of very significant elaboration.

The potential of Australia as a great wheat producing continent lay primarily in the cultivation of its red-brown earths and mallee lands on an efficient scale with suitable varieties and techniques to allow her to gain and maintain a competitive position in the world market. It was in South Australia during just this period that this situation began to take shape. Here was the first experimentation with these kinds of lands and the development of machines and methods to deal with their special problems; and here was the first wheat region on the continent to be developed with the necessary farm size, machine efficiency, and rigid commercial orientation to win a share of the world market. Though the results would only show in later years, it was here and at this time also that the first significant development of better wheat varieties and the first experiments with chemical fertilizers were initiated.

By diffusion and by farmer migration these elements and this over-all system were transferred into other regions: into Eyre Peninsula and the Murray Mallee of South Australia itself, but even earlier into Victoria, and eventually to New South Wales and Western Australia. In this way, South Australia served as the primary "culture hearth" of the modern Australian wheat industry.[12]

Within a broader perspective, South Australia was of course not a "primary hearth" at all, but only a local manifestation of a new cultural complex which was being diffused, with gross unevenness, over the world. This farming system, though it received its first elaboration in Australia in these northern wheatlands of South Australia, displayed all the distinguishing marks of the radically new European industrial age. In its scale of production,

[12] Callaghan and Millington, *op. cit.*, pp. 20–21, designate the colony as the "cradle" of the industry on the basis of South Australian solutions to four major problems: mechanization, suitable wheat varieties, the demonstration of the value of superphosphate, and the discovery of the value of bare fallow. See also Robert D. Watt, *The Romance of the Australian Land Industries* (Sydney: Angus, 1955), pp. 99–104, for a generally similar evaluation of South Australian contributions.

economic organization, technologic complex, and geographic pattern (and, no less, in the social and psychological patterns of its participants) it marked the sudden, momentary culmination of (to use Mumford's concepts) the "palaeotechnic phase" in the history of modern agriculture.

The South Australian system mirrored all the benefits and deficiencies of that era. It was geared to the mass production of a single commodity within a world-wide system of regional specialization. It employed machinery in all basic tasks, and such machines as well as cultivation techniques were the products of empirical innovations in field and factory. And the railway, the greatest symbol of this coal-iron age, was fundamental to the development and functioning of the whole system. The great deficiencies of this technological complex were its inability to deal with basic chemical and biological problems of agronomy and its dependence upon animal power. The use of horses and bullocks, and wagons and carts (and of wind and sail to export the crop) were necessary carry-overs of an earlier, "eotechnic," phase.[13] Thus, again, these years in South Australia mark a distinctive phase: the days of heavy, slow hand labor and "peasant agriculture" were past, the days of science and power machinery lay just ahead.

CHANGE

It is within this context that subsequent changes within the South Australian wheat industry can best be understood. All that has happened during the past eighty years has been an expression of the definitive character of the "neotechnic" age.

The first significant development was the discovery of the remarkable results of superphosphate fertilization. The experimentation and popularization of this innovation was the work of J. D. Custance, the first professor at Roseworthy Agricultural Col-

[13] The steam threshing engine, widely used in other wheat regions but not common in South Australia, was the most prominent application of palaeotechnic power directly to farming tasks. The many attempts to employ steam tractors for mobile field work cannot be regarded as generally successful. These were really well suited only to the great "bonanza" farms of California and the Great Plains, wherein they were a perfect expression of palaeotechnic characteristics: a ponderous, inflexible instrument geared to the simplest tasks of really mass production.

lege, and of his successor, William Lowrie.[14] The techniques of its application on farms, rather than mere experimental plots, were first worked out on Yorke Peninsula,[15] and by the middle 1890's its use was becoming common over the whole South Australian wheat belt. This single addition not only completely reversed the chronic decline in yields but helped raise them to a level higher than those which had been obtained from virgin ground.[16]

A lesser, but for a time important, factor in the improvement of yields was the development of fallow cultivation closely adapted to local soil and moisture conditions. This, too, apparently had a South Australian origin, first as a folk innovation, and then refined and evaluated by scientists.[17]

Fallowing and superphosphate were two internal improvements which did much to extricate the South Australian wheat grower from the long depression which followed so inexorably the years of expansion. By the time of World War I a new era of progress was well underway (though punctuated in 1914 by the driest year yet recorded) of which the principal manifestation was the development of two new wheat regions: Eyre Peninsula and the Murray Mallee. The colonization of these new precarious districts was a direct application of the processes and system developed in the Northern Areas, but, significantly, there was little attempt to expand once again this older area.

In the two decades following World War I this agriculture underwent more profound changes. A major innovation was the gradual development of a grain-sheep complex based upon wheat and/or barley and leguminous pasture rotations. Fallowing declined as the use of fodder crops increased. In some districts there

[14] Callaghan and Millington, *op. cit.*, pp. 91–93.

[15] Through the development of the "combine" which deposits fertilizer and seed simultaneously.

[16] *Ibid.*, pp. 143, 155; Dunsdorfs, *op. cit.*, Part One, Chapter 5 and Part Two, Chapter 1, gives a detailed description and analysis of rising yield trends.

[17] Callaghan and Millington, *op. cit.*, Chapter 7, esp. p. 115. Fallowing was important not primarily as a direct means of moisture conservation but because of the benefits of weed control, acceleration of chemical changes, and better seedbed preparation. The American system of "dry farming" caused a brief flurry of interest in Australia but was not adapted to summer-dry climates and its presumed advantages were later seriously discounted by further agricultural research (*ibid.*, pp. 114–19). On the historical incidence of fallowing and its relation to yield trends in South Australia see Dunsdorfs, *op. cit.*, especially graphs pp. 371, 373.

was a marked shift in emphasis from wheat to high quality brewing barley, most notably on Yorke Peninsula, and importantly in the Gawler Plains and Broughton districts. The grain-livestock combination not only diversified farm incomes but placed grain production within a generally high yielding, self-sustaining agronomic system which made a much more productive and efficient use of land. Thus sheep returned to these erstwhile pastoral lands in a new context and the fusion of wheat and sheep raising on the farms not only transformed the patterns of land use but must have done much to reduce the old dichotomy of economic and political interests which is so prominent a part of all Australian history.

An even more rapid alteration in the rural economy was one so commonplace over so much of the world that it needs little explanation in any summary statement. The tractor and powered machinery, truck and automobile, vastly improved the efficiency of agricultural operations and quite transformed the quality of rural life. As with all innovations, their adoption took time; tractors began to be used in the 1920's, and were almost universal by the 1940's. In their train was a whole array of enlarged and greatly improved tillage, seeding, and harvesting equipment. Railroads, of course, continued to be a vital link in marketing, but now served by trucks at one end and steamships at the other. The latest visible features of this continually evolving marketing system are the bulk handling facilities. These are still incomplete, and South Australia is the last of the Australian regions to change from the use of bags.[18]

Thus these characteristic features of the neotechnic age – the fruits of laboratory science, the internal combustion engine, and an emphasis upon carefully rationalized efficiency – came to characterize South Australian agriculture in the twentieth century. When the last Northern Areas wheat farmer to use horses finally

[18] A colorful accompaniment of that change was the departure of the last of the great wooden sailing vessels–which were suitable only for bagged grain, not bulk–from the outports of Spencer Gulf in the late 1940's–the end of what by that date could only be regarded as a remarkable eotechnic anachronism. See W. L. A. Derby, *The Tall Ships Pass, The Story of the Last Years of Deepwater Square-rigged Sail* (Toronto: Scribner, 1937), pp. 70–81, for a discussion of the reasons why South Australian wheat held out as the last commodity in world sailing ship traffic.

retired his teams in 1958, this shift in technologic phase was fully completed.

Such changes within the agricultural system were accompanied by other types of modifications in the geographic patterns of the Northern Areas. Most of these were either a filling in of the old framework or gradual alterations resulting from the impact of the use of trucks and autos. Of the first, the addition of several segments to the railway system was the most notable (Map 28). The two agricultural districts which lay beyond the fifteen-mile service belts in 1884 finally got the lines they had so earnestly sought. The Yacka district, where authorization had earlier foundered on the complex outport controversies, in the end got access to all three by a simple linking of Snowtown, Blyth, and Gladstone, which gave direct outlets to Wallaroo, Port Wakefield, and Port Pirie. To the north, the Booleroo district was eventually served by an extension of the Laura branch on through Wirrabara and Melrose to Wilmington, a decision which irrevocably ended the hopes of Port Germein for a feeder inland across the Flinders. And a half century after its first proposal, Clare finally got a broad-gauge branch from Riverton, which was later extended north to Spalding.

After World War I an interdistrict network of improved roads was gradually evolved out of the dense patterns of local rural routes, and after World War II bitumen paving was gradually extended over the main trunk roads. These new trafficways, together with the use of larger ships and mechanized loading facilities, continually narrowed the focus of grain exports upon fewer harbors and steadily reduced the use of many small outports.

Despite such new patterns of circulation and the radically new mobility of the automobile age, the geography of townships remained remarkably stable. Some crossroads hamlets have disappeared or nearly so, and some of the larger communities have somewhat increased in size, but the general pattern is nearly the same as it was eighty years ago.[19] The only really marked changes have

[19] Only four townships appear on the map today which had not already gotten an indicative start by 1881: Bute, Brinkworth, Spalding, and Booleroo Centre. The first arose late because of the delay in the agricultural development of the dense mallee lands in that district; the others are associated with later railway constructions.

been the result of mining or industrial developments extraneous to the agricultural region. The most prominent of these was the transformation of Port Pirie from simply a wheat port to a major smelting and metals export center based upon the great silver-lead-zinc mines at Broken Hill in the Barrier Ranges. The position of Peterborough (formerly Petersburg) as now the largest inland town in the North is linked to the same development and shows how rich was the prize in the vigorous contention for the terminus of the new Barrier Ranges rail line in 1884. Though beyond the reliable farming country, it became a major railway town and a trade center for much of the North East pastoral country as well. Port Augusta's growth has a somewhat similar kind of basis: new railways to the west and north across pastoral districts, with the latter also bringing coal from Leigh Creek to a large electric power station just south of the town.[20]

In the larger scheme, however, a more significant alteration has taken place: the belated triumph of centralization. In a sense this has been a superimposition rather than a complete reorientation, for much of the grain of the North still moves to the local outports. But nearly all other kinds of goods, as well as services and passenger traffic, are focused upon Adelaide. Every township is now wholly bound into the functional hierarchy of the capital.[21]

This "capture" of the North began in the later railway era, most importantly with the construction of a broad-gauge trunk line directly between Adelaide and Port Pirie.[22] Later, as part of the Commonwealth Transcontinental, a line was built from Port

[20] For a brief description and land use map of Port Augusta and a table of the functional economic structure of that city and of Port Pirie see Keith W. Thomson, "Port Augusta," *Proceedings of the Royal Geographical Society, South Australian Branch* (1954–55), pp. 21–24. The populations of these centers in 1954 were: Port Pirie 14,818; Peterborough 3,675; Port Augusta 6,985.

[21] For a detailed study, with numerous maps, of the growth of Adelaide and the present functional patterns and linkages within its trade area, see Elaine M. Bjorklund, *Focus on Adelaide, Functional Organization of the Adelaide Region, Australia,* Department of Geography Research Paper No. 41, University of Chicago (Chicago, 1955).

[22] The Yacka line connecting Blyth and Gladstone gave Adelaide its first direct tie with the Broughton district, but this was still impeded by a change of gauge. The new broad-gauge line left the main Northern line at Salisbury and passed through Two Wells, Mallala, Snowtown, and Redhill, and thus became an important local agricultural line as well.

Pirie to Port Augusta, from where it turned westward for the long traverse across the featureless Nullarbor Plain to Kalgoorlie, connecting on to Perth-Fremantle.[23] With this construction, all of the major outports were directly linked with Adelaide.[24]

This orientation was much more strongly emphasized with the development of road transport. Paved highways are still few enough to be a good measure of the relative importance of the various routes, and the recent pattern clearly illustrates how completely such traffic is focused upon the capital (Map 28, inset).

Such centralization is expressive of a whole new era in South Australian development. Faced with severe limitations on any further agricultural or pastoral expansion, and suffering heavily during the great world depression of the 1930's because of her narrow and vulnerable export economy, South Australia embarked, a generation ago, upon a major program of industrial development. True to her heritage, this has been a conscious, zealous search for a new kind of economic and social utopia following a carefully-calculated policy set forth and continuously manipulated by the government. An impressive array of modern industrial facilities stands as a measure of the success of that program.[25] Almost inevitably, such developments have been almost wholly concentrated in the metropolitan area. Thus Adelaide (together with its environs) now has two-thirds of the population of the state, and is not only its single growth center but the focus of all the fresh cosmopolitan influences of the post-war immigration,

[23] As the Commonwealth line was built on a gauge of 4′ 8½″ (the American "standard" gauge), Port Pirie became the junction of three gauges.

[24] Further, all of the narrow-gauge lines south of Port Pirie–Gladstone–Terowie were converted to broad-gauge, eliminating the break-in-gauge at Hamley Bridge. A long-range program calls for the eventual conversion of all lines in the state excepting those on Eyre Peninsula to a gauge of 4′ 8½″; see J. A. Fargher, "Railway Transport in South Australia," in Best, *op. cit.*, pp. 243–50.

[25] Among the most notable are the large automobile plant, an iron (and soon steel) and shipbuilding complex at Whyalla, a new oil refinery, and a flourishing chemical industry. The government has given top priority to the provision of electric power, industrial water, to the rehabilitation of transport facilities, and, above all, to the continuous recruitment of industry and the creation of a favorable "business climate." See Keith W. Thomson, "Secondary Industry," C. W. Bonython, "The Chemical Industry in South Australia," J. R. Dridan, "The Harnessing and Use of South Australia's Water Resources," and S. E. Huddleston, "Power Supply in South Australia," in Best, *op. cit.*, pp. 201–9, 210–15, 219–34, 235–42, respectively.

which, for the first time in Australian history, has introduced large numbers of non-British peoples into the continent.[26]

In one sense, therefore, there has been a heightening of the contrast between the capital region and the North, between a dynamic, diversifying industrial center and a stable rural area. Yet the inexorable growth of centralization, together with recent and rapid improvements in the facilities of rural life, have bound the two ever more closely together. An inevitable result has been a marked lessening of whatever degree of regional consciousness once existed in the North. While decentralization is by no means a dead political issue, opposition to Adelaide dominance is more a commonplace rural-urban controversy than one between regions discrete in the popular mind, as it was, at least incipiently, if never completely, in the 1880's. Those regional designations which are now in common use are little more than convenient locational names. Yorke Peninsula still has its obvious areal separateness; the remainder of the old Northern Areas is usually divided into the Lower North and the Upper North, referring in general to the districts lying inland from Port Pirie and Port Augusta, respectively.

In summary, these districts still comprise a recognizably separate agricultural sector, but one which now stands much more than before as but part of a larger whole, one of several production areas of the state, all of which have been increasingly focused upon the metropolis and knit ever more tightly into a typically complex, integrated modern economic pattern.

LANDSCAPE

Over the Northern countryside the marks of the past, and particularly of that brief bold era of expansion, are everywhere evident in some degree. In total it is a landscape at once Mediterranean, Australian, and uniquely South Australian.

Its Mediterranean character is wholly a product of nature: a land clothed alternately in the distinguishing seasonal changes of dress of rich winter green and sunburned summer brown. Its Australian character is a product both of nature and of man. Gum

[26] See A. J. Rose, "The Geographical Pattern of European Immigration in Australia," *Geographical Review*, XLVIII (October, 1958), 512–27.

trees and corrugated iron sheets are certainly the most strikingly apparent representations of the handiwork of each, though there are a number of details of land and life which are common to much of the continent.[27] Yet distinctively South Australian features are also clearly evident, and these are very largely the product of man. To be sure, in part the visible scene has been modeled by man working with local earth materials, but it is as much the creation of man working with distinct ideas and evolving a distinct local history.

At the outermost fringes only scattered scars of the past remain. There townships of impressive size on the older maps may have never been more than a pattern of surveyors' stakes on the land, or, if started at all, have almost literally dried up and blown away.[28] Remnants of a rotting fence which once ringed a hopeful farmer's paddock may remain; more likely such failures are recorded in an earthy palimpsest where a square of land once ploughed, abandoned, then over-grazed now stands as a near waste of bramble and weeds (Fig. 17). A bit closer in, the Marginal Lands have at times a curious archaeological appearance of an older and distant landscape: Merinos grazing over a dusty brown, sparsely-grassed surface sprinkled with the stone ruins of abandoned farmsteads in a scene that might seem more appropriate to their ancestral Castile than the Willochra. Such scatterings of hand-worked stone — a mere pile of rubble, the naked spire of a hearth and chimney, or a roofless empty shell — are the peculiar impress of South Australia's history upon her land (Fig. 18).

Townships do remain in this drought-ridden fringe, though now spaced out from one another at twice the distance or more than in the original pattern. These tend to have an unusual appearance, not a tight crossroads cluster but a dozen buildings spaced about in seemingly erratic fashion, with a main street as broad as it is long, the whole challenging the landscape interpreter to imitate the palaeontologist — to fit the tangible fragments to-

[27] For a stimulating inquiry into such details see O. H. K. Spate, "Bush and City: Some Reflections on the Australian Cultural Landscape," *The Australian Journal of Science* (May, 1956), pp. 177–84.

[28] For an interesting study of the gradual disappearance of wheat farming and of Wilson township see K. W. Thomson, "Urban Settlement and the Wheat Frontier in the Flinders Ranges, South Australia," *Proceedings of the Royal Geographical Society, South Australian Branch* (1958–59), pp. 25–37.

gether to infer the whole skeleton of the original creature, with its gross structure of boulevards, parklands, business and residential blocks (Fig. 19). Tiny stone churches, boxlike with a steep roof of battered iron sheets, are a likely part of such a community (I think of one in the Willochra). A door clumsily latched with a piece of fencing wire may allow a glimpse of a dozen tiny pews and altar or pulpit covered with a sheet to keep out the mantle of sifting red dust. Similar stone chapels dot the countryside, often empty and abandoned, relics of an age not necessarily more pious, but at least more parochial and promising (Fig. 20). All these locales lie as yet beyond the reach of paved roads, and are connected by sandy tracks, remarkably smooth at the moment of fresh grading, jarringly corrugated soon after, and utterly devoid of wayside services between towns.

At the margins of the better country, differentiation on a wider scale is apparent. Here there are numerous hamlets with only a general store, a petrol station, and, always, a pub. But more substantial communities also appear. Some of these may show some evidence of prosperity, if not progress, such as Melrose, picturesquely sited at the foot of Mt. Remarkable with a neat, compact village-like appearance which sharply reflects its distinctive anatomy: a "private" town which was never splayed over the gross skeleton of a "little Adelaide" design. An unusual characteristic of this zone is the fact that some of the larger townships show the strongest marks of decay, such as Quorn, which, with a hinterland much reduced in population and a nearly complete loss of its railway functions,[29] has a thick scattering of empty shops and houses and displays a kind of unkempt, archaic frontier charm.[30]

[29] When the government, as part of its industrialization program, fostered a great expansion of coal production at Leigh Creek on the Great Northern line between Beltana and Farina, it built a new railway (4′ 8½″ gauge) between the mines and Port Augusta which stays entirely west of the Flinders Range. The old line through Pichi Richi Pass was abandoned, as was that portion beyond Hawker. Thus the Willochra Plain is now served only by a long devious narrow-gauge line from Hawker to Quorn thence east to Carrieton and south to Peterborough—a good expression of just how "marginal" these Marginal Lands are in the modern grain economy.

[30] Sufficiently so to allow it actually to have served as a period-piece movie setting with but the slightest alterations for numerous scenes in the motion picture "The Sundowners," released in 1960.

Fig. 17 Abandoned farmland in the Willochra Plain near Hammond. (1958)

Fig. 18 The rubble of a once-aspiring township. (1958)

Fig. 19 Hammond, in the southern Willochra Plain — the legacy of the "Adelaide plan" in the "Marginal Lands." (1958)

Fig. 20 A typical country chapel in the "Marginal Lands." (Eurelia, 1958)

Fig. 21 The main street of Ardrossan. (1958)

On south into the more reliable and productive country of the Lower North and Yorke Peninsula the pattern of hamlets thickens, and the larger townships, such as Gladstone, Crystal Brook, Kadina, Balaklava, Maitland, have all the common evidences of busy farm trade centers: automobile dealers, lots full of agricultural machinery, depots for farm petrol, solid blocks of retail shops, with few vacant buildings and a few new ones. Not every community in these districts is thriving, for there is no more vivid evidence of decline than Port Wakefield, but that has come from a change in function. No longer an important junction of rail and water commerce, this first of the wheat outports is today a nearly hollow shell, and even more nearly the mere mudhole its rival ports always claimed it to be; it now ekes out a bare living from the highway traffic skirting the head of the gulf to and from Yorke Peninsula. On the other hand, Ardrossan, with its towering new barley silo (elevator) and modern mechanical loading dock, shows in its neat main street with Norfolk Island pines gracing its center parkway, that at least some of the small outports are very much alive (Fig. 21). Wallaroo presents a scene somewhat intermediate in character: alive, certainly, as a grain port with new bulk-handling facilities and with fertilizer plants serving a prosperous agricultural hinterland, but with the scars of the once-thriving smelting and mining traffic everywhere evident. Moonta, where the mines finally closed in 1923 after eighty years of operations, displays all the rubble and decay to be expected in a once-thriving industrial town now barely supported by a meagre rural trade.[31]

A growing number of new and substantial houses in most of the larger agricultural townships of these areas is good evidence of an increasing stability of settlement, and an almost complete absence of such homes in the communities of the Upper North suggests how long and difficult have been the readjustments in economy and population in that district. Yet even the most prosperous of these country townships have much in their ap-

[31] Keith W. Thomson, "The Changes in Function of Former Mining Settlements in the Wallaroo Copper Belt," *Proceedings of the Royal Geographical Society, South Australian Branch* (1954–55), pp. 48–58.

pearance that seems raw and archaic: unpaved streets, sidewalks in disrepair, weed-infested empty lots, and a dominance of antiquated and often weathered and ramshackle buildings. Such features certainly reflect the fact that this countryside has never been a really wealthy land, that good years have always been interspersed with those of drought or depression, that the amenities of ample water and cheap electricity are still not wholly commonplace. But they hint also that the era of growth, of a burgeoning community spirit has long since faded, and that the present lives within the anatomy and architecture of a past whose expectations were never really fulfilled.

In general, such features are not unexpected, for the towns in the sub-humid grain regions the world over have much in common. Yet one senses that here something more than the usual changes affecting rural life during the past generation has taken place. The enormous disparity in size between Adelaide and even the largest country townships suggests a special inhibiting factor, for, in larger perspective, it appears to be a measure of more than mere function and distance within a standard pattern of urban relationships. Here the dominance of the metropolis over its hinterland appears to be unusually strong, even for Australia where such a feature is characteristic.[32] That these grainland townships seem so heavily pervaded with the relics of the past seems likely to be but an expression in life and landscape of a dominant geographic reality of the present. Born and reared in the very time of greatest regional decentralization they stand today as the captive, stultified outposts of concentration. By its triumph in that momentous geographic controversy, Adelaide not only captured the trade and traffic of its outlying districts but has focused upon itself the whole life and spirit of the state.

This impressionistic sketch of a few landscape features has been couched in terms of settlements because, rooted in the earth but expressing the spirit of the culture, these seem to be the most revealing links between space and society.[33] Here past and present seem most intimately associated. And despite all the changes of three generations, the basic patterns of people and place in this

[32] Bjorklund, *op. cit.*, pp. 5–8.
[33] Spate, *op. cit.*, p. 183.

portion of South Australia were set nearly a century ago when the pioneer moved out upon this land and "experimented with the earth and with himself" – and much of the history and results of his efforts can still be read in the face of the earth.

BIBLIOGRAPHIC NOTE

This study is based very largely upon the official Parliamentary Papers and Debates of South Australia and upon the country newspapers and farm journals which have been cited in the notes. The legislative materials were comprehensively searched for the period 1865–85, and particular points were checked through indices in earlier or later volumes where necessary. The historic files of country newspapers in the Public Library are very nearly complete, and every issue available of every newspaper published in the region during the years 1868–84 was examined in detail, as were the weekly and monthly farm journals published in Adelaide. There was not time to make a similar survey of the daily Adelaide newspapers, though these were checked for specific matters. Other basic source materials were the official books recording the dates of survey and proclamation and other data pertaining to counties, hundreds, Agricultural Areas, and townships, and the official survey maps of hundreds and townships all of which are held in the Office of the Surveyor General. Historic maps of the hundreds were available in the Newspaper Reading Room of the Public Library. Three atlases were also very useful references: A.S. Carrol, comp., *The New Counties, Hundreds, & District Atlas of South Australia and Northern Territory, 1876* (Adelaide: E.S. Wigg & Son, 1876); *Atlas of Principal Portions of Settled Districts in the Province of South Australia, 1877–8* (Adelaide: Surveyor General's Office, 1877); and *Official Atlas of South Australia including the Northern Territory, 1885* (Adelaide: Surveyor General's Office, 1885).

Less basic but important both for perspective and many details were numerous historical and descriptive volumes, directories and gazetteers, most of which were in the Thomas Gill Collection of the library of the Royal Geographic Society of Australasia (S.A. Branch); only the most directly pertinent of these have been cited in the notes.

Although there had been no detailed study of this particular colonization phase, I wish to make it clear that without the following basic works by Australian scholars, two on early history and two on the wheat industry, it would have been quite impossible for a visiting student to have gotten a satisfactory perspective of this era and its developments. A. Grenfell Price, *The Foundation and Settlement of South Australia 1829–1845* (Adelaide: Preece, 1924), was the first balanced historical and geographical interpretation and it casts a singular clarity upon the special features of colonial beginnings. Douglas Pike, *Paradise of Dissent, South Australia 1829–1857* (Melbourne: Longmans, 1957), is an exhaustively detailed study of original sources, permeated with insight and evaluation. Both of these histories are models of research and felicitous writing. A.R. Callaghan and A.J. Millington, *The Wheat Industry in Australia* (Sydney: Angus, 1956), is an astonishingly comprehensive coverage of the topic, lavishly illustrated, carefully detailed, and authoritative throughout. Edgars Dunsdorfs, *The Australian Wheat Growing Industry 1788–1948* (Melbourne: Melbourne Univ. Press, 1956), is an elaborate descriptive and statistical analysis which was especially valuable in delimiting general historical phases and varying regional developments. My dependence upon each of these books was far greater than the few specific references in the text would indicate.

Finally, despite this necessary reliance upon library and archival resources, I would not wish to leave the impression that this has been an "armchair" study. I traveled several thousand miles within South Australia and visited, if only fleetingly, the great majority of the townships and localities mentioned. Wherever possible I have tried to relate these materials to their local settings, to get some intimate sense of people and place, and to use the landscape itself as an archive.

INDEX

The titles of the chapters and their subsections, listed in the table of contents, offer a convenient guide to general topics, therefore primary emphasis here is given to places. Note that individual Agricultural Areas, counties, hundreds, and streams are alphabetized under those respective headings.

PRINTED IN U.S.A.